Writing, Reading, and Language Growth:

An Introduction to Language Arts

RONALD L. CRAMER
Oakland University

CHARLES E. MERRILL PUBLISHING COMPANY
A Bell & Howell Company
Columbus   Toronto   London   Sydney

Published by
Charles E. Merrill Publishing Company
A Bell and Howell Company
Columbus, Ohio 43216

This book was set in Century Schoolbook.
The production editor was Elizabeth A. Martin.
The cover was prepared by Will Chenoweth.

Photos on pages 4, 27, and 84 by Ronald
L. Cramer. Photo on page 72 by Helen Han.
*Cover photo from Resource Teaching
(Charles E. Merrill, 1978).*

Library of Congress Catalog Card Number: 77-91207

International Standard Book Number: 0-675-08362-1

Printed in the United States of America

1 2 3 4 5 6 7 8 9 10/ 85 84 83 82 80 79 78

to

Barbara, Amy, Jen, and Ben

Preface

This book reflects my convictions concerning the teaching of writing and reading. While the emphasis is on children's writing, the reader will find thorough coverage of reading, spelling, and the growth of language. I have endeavored to make the book practical, to avoid jargon, and to write simply and clearly. My hope is that it will be useful to teachers and prospective teachers in elementary and secondary schools. What I have to say is based on classroom experiences with teachers and children. The examples I have used to illustrate instructional principles derive from children's work. Their relevance is indisputable, though my interpretation may be gainsaid. The book is intended to be used in language arts and reading courses at the undergraduate and graduate levels.

I believe in the language of childhood and I believe in children. I believe that language reaches its zenith in written form. Few things in life are as precious or as beautiful as the native language of childhood. Respect for its honesty and reverence for its beauty are the hallmark of the gifted teacher. Teachers must nurture the native gift of language; they must entice it out of the crevices of the mind and onto paper; they must give it the respect that is its due; they must use it to help children realize the value of their gifts. I am not ashamed of these sentimental convictions. Sentiment is, after all, a worthy emotion. It need not be barren of knowledge and wisdom. I should be greatly disappointed if my sentiment were not rooted in a knowledge of children and their language.

Acknowledgments

I wrote this book myself and am, therefore, primarily indebted to myself. I hereby acknowledge that debt. But no man is an island and most of us are not even a boulder in the middle of a small stream. This book is a travelogue of my journey on the mainland.

Much of what I have learned about writing and reading stems from close observation of my children, Amy, Jen, and Ben. Their struggles and joy, perplexities and delights have been a constant source of amusement and amazement, inspiration and insight. This book is a love letter tracing their journey to literacy.

Hundreds of Oakland University graduate students have shared their ideas and the writing of their children with me. They have invited me into their classrooms to observe and to teach. They have challenged my assumptions and inspired my interest. This book is a testament to their hopes and dreams.

Good friends in England, where I wrote much of this book, were generous in sharing their time and understanding of the British Infant School. Special appreciation goes to the administrators and staff of the Upper Poppleton Infant School who taught my children well and shared their insights without reservation. The kindness of the faculty of St. John's College in York, England was expressed in many ways. They shared their library, invited me into their classrooms, and secured my entrance into many excellent schools. Special appreciation is extended to John and Brenda Purcell, Geoffery and Kathy Summerfield, and the villagers of Nether Poppleton. This book is a testimonial to their kindness.

My colleagues on the Oakland University faculty have shared their knowledge and regenerated my enthusiasm when it was at ebb tide. Special thanks to Harry Hahn, Robert Christina, Richard Barron, Gloria Blatt, James Beers, Jane Bingham, Geraldine Palmer, and Ronald Schwartz. This book is a remembrance of their friendship.

I have had a few great teachers and friends who gave something of themselves and left their imprint on my life. Foremost among these friends and teachers are: Russell G. Stauffer, Professor Emeritus, University of Delaware; Edmund Henderson, Director of the McGuffey Reading Clinic, University of Virginia; Harold Cafone, Professor of Education, Oakland University; Dorsey Hammond, Associate Professor of Education, Oakland University; George Coon, Professor of Education, Oakland University; Bill Martin Jr., Author in Residence, Holt, Rinehart and Winston. This book is the earnest of their investment.

I am indebted to my graduate students for many of the ideas contained in chapter 12. Two groups in particular were helpful. The teachers and principals at Frost and Franklin Elementary Schools in Pontiac, Michigan, graciously tried out many of the ideas in their classrooms during the 1972-73 and 1973-74 school years. Many of the ideas were developed by students in the graduate seminar on creative writing. These students in particular deserve to be mentioned by name: Gayle Durkin, James Jarrait, Patricia Kelly, Melody Kramer, Amy Schwed, Trudie Seablom, Susan Seale, Marie Slotnic, Louise Spector, Judy Spugnardi, Karen Verhey, and Margaret Zorn.

Christine Montano and Mary Gee merit special praise for assisting me in the final preparation of the manuscript. This book is a monument to their infinite patience.

Many publishers have consented to the use of copyrighted materials. Acknowledgment of their generosity is specified in other appropriate places. This book would have been diminished without their cooperation.

Over fifty years ago, Hughes Mearns wrote *Creative Power: The Education of Youth in the Creative Arts.* His words were written long ago but his wisdom remains fresh. His love for children and respect for their often hidden talents touched my heart and stimulated my thinking. This book had its roots in Hughes Mearns' fertile mind.

Finally, I owe a special debt to Barbara. This book is the evidence of things unseen and unsaid.

Contents

1

The Nature and Nurture
of Children's Writing

Creative writing is simply an act of personal authorship. It is defined as the act of recording one's ideas in words and sentences. The term *creative* is intended only to express the idea that these words and sentences are the personal product of the child's experience and imagination. The product itself may be a letter, a story, a poem, a report, an observation, or an account. Others may judge it to be unique or mundane, dull or scintillating, thoughtful or careless, beautiful or ugly, worthy or unworthy, original or imitative. It may be fictitious or factual, expository or narrative, imaginative or documentary. It matters not how others may choose to characterize it. Any act of personal authorship should be regarded as intrinsically valuable and creative.

The purpose of fostering creative writing in the classroom is to make a contribution to each child's academic and personal growth. Growth is best fostered in an atmosphere of freedom, respect, approval, and trust. When these elements are absent from the classroom, academic and personal growth is unnaturally limited. Hughes Mearns put it best when he declared: "It is not enough to discern a native gift; it must be enticed out again and again. It needs exercise in an atmosphere of approval" (1, p. 268).

Creative writing is not a disguised talent hunt for geniuses. Nor is it undisciplined self-indulgence. It is not a plea for the eradication of meaningful and useful standards. Rather, creative writing seeks to develop standards of usage within a framework that gives first priority to children's creative urges. After children have had ample opportunity to write freely, unhindered by the necessity to conform to adult standards vaguely understood, there will be sufficient time and incentive to learn the appropriate standards and conventions of writing.

Writing is a powerful medium. Through it one can express the most private thoughts, tell an engaging story, pursue a logical argument, capture an elusive image, sort out a pocketful of ideas and retain only the most fruitful, blaspheme an enemy, entreat a loved one, relive an experience, enshrine a constitution, create a holy book. The greatest accomplishments, profoundest thoughts, loftiest ideas, and deepest feelings are recorded in written form.

No higher gift of literacy can be passed on to our children than the desire and the ability to write. Personal authorship is the summa cum laude of school accomplishments. All children can become authors, and nearly all children can learn to write independently. Classrooms where children are encouraged to write have little need for seatwork or workbooks. Children's time is spent more profitably writing about the world as they see it. The native gift of childhood language must be accorded its rightful place of honor in classrooms. It cannot be said that children's language is taken seriously in our schools until personal authorship is as natural to the child as conversation.

The native gift of childhood language is nurtured in creative writing. Without an adult figure, whether teacher or parent, to provide the powerful stimulus of approval this gift may be wasted. Childhood language needs approval, trust, respect, and freedom to experiment in order to grow.

The language of childhood contains the potential of the future author. In it lies the potential for future generations of wisdom, thought, and feeling. The child whose schooling provided many pleasant self-fulfilling opportunities for personal authorship may become the adult who uses personal authorship for the same ends. Certainly this happy outcome is more likely when personal authorship is valued and fostered among children than when it is neglected.

Without constant, enthusiastic, and thoughtful direction from the teacher, creative writing will cease. The suggestions listed here can encourage creative writing.

1. *Use children's experiences.* All children have words and experience at their disposal. You must help children understand the connection between words and experience.

   Provide a host of rich and varied experiences for the children. Encourage them to use their senses to explore art, science, movement, music, crafts, and nature. Enriching the quality of the sensory experience will enrich the language with which these experiences are described. Experience must be explored deeply and observed keenly. It must not be limited to only those things children already know or are prepared by background, predisposition, or prejudice to expect. Children who feel experiences deeply and sensitively are best prepared to write well. It is your responsibility to see that rich and varied experiences are provided for the children in your charge. The most successful teachers of writing find ways to use the common environment in an uncommon way to provoke interest and provide relevant topics for pupils to write about.

2. *Encourage pupils to write about things that are relevant to their interests and needs.* Avoid giving assigned writing topics. They are seldom

successful and rarely necessary. When it is necessary to assign topics, take time to develop interest, enthusiasm, and background knowledge. If this is done well, children may become deeply involved in the assigned topic. If all efforts fail to spark interest and imagination, it is fruitless to force children to write about something for which they can generate little enthusiasm. Better, at such times, to encourage the child to select his or her own topic.

A teacher took her class on a field trip to the zoo. On returning she instructed the children to write about their favorite animal. Instead, one child wrote a lively, humorous account of an accident he saw on the way to the zoo. The teacher accepted his offering as a satisfactory fulfillment of the assignment. Was this wise? Definitely! A sincere account of an accident, sparked by interest and imagination, is undoubtedly preferable to a forced description of a favorite animal.

3. *Develop sensitivity to good writing by reading poetry, stories, and other literature to children.* There are many resources for such literature. Among the best are the materials written and edited by Bill Martin, Jr. His Sounds of Language Series, Owl Series, and Instant Books are extremely appealing to elementary school children.

An effective writing program will provide an abundance of useful reading materials written by children. The best of these materials should be selected for reading on appropriate occasions. They not only serve as useful models for writing but also often help children feel that they, too, are capable of producing similar work.

The stories and the poems read to children often become the topic of children's writing. Furthermore, the teacher who reads to children provides models for language usage, style, and story format.

4. *Invent ways to value what children have written.* Ways of valuing children's writings may be as simple as praise for a well-written sentence or as elaborate as a young author's conference. Here are some examples of what may be done.

Share what has been written with others. Have children read their writings to the class, another teacher, the school principal, a classroom visitor, a parent, or another pupil.

Find prominent places to display stories and reports. Use bulletin boards, doors, walls, hallways, windows, and the principal's office. Teach children techniques for artistic and attractive display of their writings.

Start a class or school newspaper in which prominent space is reserved for children's writings. Be sure that every child has an opportunity to publish his or her work.

Praise children for the writings they are producing. When a particularly striking word, image, sentence, paragraph, or composition is written, show enthusiasm and appreciation for it. No sincere effort should go unrewarded.

When larger projects such as books are completed, arrange to have them placed in classroom and school libraries. In schools where much

Teachers must value what children have written. The teacher in this photograph is listening to what the youngster has just written.

The class has been doing a project on shells. Part of the project included painting and writing. This attractive display of the children's writing indicates the value the teacher attaches to this aspect of their work.

book writing occurs, library stacks bulge with the published work of pupils current and past. Not surprisingly, other children find these books interesting. Library circulation records in such schools sometimes reveal greater demand for certain books written by children than for certain books written by adults for children. In truth, some books by young authors are better written and better illustrated than many commercially produced books in school libraries. Books by children deserve greater circulation.

    Sponsor a young authors' conference or a writing fair. Such an affair is special and requires considerable planning. The basic idea is to have each child prepare a special booklet of writings for this event. Take care to help each child write and edit his or her best material for presentation at the conference. Prizes could be awarded at a young authors' conference. If this is done, care must be taken to make sure that each child receives recognition for his contribution. Usually special guests are invited to celebrate the event. When possible, a published author is invited. Special writing workshops are conducted for the benefit of the young authors. An event of this nature is a special treat to young writers and has a powerful motivating effect on them.

5. *Start the writing period with a brief warm-up time.* Many things may be done in a warm-up session, but oral discussion and sharing are the most vital. In classrooms where exciting writing is being produced, individual children are likely to be writing at any time of the day. In such classrooms there may be fewer occasions that call for warm-up time.

6. *Guide the writing personally.* Writing time is no time for you to correct papers or perform other tasks. Circulate among the children, offering advice and assistance where needed. Occasionally a child may be reluctant to write because the mechanics seem too laborious. In this circumstance an offer to record some part of the story can work wonders.

7. *Provide a number of ideas for writing for children who may have a difficult time getting started on their own.* Frequently, children who are having difficulty getting started need only an encouraging word or an idea.

8. *Write stories and poetry of your own and share them with your students.* Children need to know that writing is as exciting an enterprise for the teacher as it is for them. Teachers who write along with their pupils will be rewarded both by the writing they produce and the respect and the enthusiasm their example engenders among the children.

9. *Tie writing in with the entire curriculum.* Teachers cannot spend all their time on reading and writing. But it is possible to integrate the teaching of the skills of literacy with the so-called content subjects. Activities in social studies, mathematics, and science may provide experiences and topics that can give direction and meaning to writing.

10. *Have the children make books.* There are many occasions in writing when it is desirable to write and illustrate a more extensive piece of work than normally produced. Such occasions call for special materials and special efforts. Preparing the book cover, editing the writing, and carefully illustrating the book are motivating activities. The books

may be bound in cloth, contact paper, or other materials. The process of publishing a book (including writing, illustrating, and constructing it) gives children a positive feeling about personal authorship. A well-constructed book has the appearance of a professionally published work. Such books give children a delightful experience that generates pride of authorship.

11. *Make certain that children's writing results in outcomes or products.* Like adults, children do not write only for the sake of writing. Children's writing must be associated with tangible, concrete activities. For example, if children write a play, make certain that they have an opportunity to put on the play. If a child writes a poem, make sure that someone listens to a reading of the poem. If a child writes a book, be sure that someone reads it. If a group of children write radio commercials, have them rig up a microphone and broadcast their commercials. Children who write without outcomes soon cease their efforts or produce lifeless works. Meaningful outcomes keep motivation high and inspire renewed and vigorous effort.

12. *Start a writing center.* A writing center is an idea resource bank. It should be located in a convenient place in the room. It should be equipped with a table or two, chairs, paper, pencils, art supplies, old magazines, a dictionary, and books. In addition, it must have a file of ideas for writing. The ideas may be typed and illustrated on index cards five inches by eight inches. Instructions, examples, and the ideas represented on these cards should be brief and easy to read.

All children have something to say and sufficient command of the language to say it. This is all that is needed to be an author. Children who write about their experiences are excited for having done so. Displaying one's own ideas on paper can spark the imagination of children who normally find school chores uninteresting.

REFERENCES

1. Mearns, Hughes. **Creative Power: The Education of Youth in the Creative Arts.** New York, New York: Dover Publications, 1929, 1958 (Reprinted through the permission of the publisher).

2

Language Acquisition:
Thinking, Reading, and Writing

This chapter will consider the relationships between language and thought, writing and thinking; three major theories of language acquisition; five stages in language acquisition; methods by which language may be acquired; and the relationship between oral language and learning to read and write.

Language and Thought

Educators, psychologists, and linguists have a natural curiosity about the relationship between language and thought since a better understanding of how language and thought influence one another might enable us to teach children more effectively. The question is "Does the development of language stimulate the development of thought?"

Piaget's (16, 17) answer is that the development of thought has its roots in action and in sensorimotor mechanisms. Language serves to transmit that which is already understood. He recognizes, however, that as the structures of thought are refined, language becomes necessary in the elaboration of these thought structures. Thus, Piaget sees language as a necessary, but not sufficient, condition for the development of logical operations.

In Piaget's view, language does not organize thought, especially for the young child. Indeed, he seems to assign it a relatively minor role, at least up until the achievement of adolescence. Piaget sees the development of thought in

7

young children as stimulating language development rather than language development stimulating the ability to think.

The Russian psychologist Vygotsky disagrees with Piaget's assessment of the role of language in the development of thought. Vygotsky's (26) studies led him to assign a major role to language. Vygotsky, like Piaget, recognizes the importance of the child's interaction with the environment in the development of thought structures.

Bruner, an American psychologist, has conducted a series of studies which appear to reconcile the major differences between Piaget and Vygotsky. In Bruner's (5, 6) analysis, language serves as a major factor in stimulating the development of thought structures. He believes, however, that a variety of successful developmental experiences must occur during the period that precedes the acquisition of langue. The strategies children develop in the process of learning language become available for other types of thought maturation. As children learn language they acquire more than a set of words and sentences. Children abstract from the language learning process strategies that can be applied to other types of learning. Since language learning is an abstract process governed by rules, the generalization of strategies learned are useful, for example, in learning to read and write. As children develop, language becomes instrumental in helping to direct thought by enabling children to abstract elements of their experiences and to organize and classify them into increasingly more sophisticated thought structures.

Earlier, we asked the question, "Does the development of language stimulate the development of thought?" A balanced view of the works of Piaget, Vygotsky, and Bruner suggests that language acquisition does have an influence on the intellectual development of children.

Piaget's concepts would lead us to develop activities and experiences that emphasize many opportunities to experiment within the physical and social environment. Thus, arts and crafts, movement, music, drama, play, object manipulation, and other direct participation activities would be heavily stressed in both group and individual settings. These experiences would serve both as language motivators and as experiences that give language concrete and direct referents in the physical and social environment.

Vygotsky's concepts would lead us to recognize the usefulness of the teacher's role as an adult language model interacting with the children as listener, speaker, questioner, language model, and friend. The teacher's role would be to extend and expand children's thinking beyond the limits they may have constructed for themselves. Vygotsky's ideas would also lead us to stress the importance of a classroom where children can talk to one another and to themselves. Opportunities for imaginative play, role playing, and experimentation where the child is an active participant would be emphasized.

Bruner's concepts would lead us to design activities and experiences where children actively experiment and interact with the physical and intellectual world on their own terms. We would expect that the general rules that govern children's language learning could be applied to other forms of learning. Consequently, the reading and writing program would exploit the natural relationship that exists between oral and written language. Discovery learning and problem solving would be emphasized throughout the curriculum. The major objective of all teaching and learning, beyond whatever immediate pleasure and practical ends it might serve, would be that it serves the learner in the future.

Despite the slightly different outlook each of these three psychologists places on the relationship between language and thought, the educational implications derived from their work have much in common. The reason for this commonality lies in the central role each assigns to discovery learning and the active role of the child in the learning process.

Writing and Thinking

Writing focuses thinking. Talking is less effective in focusing thinking, although this may vary from person to person. In writing, one's thoughts are laid out in a linear fashion. Therefore, it is easier for ideas to be arranged and rearranged until a clearer thought structure is constructed. Written thoughts can be manipulated more easily than verbal thoughts. Consequently, writing can be an aid to clear thinking. Perhaps Bacon had this process in mind when he wrote, "Writing maketh an exact man."

Writing enables us to lay out our thoughts on a topic in such a fashion that we can examine them closely. Once the initial writing task is completed, we can begin clarifying our thoughts through organization, refinement, and expansion.

Writing provides a medium for those children who are or will become writer-thinkers. The writer-thinker is one whose thoughts are best clarified, refined, and expanded through the medium of writing. An effective writing program can give children the opportunity to explore the connections that exist between writing and thinking.

Three Theories of Language Acquisition

Many theories have been put forth to account for the unique facility of language among humans and how it is acquired by young children. The three most commonly cited explanations may be classified as the behaviorist, the nativist, and the cognitive theories of language acquisition. Within each of these broad categories considerable difference of opinion exists between one theorist and another.

Behaviorist Theory

Behaviorist theory generally holds that a child initially learns language by imitating the language of adults. The child's language is gradually shaped to adult norms because adults reward the child's successive approximations of their own language. Behaviorists usually explain language acquisition in terms of key concepts such as reinforcement, generalization, imitation, successive approximation, and mediation.

Skinner (19) explains language learning in terms of the reinforcement of imitative behavior. For example, an infant's random babblings begin to sound more and more like adult speech because adults reinforce the child's successive approximations of their own adult speech. Through the process of reinforcement, successive approximation, and generalization, the child's language is gradually shaped and extended to adult norms.

Other behaviorist theories place less emphasis on reinforcement, imitation, and generalization. Braine (3, pp. 1–13) emphasizes the role of contextual generalization. According to this principle, the child makes generalizations about certain sets of language items occurring in certain contextual positions. Athey (1, pp. 16–110) has summarized the contextual generalization concepts in these words:

> Context generalization is the process whereby the child, having established the meaning of a pivot word, is able to expand his repertory of intelligible utterances considerably. It is not essentially different from stimulus or response generalization except that it takes place across temporal positions. For example, upon hearing, "Will you/go to the store?" the child observes that "you" occurs in the first half of the sentence and "go" in the second half. "You" and "go" are then carried into new analogous contexts by the process of context generalization, enabling the child to construct longer and longer sentences. This process explains his linguistic productivity. (p. 22)

Staats and Staats (25), in addition to the usual concepts of reinforcement and generalizations, emphasize the role of mediation in language learning. Mediated responses are described by Athey (1, pp. 16–110) in this way:

> Mediated responses are names, labels, or linguistic responses which mediate between stimuli and behavior (Jensen, 1966). Mediation is derived from simple S-R associations in which one stimulus elicits several responses, or several stimuli elicit the same response, or a response in one situation is a stimulus in another situation. Mediation is thus held to account for much complex linguistic and cognitive behavior (Staats, 1968). (p. 23)

Critics argue that behaviorist theories of language acquisition are incapable of explaining its most interesting and crucial aspects. For example, many of its key explanatory concepts have been criticized as inadequate, vague, or, as in the case of imitation, playing only a minor role in language acquisition.

The most controversial and influential critique of behaviorist language theory is contained in Noam Chomsky's (9, pp. 26–58) review of Skinner's *Verbal Behavior*. Chomsky charges that the most significant things to be learned about language are to be learned from the study of children's language, which is inadequately represented in Skinner's account. He further argues that the step called generalization in behaviorist theory includes just about everything of interest in language acquisition. Yet this key concept is only vaguely defined and never empirically shown to be the key to language acquisition in children.

According to Wardhaugh (27, pp. 168–94), educators are especially likely to be disappointed in behaviorist theories of language acquisition because the child plays such an insignificant role in many of its theoretical formulations.

Nativist Theory

Language is a biological endowment unique to the human species, Lenneberg (13) has argued. He is joined in this belief by McNeill (15) and others. The nativist, or biological, theory of language acquisition is based on the belief that the human nervous system is innately predisposed, through the evolutionary process, to the development of language. Maturation in language development parallels related growth in thinking and motor ability. Assuming the absence of some massive abnormality or injury, every child will naturally and rapidly learn to speak whatever language he or she is exposed to. Learning to talk is as natural and inevitable as learning to walk. The nativist theory emphasizes what occurs inside the child whereas the behaviorist theory emphasizes the role of events in the child's exterior environment.

Lenneberg has presented a number of arguments supporting the notion that the human ability to acquire language is due to biologically inherited capabilities. His evidence is based on normal and abnormal language development in children, as well as evidence which suggests the possibility of an innate biological capacity for language, unique to the human species. Lenneberg (13) has cited the following evidence to support his theory:

1. *Language is unique to the human species.* While it is apparent that animals can communicate in some interesting and even complex ways, there is no evidence to show that any nonhuman species has learned to communicate using the complex syntactic properties of human language. The learned behavior of parrots, pets, and chimpanzees shows only a superficial resemblance to human language.
2. *Every human language is based on similar universal principles of semantics, syntax, and phonology.* This is sometimes referred to as the principles of linguistic universals, an argument that maintains that certain features of language and language learning are universally similar in key respects.
3. *The developmental schedule for languge learning is uniform in all cultures.* In all cultures, for example, children have mastered the essential elements of their native language between the ages of four and six.
4. *Language is learned with such ease and is so deeply rooted in humans that children learn it even in the face of enormous handicaps.* Even blind, retarded, and criminally neglected children learn to speak and often with only a minimal delay.
5. *There is evidence that language learning is related to certain anatomical and physiological correlates.* There is reason to believe, for example, that certain parts of the human brain contain specialized structures for the production of speech, and these structures are apparently species specific.

The theory of biological endowment for language ability has gained a considerable following in recent years. Perhaps this trend is at least partially attributable to the failure of psychologists and linguists to adequately account for recent linguistic observations, particularly the existence of language universals, in any other satisfying way.

The nativist theory of biological determination of language acquisition must be taken seriously. However, like other theories, it leaves some basic matters unexplained. For example, the theory does not adequately account for the actual mechanisms of language acquisition except in a general way. How the child moves from biological endowment to actual linguistic performance is not adequately explained.

The fact that environmental factors are relatively unimportant in nativist theory (since children are presumed to possess certain general language abilities before specific elements are ever produced) tends to make the theory considerably less interesting to educators because it seems to negate the importance of applications of language learning processes to reading and writing.

Cognitive Theory

The cognitive theory of language acquisition is similar to the nativist theory in that it postulates innate structures which make language learning possible. However, the cognitive theorist claims that universal thought structures, rather than linguistic universals, account for the capacity to learn language.

Slobin (20), for example, seems to suggest that the child may be preprogrammed, in effect, with such cognitive abilities as short-term and long-term memory facility, information processing capacities, and cognition of the categories and processes of human experience. These factors, along with other developing cognitive abilities, determine and control the pace of language acquisition.

Similarly, Cromer's (11) research indicates that as the children increase their cognitive ability they free themselves to learn and express new language abilities. Having developed the necessary cognitive structures, children immediately extend their linguistic performance in concert with their newly developed cognitive ability.

Cognitive theorists, such as Piaget, Vygotsky, and Bruner, have not been primarily concerned with describing a language acquisition theory. Rather, they have concerned themselves with the development of a theory which accounts for cognitive development. Consequently, they have discussed the mechanisms of language acquisition mainly in terms of how it is acquired. Athey (1, pp. 16-110) has responded to this tendency with the following critique:

> Perhaps the greatest criticism of cognitive models is that they fail to account specifically for the facts of language development. It is not so much that linguistic facts are incompatible with the models as that they seem irrelevant to them. Yet the cognitive and language functions are so interdependent, and their developmental paths are intertwined. It is difficult to see how a theory in either area can be considered adequate if it fails to take account of existing theories and facts in the other. (p. 44)

Cognitive language theorists tend to interpret linguistic data consistent with the view that general cognitive development determines language acquisition. Like the nativists, they postulate inborn capacities. But whereas Lenneberg would emphasize a set of linguistic universals as the crucial inheritance, cognitivists, such as Slobin, prefer to posit a set of inborn cognitive mechanisms which enable the child to process linguistic information gleaned from the environment. The cognitivist view is compatible with the interests of most educators and the aims of many psycholinguists, for it leaves room for environmental influences on language acquisition. Cognitive theory makes the search for applications from language acquisition to reading and writing a sensible and plausible concern.

Stages in the Language Acquisition Process

Nativist and cognitivist theories of language acquisition assume that children acquire their native language because they have an inborn preference for language or at least the neurological apparatus that makes its acquisition all but inevitable. Even so, theorists from all areas would acknowledge that events which occur in the children's environment have some impact on the actual acquisition of, and continued growth in, language.

The acquisition of the basic structure of oral language is fully acquired, according to various investigators, somewhere between ages four and six. While there appears to be some continued language refinement after age six, this process may be regarded as somewhat different from initial language acquisition. Certainly, growth in knowledge of language meanings continues through life.

How do children interact with the fully acquired language of the adults and older children who surround them? It is believed that children pass through several stages in their language development. While these stages are neither precise nor uniformly acknowledged they may be roughly outlined as follows.

Stage One

This is a prelinguistic phase where babbling and random experimentation with sounds occur. During this stage children produce all of the sounds relevant to their native language as well as sounds significant in languages other than their own.

Stage Two

This stage marks the beginning of recognizable language behavior. The child responds to verbal language signals and begins to produce sounds to express needs. Later, the child begins to produce one word utterances such as *bye-bye, da-da, ma-ma*. As the child gains greater control over his vocal mechanisms and continues his mental development, there is a corresponding increase in his clearly recognizable and meaningful vocabulary. The one word utterances are often sentence-like in terms of their meaning. For example, the utterance *milk* may mean that the child wants milk or may simply be a naming function. Verbs are used less frequently than nouns in this stage. Words uttered often have concrete referents or associations with referents that are present in the observable environment.

Stage Three

This stage marks the beginning of expansion and delimiting of speech so that it sounds more like adult speech. The child expands his utterances from one to two and three word utterances. His speech becomes more precise in that he expresses his needs and desires more specifically. Thus, while the child is expanding the length and content of his expressions, he is, at the same time, continually refining his ability to use language that more closely fits the context of the situation in which the language is uttered.

The two and three word utterances characteristic of this stage have been described as *telegraphic* because of the preponderance of nouns and verbs over function words (articles, prepositions, conjunctions, and auxiliary verbs). An analysis of these two and three word telegraphic utterances by Brown and Bellugi (4, pp. 133-51) led them to conclude that these words are used because they are the class of words which carry the greatest meaning and hence are most effective for communication.

A young child's language at this stage suggests that it is governed by rules and contains the most essential elements of mature language. Meaning is its most notable characteristic.

Stage Four

This stage is marked by the acquisition of syntactic structures of language, the induction of rules for generating these syntactic structures, and the rapid expansion and acquisition of new vocabulary items. According to Pflaum (16), these changes are manifested in such events as increasing length of sentences and the use of negative sentences, questions, and verb forms such as *ed, ing*, and transformations.

During this stage an interesting phenomenon occurs with the use of irregular verb forms. For example, the child may move from saying *He ran* to *He ranned*. This event signals that the child is developing the concept of past tense and is overgeneralizing its applications. Before this occurrence, the correct *He ran* most likely represents a naked memorization or imitation derived from adult speech models. Later, the child sorts out the regular and irregular forms without difficulty or residual damage to his language facility. The naturalness of this trial and error behavior provides a worthwhile object lesson for adults and teachers concerning notions about correct and incorrect language. In language learning, as in other types of learning, mistakes are relative events and ought to be viewed for their positive contribution. Unfortunately, errors are often regarded by educators as wholly negative events. This attitude is wrong and may seriously impede learning.

This stage of language development is a delightful and astonishing one. Language often appears to explode from immaturity to a maturity that is rapidly approaching adult norms.

Stage Five

When a child attains this stage he has, for all intents and purposes, internalized the grammar of his native language. The child's vocabulary is extensive and he is able to generate grammatical sentences he has never heard or uttered before. Smith et al. (24) calls this the *automatic stage* and describes it in this way:

> At the time he reaches this stage the child is greatly increasing the quantity and effectiveness of his language. His language has moved rapidly from highly individual attempts at communication to an idiolect that falls well within the norms of his community's dialect. Whatever this dialect is when he has reached the point of automatic control over it, it is adequate to meet the communicative needs common to persons of his age in his immediate society (p. 25).

In spite of the extensive control which the child has over his language at this stage, it should be remembered that there is some evidence which suggests that further refinement continues, as Carol Chomsky's (10, p. 443–48) study has shown. The continued refinements and the constant growth of vocabulary do not detract, however, from the language power that school age children possess. Their language mastery is firmly established by the time they enter school.

The five stages of language acquisition should be regarded as an attempt to organize and interpret the welter of data bearing on language development. These stages represent a reasonable approximation of growth stages in language development. To the extent that they help us organize our thinking about children's language learning, they may prove useful. If, on the other hand, we take them to be rigid, empirically established stages, we shall inevitably misunderstand and perhaps misuse them.

Environmental Influences in Language Acquisition

Certain environmental influences may help account for the astounding language facility which children develop in a relatively short period of time. There are no definite answers but there are some mechanisms which may consitute at least a partial explanation for language development. The reason for trying to determine what environmental influences help the child to acquire language is the hope that this knowledge may be applied to the teaching of reading and writing and other literacy skills. Three environmental influences or mechanisms that may aid language acquisition are imitation, expansion, and meaning.

Imitation

One way children may acquire language is through imitation of adult language models. Behaviorist theories of learning place considerable emphasis on some type of imitative or modeling behavior in language learning. It does sometimes appear that children imitate adult language. Usually these imitations are reductions of larger sentences to a few essential words. The question naturally arises as to whether these are imitations or simply utterances generated by a set of rules. Ervin's (12) study indicated that there are few direct imitations in children's speech and concluded other factors must be used to acquire language. Braine's (3, pp. 1–13) research similarly argues for the necessity of some other factors to account for language learning.

Despite these pessimistic views on the efficacy of imitation in language learning, most of the arguments against imitation reduce to a skepticism about its adequacy to explain language learning by itself. McNeill (14), for example, does not deny the importance of models but argues that simple imitation is inadequate to explain language acquisition. It seems inconceivable that imitation of some type, at some time, does not account for some language learning. The language in the child's environment must serve as some sort of model, and modeling is a form of imitation. Presumably, therefore, imitation plays some role in language learning, although its role is apparently not a major one.

Expansion

It has been suggested by Brown and Bellugi (4, pp. 133–51) that adult expansions may serve as a method by which the child obtains information that facilitates language growth. Expansion of a child's language occurs when an abbreviated statement such as *papa away* is repeated by an adult in an elaborated or expanded form, for example, *Yes, papa has gone away.* Presumably the child obtains from this expansion, which occurs frequently and naturally between parent and child, information about how his abbreviated speech is described in mature adult speech.

The evidence regarding the effectiveness of expansions in facilitating language growth is mixed. McNeill (15) indicates that expansion was effective when expansions were limited to those statements that the responding adult fully understood. On the other hand, Cazden (8) reports that modeling well-formed sentences that were comments on the child's utterances proved more effective than simple expansion.

While the evidence on the usefulness of expansion is uncertain, one is tempted to suspect that such a natural process must have some positive effect on language acquisition. Slobin (23) poses this suspicion when he says:

Until the necessary data is amassed I would still like to believe that when a child hears an adult expansion of his own speech he learns something important about the structure of his language (p. 443).

Meaning

Linguistic studies of children's acquisition of language have focused almost exclusively on the acquisition of syntactic and phonological competence. More recently, meaning is beginning to be considered in relation to how language is acquired. Since language is instrumental in conveying understanding, directing purpose, and determining behavior it is logical that this renewed focus on meaning should begin to assume some importance in language acquisition studies.

Slobin's (22) review of Russian language development studies suggests that children acquire language structures according to their relative semantic difficulty rather than their grammatical complexity. Bloom (2) has suggested that a child's level of meaning competence is more fully developed than the surface structure of his speech.

Unfortunately, few empirical studies exist that elaborate on the role that meaning may play in facilitating language growth. One suspects, judging from the more general cognitive development studies of Piaget, Vygotsky, and Bruner, that meaning plays a most crucial role. Furthermore, the likely impact meaning may have on expansion, modeling, and imitative mechanisms should not be discounted. Surely these mechanisms carry meaning as well as syntactic information to the child. Bloom (2) says that a child's linguistic and non-linguistic experiences, along with his cognitive perceptual development, operate together to influence a child's language competence. One cannot help but recognize the logic of this assertion.

Imitation, expansion, and meaning have been considered as possible environmental influences on language acquisition. Research evidence bearing on the effectiveness of these mechanisms is inconclusive. It seems reasonable to conclude that interaction between the child and the adult has some influence on language growth. Furthermore, the richness and quality of child-adult social, linguistic, and cognitive interaction may prove to be the most important variable of all.

The behaviorist and cognitive theories of language acquisition leave considerable room for environmental influence on the language competence a child may develop. Some interpretations of the nativist theory of language acquisition also support this view. Language exists, after all, in both a social and biological context. To consider language exclusively as a biological inheritance, as some nativist theorists do, is unrealistic. It is equally unrealistic to exclusively consider language a social invention solely determined by environmental influences, which some behaviorist theorists do. When the full story of language acquisition is known it seems reasonable to expect that a significant role will have been assigned to biological inheritance. Most likely this inheritance will take the form of neurological and physiological structures that make language acquisition possible only in humans. At the same time, that story is also likely to reveal that societal and environmental influences aid language acquisition and direct it along certain paths governed by the general laws of learning unique to humans.

Connections Between Learning Oral Language and Learning to Read and Write

The task of educators is to interpret and apply the information supplied by linguistic, psychological, and educational research. It is, therefore, appropriate to conclude this chapter with a section that does just that. We can apply what is known about the acquisition of oral language to the teaching of reading and writing. One way of doing this is to examine the connections that exist between native language acquisition and learning to read and write. The purpose of this examination is to extrapolate possibly fruitful ways of approaching reading and writing instruction based on information about how children learn oral language. Carroll (7) and Wardhaugh (27, pp. 168–94) have made similar examinations in the past.

Oral Versus Written Language

Native language learning is primary and oral whereas reading and writing are secondary and written. Historically, oral language came first. Written language is based on an oral language tradition. While there may be some inborn capacity to learn oral language, no one would seriously argue that there is a biological predisposition to learn to read or write.

Since written language is derived from oral language, one would expect this relationship to influence the attainment of literacy. First, enrichment of oral language would have a beneficial influence on the successful acquisition of reading and writing skills. Therefore, schools would have to direct their efforts toward the enhancement of children's oral language environment. These efforts would require providing children with a wealth of linguistic and nonlinguistic experience designed to enhance conceptual, perceptual, and cognitive growth.

Second, reading and writing should be taught in a way that maximizes opportunities for observing the intimate connections between oral and written language. The more personal this connection is for each individual child, the greater the likelihood that literacy skills will be successfully learned. Recording a child's language and using it to initiate him into reading and writing instruction is the most direct way to maximize the observable relationship between oral and written language. This process is discussed in detail in chapter 3.

Natural Versus Unnatural

Native language learning occurs in a natural, informal, high stimulus environment. Reading and writing instruction, on the other hand, often takes place in an unnatural, formal, and low stimulus setting. Native language learning uses no preprogrammed materials, books, teachers, or planned curriculum. Learning happens naturally. It happens partly because the child is preprogrammed to learn oral language and partly because the child is constantly exposed to what he is destined to learn. Adults and older children provide this exposure through natural conversation and encouragement in informal settings. The surrounding oral language stimuli are not scoped and sequenced into bite-sized bits. The assumption is that the child will extrapolate the rules of the language system, pace his own learning, and devise his own strategies. The possibility of failure is never entertained. Rather it is assumed that success is inevitable.

In learning to read and write everything is done quite differently. Rightly so, to a degree, for the processes are not totally analogous. Still, it is possible to imitate to some degree the circumstances surrounding oral language learning. Schools can construct a setting where the following conditions exist: (1) children are read to frequently, (2) oral language is recorded for initial reading purposes, (3) oral language is honored and encouraged, (4) art, music, drama, and other art forms are part of the literacy program, (5) books and other printed materials abound, (6) oral and written language stimuli surround the child, (7) failure is regarded as an imposter, (8) individual learning paces are understood and encouraged, (9) literacy instruction is personalized, lively, and enjoyable. Teaching and learning must be done in an atmosphere that is relaxed so that children can learn at a pace that suits their intellectual and emotional make up. A natural, informal, and high stimulus reading-writing environment similar to the oral language environment can and should be duplicated.

No Stress Versus Stress

In oral language learning there is little or no stress on the learner whereas the circumstances accompanying the teaching of reading and writing are often stressful and frequently produce anxiety in the learner. Stress interferes with learning and produces anxiety when it is excessive. Fortunately, undue stress is seldom placed on children as they are acquiring their native language. There is good reason for its relative absence. Few children fail to learn to talk. This fact seems to induce patience in parents and confidence in a successful outcome. Thus, ready acceptance of individual differences in language acquisition flourishes among most adults who furnish the child's early language environment.

Consider how different the environment is in which a child acquires the skills of reading and writing. Schools are typically organized in a way that takes little note of maturational differences among children. Furthermore, teachers and parents typically expect at least one year's progress in reading and writing growth for each year in school. The child who fails to reach this mythical norm may be subjected to all sorts of pressures that lead to anxiety, rebellion, apathy, discouragement, and other stress reactions. Whether or not a child is subjected to these pressures depends on the behavior of teachers, peers, parents, siblings, and the teaching methods and materials used. But for many children failure is predetermined by the circumstances the school creates and by failure to recognize individual differences in readiness to learn, learning rates, and achievement potential. The child who gets off to a bad start in reading and writing, usually through no fault of his own, comes under severe stress generated by the system of which he is the innocent victim. Anxiety and its companion, failure, begin to build a barrier which further impedes learning. Thus, a vicious cycle is created from which some children never escape.

Some lessons may be drawn from the relatively low anxiety levels in oral language learning. Anxiety levels can be greatly reduced in the teaching of reading and writing. Above all, there must be a recognition that the acquisition of reading and writing skills is a highly individual process. Excessive competition, ability grouping, lack of patience, rigid grade levels, parental and teacher ignorance of developmental processes, and inappropriate instructional materials and techniques are among the major factors that lead to failure in reading and writing. Each of these factors is an environmental condition and, hence, can be changed by teachers, schools, and society. Not all of them are easily changed by an individual teacher, but some are within the *sole* jurisdiction of an individual teacher. Other factors are within the realm of the teacher's persuasion and influence. Educators must work jointly toward modification of environmental circumstances that lead to failure in reading and writing if we are to apply the lessons imparted by the ready way children learn to speak their native language.

Receptive Versus Expressive

Reading and writing are parallel and related processes. Reading is a *receptive* language process. Its counterpart in oral language learning is listening. Writing is an *expressive* language process. Its counterpart in oral language learning is speaking. Reading and writing complement one another in the same way that talking and listening complement one another. Each process mutually strengthens and extends the other. Yet, reading and writing are seldom taught within the same time frame, nor is their intimate relatedness recognized for teaching purposes. Some children are in the fourth grade and are effective readers before serious writing commences. For many children, writing is simply never a serious part of their education. This is indeed unfortunate, for to fail to teach reading and writing in a way which recognizes and takes advantage of their mutually strengthening properties may seriously retard the acquisition of one or both language processes. It is especially important that reading and writing begin in the early primary grades.

That the two processes can be taught within the same time frame and in a manner that takes full advantage of their intimate relatedness is indisputable. There are many classrooms and schools where this is effectively done.

Immediate Versus Delayed Gratification

Oral language learning fulfills an immediate, vital need to communicate whereas reading and writing do not. The benefits of speech are immediate, rewarding, and relevant. The benefits of learning to read and write appear less vital, rewarding, and relevant because the rewards and relevance that attach to reading and writing are less tangible than they are for oral language learning.

What we may learn from this difference is the necessity of making the acquisition of reading and writing skills a more rewarding and relevant activity. Reading and writing instruction should emphasize the fun and practical benefits that can be derived from using these skills in the present as well as the future.

Oral and Written Language Acquisition

Spoken language is governed by rules. It has a structure that governs pronunciation, meaning, and the generation of sentences. Written language is also governed by rules.

In order to read and write, children must learn the rules that govern written language, including pronunciation, spelling, organization, and interpretation. Normally, the rules that govern written language are formally taught. But is this necessary? Perhaps reading and writing instruction should proceed on the assumption that sufficient exposure to written language stimuli will result in the inductive discovery of many of the rules that control it. Perhaps there is too much formal teaching of rules in reading and writing instruction. An inductive approach in which children are encouraged to explore and experiment with written language would require a greater toleration of trial and error and wrong paths taken than many teachers are accustomed to allowing. This approach would demand enormous faith and patience, but it might prove more fruitful than the rule-oriented methods currently used in teaching reading and writing skills.

There are significant differences and similarities between learning oral language and learning to read and write. Some of the differences exist because of inherent differences between the two processes. Others exist because of arbitrary choices made by schools and society. It is the arbitrary differences that should be modified to make the teaching of reading and writing more parallel and related to the manner in which oral language is acquired.

It may be true that oral language is, in certain respects, unique behavior in which biological predisposition plays some role. To the extent that this is true, the learning conditions cannot be precisely duplicated. Computers may never precisely duplicate the functions of the human brain. However, this circumstance does not deter scientists from learning as much as possible about how the human neurological system works and applying the information gained to develop better computers. Just so should educators continue to learn as much as possible about oral language acquisition and apply the information gained to the teaching of reading and writing.

SUMMARY

This chapter has examined six factors related to language acquisition among children, including (1) the relationship of language to thought, (2) the relationship between writing and thinking, (3) three major theories of language acquisition, (4) five stages of language acquisition, (5) environmental influences on language acquisition, and (6) the relationship between oral language acquisition and learning to read and write.

Vygotsky argues that language stimulates the development of thought structures in children whereas Piaget emphasizes the notion that the development of thought stimulates the growth of language. While Piaget and Vygotsky have come to different conclusions on this matter, Bruner has attempted to reconcile these differences. He stresses that, while language does stimulate the development of thought, the strategies learned during the language learning process are useful for other types of thought maturation.

Writing influences thinking. Hence, ideas committed to writing are more amenable to transformations of thought than is oral language. These transformations are accomplished through expansions, extensions, refinements, and organization.

The three major theories of language acquisition are behaviorist, nativist, and cognitivist. Behaviorist theory holds that language is learned primarily through imitation of adult language models. Behaviorists postulate concepts such as reinforcement, mediation, succesive approximation, and generalization to account for language learning. Nativist theory asserts that language is acquired because of a uniquely human biological capacity to learn language. This theory relies heavily on evidence which suggests that certain features of language and language learning are universally similar in key respects. Cognitivist theory postulates innate thought structures which make language learning possible, rather than an innate predisposition for language learning per se. Thus, universal thought structures, rather than linguistic universals, account for the capacity of children to learn language.

Five stages in the development of language have been suggested. These stages begin with a prelinguistic babbling stage and end in fully developed language somewhere between the ages of four to six. The concept of stages in language acquisition is a helpful and convenient way to organize and interpret the conflicting information bearing on language development. However, it should be remembered that these stages are approximations, not empirically established categories.

Three environmental influences on language acquisition were discussed, including imitation, expansion, and meaning. There is some evidence to indicate that imitation, expansion, and meaning may play some interrelated role in early language acquisition. However, the precise way in which these factors interrelate and impinge on language acquisition is unknown. The current status of research in this area is so uncertain that even the major terms are inadequately defined. Hence, agreement as to the role each of these environmental factors may play in language acquisition awaits future clarification.

Finally, the relationship between learning oral language and learning to read and write was examined. It seems clear that a better understanding of the manner in which oral language is acquired will lead to more effective strategies of teaching the secondary language processes of reading and writing.

REFERENCES

1. Athey, Irene. "Language Models and Reading." **Reading Research Quarterly** 7 (1971).

2. Bloom, L. **Language Development: Form and Function in Emerging Grammars.** Cambridge, Mass. M.I.T. Press, 1970.

3. Braine, Martin D. S. "The Ontogeny of English Phrase Structures." **The Language** 39 (1963).

4. Brown, Roger, and Bellugi, U., "Three Processes in the Child's Acquisition of Syntax." **Harvard Educational Review** 34 (1964).

5. Bruner, Jerome, Oliver, R. R., and Greenfield, P. M. **Studies in Cognitive Growth.** New York: John Wiley and Sons, Inc., 1966.

6. Bruner, Jerome. **The Process of Education.** Cambridge, Mass.: Harvard University Press, 1966.

7. Carroll, John B. "Some Neglected Relationships in Reading and Language Learning." **Elementary English** 43: 577–82.

8. Cazden, Courtney B. "Environmental Assistance to the Child's Acquisition of Grammar." Unpublished doctoral dissertation, Harvard University, 1965.

9. Chomsky, Noam. "Review of B. F. Skinner, **Verbal Behavior.**" **Language** 35 (1959).

10. Chomsky, Carol. "The Acquisition of Noun and Verb Inflections." **Child Development** 32 (1968).

11. Cromer, R. "The Development of Temporal References during the Acquisition of Language". Unpublished doctoral dissertation, Harvard University, 1968.

12. Ervin, Susan M. "Imitation and Structural Change in Children's Language." **New Directions in the Study of Language.** Edited by E. H. Lenneberg. Cambridge, Massachusetts: M.I.T. Press, 1964.

13. Lenneberg, Eric H. **Biological Foundations of Language.** New York: John Wiley and Sons, Inc., 1967. (Reprinted by permission of John Wiley and Sons, Inc.)

14. McNeill, David. "Developmental Psycholinguistics." **The Genesis of Language: A psycholinguistic approach.** Edited by F. Smith and G. A. Miller. Cambridge, Massachusetts: M.I.T. Press, 1966.

15. McNeill, David. **The Acquisition of Language: The Study of Developmental Psycholinguistics.** New York: Harper and Row, 1970.

16. Pflaum, Susan W. **The Development of Language and Reading in the Young Child.** Columbus, Ohio: Charles E. Merrill Co., 1974.

17. Piaget, Jean. **The Language and Thought of the Child.** New York: Meridian Books, 1955.

18. Piaget, Jean, and Inhelder, B. **The Psychology of the Child.** New York: Basic Books, Inc., 1967.

19. Skinner, B. F. **Verbal Behavior.** New York: Appleton-Century-Crofts, 1957.

20. Slobin, D. I. "Comments on Developmental Psycholinguistics." **The Genesis of Language: A Psycholinguistic Approach.** Edited by F. Smith and G. A. Miller. Cambridge, Massachusetts: M.I.T. Press, 1966.

21. Slobin, D. I. "The Acquisition of Russian as a Native Language." **The Genesis of Language: A Psycholinguistic Approach.** Edited by F. Smith and G. A. Miller. Cambridge, Massachusetts: M.I.T. Press, 1966.

22. Slobin, D. I. "Imitation and Grammatical Development." **Contemporary Issues In Developmental Psychology.** Edited by N. S. Endler, L. R. Boulter, and H. Oscar. New York: Holt, Rinehart, and Winston, 1968.

23. Smith, Brooks Kenneth Goodman, and Meredith, R. **Language and Thinking in the Elementary School.** New York: Holt, Rinehart and Winston, Inc., 1970.

24. Staats, Arthur W., and Staats, C. K. **Complex Human Behavior: A Systematic Extension of Learning Principles.** New York: Holt, Rinehart, and Winston, 1963.

25. Vygotsky, L. **Thought and Language.** Cambridge, Massachusetts: M.I.T. Press, 1962.

26. Wardhaugh, Ronald. "Language and Beginning Reading." **Reading Research Quarterly** 7 (1971).

3

Helping Children Record Their Language and Their Experiences

It is a cliché to note that the components of language arts are interrelated, but the statement is nonetheless true. Any program of literacy instruction which ignores this fact cannot develop fully literate children.

Therefore, if one wishes to develop an effective language arts program in the elementary school, one must teach reading and writing as a unity. An effective reading program should lead naturally and quickly to an effective writing program. One approach to reading instruction that is designed to accomplish this task is the Language Experience Approach.

The Language Experience Approach utilizes each child's ability to communicate his or her experience through oral and written language and through whatever artistic and dramatic talents he or she may possess. The child is taught to read through recording and reading the language he uses to describe his experiences. Each child's language becomes his or her personal primer for initial reading instruction.

The two words *language* and *experience* are not the exclusive property of this approach, since all reading approaches depend, more or less, on the utilization of a child's language and experience. However true this may be, the term *language experience* has come to be associated with a particular way of teaching reading. The term is sufficiently descriptive to represent fairly a set of procedures which tie reading and writing instruction together in a natural way.

Most children begin school eager to read. Those who can read are usually eager to demonstrate their accomplishment. Those who cannot read are usually ready to try. Therefore, an early start should be made. The object at the start is to show pupils that reading is easy and natural. A good way to accomplish this is the experience story that is dictated by the pupil and recorded by the teacher.

Most children who are unable to read are unable to write independently. Even those who are able to read fluently experience difficulty with independent writing in the beginning stages. They are still struggling with the skills of manipulating pencil and paper, forming letters, and spelling words. Obviously, this impedes fluency in independent writing. Therefore, it is necessary to find some means of bridging the gap between the child's wealth of oral language and his initial dearth of independent writing skills. Recording children's language by means of pupil-dictated accounts provides the bridge.

The recorded story mirrors the child's talk and introduces him or her to the concept of authorship. Recording the child's language as the experiences are described serves two basic needs in literacy instruction. First, it provides the most relevant possible material for initial reading instruction. Second, it makes instant authorship possible during that period when the child is still acquiring prerequisite skills for independent authorship. Recording children's language builds in their ability to give a coherent account of their experiences. They are authors and they can write. This sense of mastery is invaluable when the more difficult task of independent writing begins.

Recording a child's observations may take place in a number of different ways. They will be considered here in the logical order in which they are most likely to be used in the classroom: (1) recording through artistic expression, (2) recording group accounts of experiences, (3) recording individual accounts of experiences, and (4) recording with mechanical devices.

Recording Through Artistic Expression

Before children are capable of recording their ideas through the more abstract medium of print, they are able to represent their impressions of the world in the concrete forms of art and drama. Many good British infant schools have discovered the value of art and drama to an extent that few American schools can match. The most exhilarating classrooms I have ever seen were just outside London. Entering them was like entering a modern art museum. Fantastic dioramas, charts, puppets, clay sculpture, and pictures of every sort covered the walls and ceilings and every available nook and cranny. One American teacher, upon observing this display, inquired how time was found for the academic program. Her question capsulized an attitude typical of many American educators who delegate art to special teachers.

Art and drama are often considered by American educators to be good if one has time for frills or extras. Nonsense! A proper concern for artistic expression allows children to use their senses so that they may build a varied and rich base of experience. In turn, this base of experience enables children to know themselves and their world better. When children are encouraged to express their thoughts through clay, drama, movement, paint, fabric, or crayon, their readiness to write or read or talk or think is enhanced. These experiences have a positive effect on the quality of academic work.

Children learn best when they have closely examined and observed the world around them. No child yet has learned science exclusively from a textbook. Children must manipulate, observe, and conduct scientific experiments. Then they will learn science, for they have built, through the senses, a base of scientific experience. This observation implies that teachers must think less in terms of subjects and more in terms of experience which children enjoy and learn from simultaneously. Clearly, such thinking requires the teacher, through inventiveness and imagination, to arrange the classroom environment in a way that maximizes the use of the senses.

Artistic expression can be encouraged in many ways. Children can be asked to write a picture book which describes an experience the teacher has planned. They can be encouraged to present a social studies report using artifacts created from clay, construction paper, and papiermâché. They can be allowed to interpret a book, play, story, or song through the use of dramatic movement. They may be shown how to work out their math problems with charts, audiovisual materials, and manipulatable objects. They may be asked to illustrate a sequential event with a comic strip format. They may create a composition about their school with a camera as their artistic instrument. There is no subject or academic skill which cannot be enhanced by approaching it through some artistic medium. The limitations are only those which teachers artificially impose on themselves. Time-honored but invalid excuses such as, "It can't be done," or "It shouldn't be done," or "I don't know how" simply will not suffice. There are many classrooms where it is being done.

The child at the easel has just completed a painting. Later she will be encouraged to write about her work. Drawing, painting, crafts, and drama are important in their own right, but one could easily justify them on the basis of their academic contribution as well.

Recording Group Accounts of Experiences

Just as it is possible and desirable for children to record their experiences through artistic expression, it is also possible and desirable to record children's language using group procedures.

Group accounts may be recorded for the entire class or for a group within the class. A prewriting stimulus should be planned as a shared group experience to catch the attention and hold the interest of the group. This planned stimulus may simply mean bringing into class a turtle, hamster, chick, rabbit, novel toy, an unusual book with pictures, a simple science experiment, or a classroom guest. Or it may require taking the children out of the classroom to explore the different colors of green or the different types of insects to be found in the grass.

The creative teacher will find the time devoted to sharing experiences a challenging opportunity to broaden children's horizons and to heighten their sensitivities. This shared prestory experience encourages oral language and pupil thinking as the children talk about the stimulus. Of course, they must have an opportunity to touch, see, smell, taste, or hear the stimulus. They must have an opportunity to use all the senses that are appropriate for the occasion.

The group story below was written by a first grade class. They had been studying Japanese customs. On the occasion of this story the children ate with chopsticks for the first time. They wrote this story:

CHOPSTICKS

Chopsticks are used for cooking. Sometimes you use them in Chinese and Japanese restaurants. The Japanese use them for eating rice. Today our class will eat with chopsticks. Chopsticks are fun to eat with. Chopsticks are easy to experience with. We learned how to use chopsticks.

After an experience such as the one above has been explored and discussed, the teacher records the story in manuscript writing on a large piece of paper mounted on an easel. If the stimulus period has been successful, pupils will eagerly offer their observations. The teacher should encourage as many children as possible to each contribute a sentence or two to the recording.

Throughout the recording process, the integrity of the child's language must be maintained. This means that the language of the child is recorded precisely as given. For example, if the child says, "I seen a pretty bug with green legs," the teacher must not change the word *seen* to *saw*. The grammar lesson may be attended to at another time if one feels that grammar lessons, as such, are appropriate. To change the language destroys the integrity of the child's production and introduces a visual configuration which is different from that which was said. When the child reads his sentence back, in all likelihood, he will say it as he originally offered it. The language a child uses reflects the habits of a lifetime. The child's language represents a personal reservoir of emotion and knowledge. It must be treated with the respect it deserves, or the child will cease to use it in the classroom. Misrepresenting, demeaning, or misusing a child's language may render null and void his most efficient and effective learning medium. It is extraordinarily wasteful to deprive both the teacher and the child of this indispensable asset for learning. If the language of the classroom is different from the language of the child, effective schooling and other societal influences will eventually improve this difference. Refusing to acknowledge a child's language as acceptable for learning beginning literacy skills is bad pedagogy and worse psychology.

Appropriate punctuation and form should be automatically incorporated as the story is recorded. Story titles may be added either before or after the story is recorded, depending on the group's preference. As the teacher writes each word, he or she says it aloud. When each individual sentence is completed, he or she reads it back for all to hear. Occasionally a student may ask to have his or her sentence modified. This request should always be honored.

Immediately after the story is recorded, the teacher reads it back to the group, pointing briefly to each word. Then the entire group reads the story in unison with the teacher as he or she points again to each word as it is said. Care should be taken to maintain a conversational rhythm in the rereading.

Following the rereading, each child is asked to represent the story through some medium of artistic expression, usually by drawing or painting a picture. As the children illustrate their story, the teacher moves about the room writing the story title and the pupil's name on each paper. These group stories may be read again the following day and children encouraged to read these stories to each other.

The Individually Recorded Account of a Child's Experience

Children enjoy dictating personal accounts of their experiences. Furthermore, they take a great pride in their recorded writings. The pride that children take in personal authorship, even through dictation, is an emotion which teachers can use to get children off to a fast and successful start on the road to literacy. The wise teacher understands this and provides meaningful outcomes for writing projects. The range of topics, diversity of length, complexity, and sophistication of personally dictated accounts are shown in the following examples:

MY JOB

I would like to be a nurse. I would give people shots. I would give them baths. I would work at the hospital. I would get ten dollars a day.

Heidi
first grade

IN MY HOUSE

I like my mother to clean up the house and wash the dishes. I watch her. She washes the table. She makes our beds. She mops the floor. She washes the windows. She cleans the bathroom. My daddy paints the house. He cleans off the high windows. I helped him move the furniture.

> Stephen
> first grade

I'M NOT REALLY ME

I'm not really me. I'm a Bonneville. When they twist my steering wheel, it hurts my nose. When they smack their hand on the horn, they hurt my poor old dashboard. The children jump up and down on the seat and then they stop to full me up. The gas stinks. A little oil here and a little oil there and I shout, "I can't swim." My mother woke me up just as the good part came, for it was another dream.

> Tim
> second grade

FARM TRIP

We went on a hayride. I saw a horse and a cow. I saw a goat. I saw a baby lamb. I saw a king goat.

> Travis
> first grade

I know what a fish does.
It swims.
It eats.
It lays eggs.
Maybe it makes a nest.
I know what a fish does.

> Derek
> first grade

MY TRIP

I had fun when I went to my Aunt's house. I played with my friends there. I said to my friends, "Let's go play over at the creek." We went over to the creek and found a fort.
We were trying to get in and there wasn't a door. So we went all round the fort and we tried to get up and we fell. We found some boards and we climbed up on the boards and got on the roof. The roof fell apart.
We got in the fort and I said, "Let's get out of here before the kids come back." Before we knew it, there was another entrance. Come, let's go out that entrance." I said. We went to the creek and found fossils.
My friend found a fossil that looks like a lion's tail. "Oh, boy! I wish I could have that," I said. He was the lucky one. Then he

found another one that had one layer and then another with lines on
it. Then I found an arrowhead and another arrowhead. Then I asked
his dad if they were arrowheads. His dad said yes. I asked my dad
and he said no. Then I found lots of limestones. When we got home
I found out that they were Thunder Eggs and a Petosky Stone.
Then I got down my geology set and I weighed the petrified wood,
tusk shell, and my agates from Mexico and Brazil.
I found a stone that was from a dinosaur. I said, "That isn't anything," and I threw it down and looked in my book and found it
was a dinosaur bone.

Jim
second grade

The preceding accounts were dictated by first and second grade children.
They do not, by any means, represent the best or the worst of typical first and
second grade language. Most of the children in these schools come from low or
middle income families. These stories illustrate the wealth of language and experience common among children in cities throughout America.

Personal authorship, through dictation, establishes for the child an
immediately observable relationship between the spoken and written word.
There is no faster or more effective means of laying bare the mystery of print
than individual dictation. Furthermore, the teacher can be certain that the
child will fully understand the vocabulary and the concepts contained in this
beginning reading material. Why? Because every word and concept recorded
has been processed directly through the mind of the child who dictated it. There
is a built-in certainty that the material will be relevant. No other material has
this guarantee.

In classrooms where personal authorship has been well established,
children eagerly anticipate their opportunity to dictate. Children sometimes
feel neglected, and seldom hesitate to tell you so, when they have been unable
to dictate.

Getting individually dictated accounts requires careful planning and organization. Individually dictated accounts can be started soon after the
children have had several opportunities to record their experiences in group
situations and the teacher judges that a child has acquired some facility in
describing experiences. At first the efforts of some children may seem meager
but normally fluency rapidly increases. For most children, fluency is present
from the start.

Personal authorship through dictation has many pedagogical advantages
which makes it an ideal method for introducing the beginning reader, or the
older child with a history of reading failure, into the world of literacy. Lee and
Allen (1, pp. 5-7) have succinctly expressed an important language experience
concept in the following statement:

What a child thinks about he can talk about. What he can talk about can be
expressed in painting, writing, or some other form. Anything he writes can be
read. He can read what he writes and what other people write. (pp. 5-7).

As in group recording, it is wise to plan a stimulus session, especially in the early stages. The stimulus session may be conducted in the same way as described for group recording. Once the children are comfortable with dictation the teacher will discover that they are eager to dictate accounts of their personal experiences. When this happens, planned stimulus sessions may be conducted less frequently. However, it should not be assumed that this happy condition will prevail for all children. Consequently, those who need the oral language sharing experience fostered by the stimulus sessions must continue to have it.

Teachers sometimes prefer to deal with one group at a time when obtaining individual stories. If so, it is wise to

1. gather a group of children in a designated area in the room,
2. present the stimulus,
3. provide meaningful work for the children who are awaiting their turn to dictate and,
4. take one child at a time aside from the group and record his or her account.

Dictating sessions should be private. This reduces the pressure on the child and usually gives better results. If the child is having difficulty dictating, the teacher can suggest possible ideas or ask questions to stimulate thinking. Sometimes a child is not prepared to dictate. The teacher may suggest that he dictate later or ask the child to illustrate his idea and add the words later.

The individually dictated stories are recorded in manuscript printing or are typewritten. When the individual story has been completed, it is taped into a composition notebook. The recorded account is then illustrated on the opposite page.

The following procedures are recommended for the rereading of a dictated account.

1. The teacher reads back what the child has said, or the teacher and child may read the account together if the child is able to do so.
2. The child returns to her desk or other suitable work space and underlines the words she knows.
3. When the child returns to her desk she illustrates her story. These illustrations are intended to express the child's artistic ability and choice of attributes to represent the concepts her story contains. Sometimes children are encouraged to draw or paint before dictating. Often this reversal of the process is helpful to the child who is reluctant to dictate.
4. The next day the group is reassembled and each child is asked to read her story to the group. If the child needs help in the rereading, the teacher should immediately provide it.
5. On the third day the child returns to the teacher and reads her story again. The teacher and child may then decide which words she knows sufficiently well to be included in her word-bank. The word-bank is a

collection of words learned from the experience stories (2). These words are subsequently used in teaching word recognition skills and in other word exploration activities.

As with all teacher ideas that may be new for a particular teacher, personal authorship through dictation may prove to be a challenging task to manage effectively. A few tips that will facilitate the process are in order.

1. *After becoming familiar with the process, train others to help with the recording.* An aide can be trained to record dictated accounts. If an aide is not available sometimes a parent can be persuaded to help. Upper grade children can also be trained to be competent recorders. This idea has the advantage of providing needed help while also giving a meaningful educational experience to the upper grade child.
2. *Set up a rotating schedule of dictation.* Various plans are possible, depending upon the teacher's objectives, frequency of dictation desired, and scope of the total reading-writing program. While various schedules are possible, Table 1 outlines a three day sequence. Alternatives include four, five, and six day sequences.
3. *Study authoritative materials from various sources to become better acquainted with the necessary procedures.* The most useful resource available is Russell Stauffer's book entitled *The Language Experience Approach to the Teaching of Reading* (2). Articles describing the Language Experience Approach may be found in many professional journals and magazines.
4. *Find a colleague who is currently using the Language Experience Approach.* If no one is available, try to persuade a colleague to try the procedure with you. It is invaluable to have someone to consult with when things are not going as expected.

Recording Experiences on Tape and Film

The use of tape recorders, cameras (movie and still), and television can add a special dimension to the recording techniques that may be used with children. Each of these means of recording will be considered.

Audiotape Recorders

There are several varieties of audio recording that may be used by young children. The most popular and easy to use is the cassette tape recorder. There are a variety of machines available, many of which can be operated easily by first graders.

A youngster's first experience with audio recording is always an interesting one to observe. Children are usually surprised at the sound of their voice

TABLE 1
Three Day Schedule for Recording Individual Accounts

	First Day	Second Day	Third Day	Fourth Day	Fifth Day
Group 1	1. Teacher records 2. Teacher and/or child rereads account	1. Child rereads account with appropriate teacher help	1. Final rereading of story account 2. Child receives word cards for words he or she knows		
Group 2		1. Teacher records 2. Teacher and/or child rereads account	1. Child rereads account with appropriate teacher help	1. Final rereading of story account 2. Child receives word cards for words he or she knows	
Group 3			1. Teacher records 2. Teacher and/or child rereads account	1. Child rereads account with appropriate teacher help	1. Final rereading of story account 2. Child receives word cards for words he or she knows

and intrigued with the novelty of the process. A good way to introduce young-sters to its possibilities is to record their conversations or to tape a teacher-narrated account for them to listen to. Once the children learn to operate the recorder, the teacher may suggest recording individual accounts to be played back to the class. The teacher will want to provide adequate support in this initial venture to assure a successful beginning.

The cassette recorder may be used for many different purposes and activities. The following list suggests some of its uses.

1. *Recording individual experience stories.* Although it is normally best to transcribe experience stories directly into print while the youngster observes, there may be occasions where this is not possible. On such occasions the child records the story. Later, the teacher or an aide transcribes it. The youngster may then reread the story and compare the audio version with the printed version. This provides good practice in matching sounds to print and may be helpful to those youngsters who have some difficulty remembering their dictated statements. This procedure is somewhat cumbersome and sometimes causes too long an interval between dictation and rereading. Therefore, it is not a satisfactory substitute for on-the-spot recording of children's language. Nevertheless, on those occasions where the teacher judges it to be necessary or desirable, the tape-recorded experience account may be an appropriate and valuable experience.

2. *Recording group oral and written material.* Often teachers encourage two or more children to write short plays, skits, commercial messages, jokes and riddles. Recording these materials usually provides extremely useful feedback to the group. Such experiences require considerable time and teacher patience. However, when children are given proper supervision and support in such endeavors, the results are usually rewarding.

3. *Recording material for self-instruction.* Adults sometimes discover that talking about an idea is helpful in clarifying thought. Youngsters may be encouraged to talk their ideas into a recorder, listen, rearrange, and record again. Recording in this fashion tends to develop fluency and spontaneity in oral language and thought, as anyone who has recorded letters and other materials knows. Initially, such recording experiences are likely to be halting and disjointed. Later, as familiarity and experience with recording develops, one normally experiences greater lucidity and fluency of thought and speech. This same phenomenon is likely to occur with youngsters as well. Hence, the teacher must give the child sufficient time to overcome the normal reticence and difficulty he or she may initially experience.

4. *Recording material for group and individual skill practice.* Teachers who commonly utilize listening stations as part of their weekly instruction normally depend on commercially prepared or teacher prepared materials. The older or well advanced child may be a useful helper in

preparing such material. For example, if a lesson consists of listening to a story and doing follow-up activities, selected children may be given the responsibility of preparing such a lesson. This is a valuable educational experience for the youngsters charged with the responsibility. It is also helpful to the teacher and youngsters who will eventually use these materials at the listening center.

There are many other possible uses for audio recording. One of the most popular is a device called a Language Master® . This machine usually comes with prepackaged lessons of various types. However, one can record on these machines as well as listen, and this may be its most valuable use.

There are limitations and disadvantages to audio recording. One of the most obvious and annoying is the mechanical failure commonly experienced. Other practical difficulties also arise. Some children may be too shy or inhibited to utilize recording effectively. This problem sometimes arises from initial uncertainty and is usually easily overcome. Teacher sensitivity is needed to insure profitable use of any technique, however, and audio recording is no exception. These difficulties serve only as a challenge to the thoughtful teacher who wishes to extend the variety and effectiveness of recording children's language and experiences.

Videotape Recording

In recent years it has become increasingly feasible for schools to own and operate their own videotaping systems. Many schools, in fact, own such equipment and make regular use of it. The early generation of cumbersome, difficult to operate, easily broken machines has been replaced with highly compact, portable, easy to operate systems.

Video recordings can be used to enhance all aspects of the curriculum but, in particular, they lend themselves to a supportive role in the writing program. There are many activities related to the writing program for which videotaping may be used.

Writing and producing plays is one use of a video tape. A very effective way to motivate the writing of plays, character sketches, and skits is to announce that each team or group who writes a play will have an opportunity to videotape their production. Using the recorder to tape rehearsals is also an effective way to get children to understand the necessity for rewriting. As children view their dramatizations on tape they are able to see their writings take lifelike forms. This provides a dimension of realism that other media cannot hope to match.

Improvised drama may be preferred among younger children. A group or an individual may perform a pantomime scene, tell a joke, or share an experience which is recorded and later viewed. After recording on video tape and viewing the replaying children may then wish to write or dictate about the experience. The advantage of using the video recorder in this manner is that it requires less planning and a shorter period of time to complete. Also, improvised drama is more likely to be within the capabilities of primary grade children. Of course, some primary grade children are quite capable of writing plays and producing them effectively. Hence, it is a matter for each teacher to judge whether to use improvised dramatization and write or record later, or whether to have the children write or record plays and then dramatize. Both are effective ways to tie writing and drama together using videotaping as the medium for recording children's experiences.

Recording With Film and Camera

Photography is an intriguing way to teach children how to use visual materials to communicate meaning. The activity can be structured to include planning, organization of ideas, arrangement of visual elements, group decision making, oral communication, sequencing, and writing.

1. *Using still photography.* Still photography is the simplest form of photography to use with elementary school children. It is also relatively inexpensive since the only materials needed are a simple camera, black and white film, and funds for processing the film. In order to teach children how to combine photography and writing the following sequence of events may be used.
   a) Divide the class into small groups. Provide each group with a set of pictures taken from magazines or other sources. Have the children decide how they would like to arrange their pictures to communicate an idea. When they have completed this task each group may be asked to elaborate upon their idea either orally or in writing.
   b) Tell the children that a camera is available for them to take their own pictures. Have them plan the sequence of pictures needed to communicate whatever idea they have chosen.
   c) Send each group out to take pictures needed to illustrate their idea. No group should be allowed to begin this step until they have provided satisfactory evidence of a plan for communicating their idea.
   d) Develop the film and return the photographs to the group. This step may take two or three days. The delay seems to have little effect upon the children's enthusiasm or motivation. The heightened anticipation that waiting for the pictures provides can, in fact, be used to advantage by the thoughtful teacher.
   e) Reassemble the group and have them arrange their photographs in a manner that best illustrates the idea they are seeking to communicate. The decision-making required here may involve considerable debate and some departure from the original plans.
   f) Have each group begin writing or dictating the textual material required to complete the idea they intend to communicate. This

should be a team effort. Team efforts sometimes require specialization. For example, a group may wish to appoint a writer, an editor, and a layout person.

g) Make booklets in which to display the pictures and text. The sophistication with which the text and visual elements are arranged is partially dependent upon the grade level of the children. At the first or second grade level, for example, there may simply be a photograph pasted on a page with accompanying textual material below. With older children other arrangements may be attempted. The text itself may be printed by the children or typewritten.

Below is a story photographed and written by two second grade children. The story (without the pictures) was written following the guidelines described above. The story is reproduced exactly as it appeared in the original booklet.

HALLOWEEN SAFETY

Picture One

We are writing this book so you will know what to do and what not to do on Halloween night. If you get some candy don't eat it when you are still walking because it might be poison. So when you get home ask your mother to look at your candy or you might get killed. So ask your mother if she will look at it. You would not want to get killed.

Picture Two

When you come to someone's house you say trick or treat may I have something good to eat. Then the mother will give you some candy. After she does you do not walk away. You say thank you very much and then you go away.

Picture Three

You have to put halloween things on your window because it won't look funny and scary. So when it is halloween night please put things on your window or kids won't like your house very much. So maybe someone has things on their window and you are next to that house and you don't have anything on your window. No one will go to your house. So put things on your window. People will like it if you do. I really think so.

Picture Four

This girl is ten and she can cross the street because she is older. But if she gets run over by a car it will be her fault. If you are six do not cross the street. You can go with your father but if you get run over it will be the car's fault because the cars should stop sometimes too. Just be careful.

Picture Five

If you want to go trick or treating you better dress warmly or you might catch a cold and have to come right back home and go to bed. So dress warmly because you would not want to go to bed and not get any candy. So all the time put a coat on or put something on because you want some candy don't you?

Picture Six

Make sure your mask is off because somebody could run over you. So don't wear your mask across the street. You want to have fun on Halloween don't you? So take off your mask.

Picture Seven

Don't soap the windows or you will have to clean the windows and you will not like it one little bit. I did not tell my mother that I am going to soap the windows. I came home and I got it.

Picture Eight

Don't soap the windows or you will get it and it is not nice. What if someone soaped your windows you won't like it. If a girl or boy sees you you will have to clean the window. You will not like that.

Picture Nine

Don't talk to strange people because they could kill you. But some are very nice like that man. (Picture of school principal—apparently no stranger was available.)

Picture Ten

We had to tell our mother that we are going to get some candy. She said "OK but be careful." Always let your mother know where you are going.

Picture Eleven

You should say thank you when someone gives you some candy. It is nice to say thank you too. Then when you say thank you they will say welcome. Never say bad things.

Susen and Suanne
Second grade

Still photography and the writing projects that stem from it are easy and inexpensive to implement. There are other forms of recording with film that are more complex and, in some instances, a bit more expensive.

2. *Using moving pictures.* Many teachers have discovered that making moving pictures is not as difficult and expensive as it might first

appear. Usually the equipment needed can be obtained from interested parents or from school resources. The children themselves can sometimes raise the necessary money to defray film and processing costs.

Making moving pictures requires careful planning and some experimentation. Each class member can be given some assignment in the production of the film. There must be writers, actors, directors, and technicians. The first decision required is what film to make. Since writing is tied into the project, a script must be written. Once the script is completed, decisions must be made regarding how and where the film is to be shot.

One group of fifth graders in Pontiac, Michigan decided to produce a film about Dracula. They obtained the use of a farm house and the surrounding grounds as a location for filming. Plans need not be this elaborate but sometimes special occasions call for special effects. After the film was shot, a group of individuals edited the film. When the film was finished they held a premier showing. It turned out very well. The film was shown to parents, other classes within the school, and, of course, over and over again to the children who created it. Such a production requires fairly elaborate planning, writing, and rehearsal. The children were thrilled with their creative efforts and the activity was very much worthwhile.

3. *Using filmstrips.* A relatively simple way to make films is to make filmstrips. Blank filmstrip is commercially available and can sometimes be obtained free from certain commercial photography establishments. Filmstrip-making kits are also commercially obtainable. However, it is much more economical to buy a large roll of blank filmstrip material than to purchase these kits. The kits are much too costly for the amount of material provided.

The teacher should introduce children to filmstrip-making by showing a filmstrip he or she has prepared. This step is advisable for two reasons. First, it introduces the concept of filmstrip-making to children in a manner which can be easily understood. Second, it familiarizes the teacher with the steps required to produce filmstrips. The process of making filmstrips is quite simple. The following steps outline the procedure required to make filmstrips and indicate some of the problems likely to be encountered during the process.

   a) Provide each child with a piece of paper laid out in boxes the same size as each frame on a filmstrip (see illustration). Have each child plan out the entire sequence of the filmstrip on this layout paper.

   b) Use soft-lead colored pencils or felt tip pens for writing or drawing on the film. Older children may prefer using india ink and quill pens. The writing on filmstrip is easily smudged, so care must be taken. Usually, one side of the film is duller than the other. The dull surface is much easier to write on.

   c) Encourage children who cannot write in the small space of a filmstrip frame to use several frames for their pictures and

Layout		Paper
1	8	15
2	9	16
3	0	17
4	1	18
5	12	19
6	13	20
7	14	21

Frames ➞ 1 . . . . .   First six inches
2 . . . . .   left blank for
3 . . . . .   leader into
4 . . . . .   the projector
5 . . . . .
6 . . . . .
7 . . . . .

words. Using more than one frame presents little difficulty in projecting. These films may be shown on a regular slide projector or on an overhead projector. First and second grade youngsters have been successful with filmstrip-making. Sometimes their drawings and words are difficult to decipher, but they are usually delighted with their work.

d) Provide each youngster with an opportunity to project and narrate the filmstrip for the rest of the class. Few projects will generate greater enthusiasm for sharing. This sharing step may be the most important part of filmstrip making.

e) Encourage older children to produce filmstrips for younger students. Intermediate grade children enjoy writing filmstrip stories, comic strips, illustrated math, social studies, science concepts, and other instructional and entertaining sequences for young children. Such experiences are profitable educational experiences for both younger and older participants.

4. *Use Polaroid cameras.* Polaroid cameras are an excellent instrument to use to motivate writing. They can be used for essentially the same purposes as the instamatic camera described earlier. The one different factor is the opportunity to obtain the finished photograph immediately. This speeds up the process and provides a flexibility not possible with ordinary cameras. It is emphasized, however, that immediate availability of the finished photograph does not appear to be an essential element in the successful use of photography to enhance writing activities.

SUMMARY

Most children who are unable to read are unable to write independently. Even those who are able to read fluently experience difficulty with independent writing in the initial stages. They are still struggling with the skills of manipulating a pencil and paper, forming letters, and spelling words. Obviously, this impedes fluency in independent writing. Therefore, it is beneficial to reading and writing growth to bridge the gap between the child's wealth of oral language and his temporary lack of independent writing skills. Recording the child's language provides the bridge.

The recorded story mirrors the child's *talk* and introduces him or her to the concept of authorship. Recording the child's language serves two basic purposes in literacy instruction. First, it provides the most relevant possible material for beginning reading instruction. Second, it makes instant authorship possible during that time when the child is still acquiring the prerequisite skills for independent authorship. Recording also helps children give an account of their experiences in a coherent fashion. They are authors and they can write. This sense of mastery will be invaluable to children when they begin the more laborious task of independent writing.

Recording children's observations about their world may take place in a number of different ways, including: (1) recording through artistic expression, (2) recording group accounts of experiences, (3) recording individual accounts of experiences, and (4) recording through mechanical devices.

REFERENCES

1. Lee, Doris and Van Allen, R. **Learning to Read Through Experiences.** New York: Appleton-Century-Crofts, 1963.
2. Stauffer, Russell. **The Language Experience Approach to the Teaching of Reading.** New York: Harper and Row, 1970.

4

Getting Children Started on Independent Writing

Children must be prepared for writing their first independent story. If they are not properly prepared the results will be disappointing for the children and the teacher. This chapter will consider the salient features essential to getting children started in their first independent writing experience. This goal will be accomplished by (1) analyzing the first independently written stories of five first grade children and explaining how these stories came to be written, (2) discussing the significance of the first independently written story, (3) considering three basic prerequisites for independent writing, and (4) giving and receiving words and experiences.

First Independently Written Stories

The six stories below were written by five first grade children. The stories were written in early November 1973. The teacher had been recording dictated stoies for about six weeks prior to the writing of these stories:

Story as Written	Translation of Story
My Dad And me wr bltting a Hos it was A Big Hos.	My dad and me were building a house. It was a big house.
David	David

I play in the grass And I play wih my frads And I play wih Debbie.	I play in the grass. And I play with my friends. And I play with Debbie.
Mary	Mary
Wane the poho	Winnie the Pooh
Wan evng wane wt iut to get some hane he kalimd and kalimd for hane he fnd hane.	One evening Winnie went out to get some honey. He climbed and climbed for honey. He found honey.
John	John
My Dad is nice My Mom is nice My sistrss is nice	My dad is nice. My mom is nice. My sisters are nice.
Danielle (first story)	Danielle
I like to play on the siweing with my bruthrs and Sistr.	I like to play on the swing with my brothers and sister.
Danielle (second story)	Danielle
I kak My had I fel off the bed My Mom tok Me to the hsptl.	I cracked my head. I fell off the bed. My mom took me to the hospital.
Nathalie	Nathalie

One day, while visiting in the classroom of these five children, I asked the teacher if her children had tried independent writing as yet. She replied negatively, indicating she did not believe they were ready. I then asked her to point out five children who were able to do some reading and who had been recording stories regularly. She suggested the five children whose stories appear above.

I gathered the children around a table and started their first independent writing session by asking, "Have any of you written a story by yourself?" Their chorus was unanimous: "We don't know how to write by ourselves." Nevertheless, I felt confident they could. They were much less confident. One boy asked, "What could we write about?" This query gave me an opening, and so we discussed his questions for about five minutes. Together we concluded that they should write about something that had happened to them recently. If this writing episode had not occurred on the spur of the moment, it would have been better for me to present a specific writing stimulus. But there was no time for that, so I played it by ear.

When I was assured that everyone had something to write about, I said, "There will probably be some words you want to use but don't know how to spell. When this happens I'll help you." I knew there would be many such words and I wanted them to tell me when they needed help so that I could personally instruct each child how to proceed. There were many words they did not know how to spell as their stories abundantly testify. Here is an example of what I said and did with each child when they asked for help in spelling a word:

Teacher: What is the word you want to spell, John?

John: *evening*

Teacher: What is the first sound you hear in evening? (I then pronounced *evening* with a slight but not distorted emphasis on the first sound.)

John: *e*

Teacher: Good. Write the *e*. What is the next sound you hear in *evening*? (This time I emphasized the second sound.)

John: *v*

Teacher: That's fine. Write the *v*. What is the last sound you hear in *evening*? (This time I emphasized the last sound.)

John: *ng*

Teacher: That's excellent John; *e-v-n-g* is very close to the way *evening* is spelled. You did an excellent job on that difficult word. Now, I want you to do the same thing the next time you have a word you don't know how to spell. If you need help again, let me know.

This procedure was repeated as often as necessary for each child. Gradually, some of the more confident children began to try the process without my help. Others needed my help throughout the writing of their first story. Some children catch on to this procedure and do it well from the beginning. Others, especially those who are overly concerned about making mistakes, take longer. The teacher must remain patient and supportive while children acquire sufficient independence to proceed on their own. When this stage is reached children can write independently using any words in their speaking vocabularies. Teachers who are worried about the influence this process may have on future spelling habits should refer to chapter 8 where this matter is discussed in detail. In brief, the influence is beneficial, not harmful, to spelling habits.

Forty minutes later, when the children had completed their stories, I suggested that we all go to the principal's office and read the stories to him. The principal, an extremely supportive administrator, was delighted and asked for copies to put on his bulletin board. Later, this was done. The children were proud of their work and, incidentally, pleased to visit the principal's office with something good to report. When we returned to the classroom the teacher had the children read their stories to the class. It was a proud moment for them. As I was leaving, the children asked if I could come back later in the week and do another story with them. Their achievement not only gave them positive feelings about themselves, but set off a spark among the other children. Several wanted to know when they could write a story.

A word should be said about the amount of time spent working with a relatively small group of children. The classroom teacher would normally have to carry out alone the procedures described. Can this time be justified? The answer depends on each teacher's assessment of the importance of learning to write independently and the understanding of the contribution it will make to the children. Teachers commonly spend large chunks of time teaching reading with small groups of children. When teachers realize that they are responsible for full literacy and that each branch of language arts contributes significantly to the others, they will recognize the need for proportioning their instructional time among the various language arts. In the long run, writing will strengthen and hasten the progress children make in their reading development. There is no sensible alternative to spending whatever time may be required to achieve the essential goal of teaching children to write effectively.

The Significance of the First Independently Written Story

The process children go through in writing their first stories is more important than the stories they produce. In these first stories discussed in this chapter, the children were struggling against a host of difficulties that most adults have long forgotten. Consider the difficulties they faced:

1. Their spelling skills consisted of a few sight words and two months of phonetic training in reading. They had received no formal training in the mechanics of writing. Yet they were asked to write a story and to spell as best they could any words they wished to use.
2. They had been learning to form the letters of the alphabet for only two months. It was still difficult for them to form some of the letters.
3. Previously, their ideas and words were recorded for them. Now they were their own recorders. This new mode of communicating their ideas required a new set of habits and skills.

When we allow for the difficulty and newness of the task we must consider the stories these five children wrote as quite remarkable. Their remarkableness stems not from their content, but from the effort their writing represents for these children. Therefore, the relevant question is not, "How good are these stories?" Rather, the important questions are, "Did the children enjoy their first independent writing experience?", and "Did they learn something important about the process of independent writing?" The answer to both questions is *yes*.

There are several interesting characteristics of these six stories that should be recognized. Sherlock Holmes was fond of pointing out to Watson that it is not what we observe that is important, but it is the meaning of what we observe that makes a difference in our ability to understand events that transpire daily before our eyes. It is the meaning of what you have no doubt already observed that I wish to comment further upon.

1. *The stories written by John, Nathalie, and David are well structured and the most interesting.* They also have the highest percentage of spelling

approximations, a circumstance that is not accidental or coincidental. They are more interesting stories precisely because these three children were not intimidated by the demands of spelling. Consequently, they were more willing to use whatever words were required to serve the purpose of their stories. These children subordinated the mechanics of writing to content, and the result was better writing.

2. *Danielle's first story and Mary's story are the least interesting in terms of structure and content.* They are also the two stories with the highest percentage of correctly spelled words. Again, this circumstance is not accidental or coincidental. These two girls were the most inhibited about using words they could not spell. Notably, Danielle's second story is more interesting than her first. There are more spelling approximations in her second story than in her first. The lesson is clear. To write effectively, children must be able to use whatever ideas, words, and experiences are available to them. If our teaching methods restrict the flow of words and ideas, then writing will certainly be impoverished. Children who are just beginning to write have an abundance of ideas and words to use. Research estimates that children of first grade age typically know between 6,000 and 12,000 words. They can spell only a tiny fraction of that total. When spelling and other mechanical concerns are removed as a central constraint, writing becomes immediately possible.

Skills That are Prerequisite to Independent Writing

To begin independent writing, a child must be able to talk, form the letters of the alphabet, and associate letters with speech sounds.

Talking

A normal child of school age speaks his or her native language fluently. Some children have a larger vocabulary and express themselves more clearly than others. Such differences are normal. Occasionally, a child may appear to be nonverbal or deficient in language development. Often this apparent deficiency is not a real one. For example, shyness may prevent a verbally fluent child from expressing himself in certain environments. Similarly, cultural language differences may inhibit some children from using their language freely. This is particularly true if they sense some hostility toward their different language habits.

Almost all first grade children possess sufficient language ability to enable them to write the first day they enter school. If the teacher is willing to record their conversation, they can become authors immediately. While this is not independent writing, it is an important step toward independent writing. Of the three prerequisite abilities necessary to independent writing, talking is the only one that need not be taught. It must, however, be encouraged. Because children *can* talk does not necessarily guarantee that they *will*. There are certain kinds of classroom experiences and environments that place a premium on meaningful verbal interchange between and among children and teachers. On the other hand, there are classroom experiences and environments which restrict and inhibit meaningful talk. Both situations are invariably determined by the quality, sensitivity, and effectiveness of the teaching and the environment created for teaching.

Writing the Letters of the Alphabet

In order to write independently a child must be able to form letters either in cursive or manuscript printing. Experience suggests that it is simpler for first graders to learn manuscript rather than cursive writing. The teacher should begin the task of teaching children to print early in the school year. With proper instruction and motivation most children will learn to form letters sufficiently well to begin independent writing within a range of two to four months. Instruction and appropriate practice should continue throughout the year as needed but with decreasing intensity. Handwriting practice should be limited to short periods of time suitably spaced throughout the week. Both group and individual instruction should be provided as needed. Individual instruction can be accomplished informally by circulating among the children during practice sessions helping them with letter formation and other essential details.

Whatever system of handwriting is chosen should be functional and simple. Sometimes the practice materials provided by a commercial system are useful. However, the teacher may find his or her own ideas quite as useful, particularly if they are closely related to meaningful writing. It must be kept in mind that handwriting is taught so that children can become independent writers. Consequently, neatness, legibility, penmanship, and other handwriting concepts must be subordinate to this goal.

Associating Letters With Speech Sounds

Before children enter school they learn to distinguish a laughing sound from a crying one, the sound of the wind from a siren, an angry voice from a friendly one. They have also learned the sounds of language. The proof is that they can talk. Children who have learned to talk have mastered the phonology of their language. It does not follow, however, that the typical first graders can automatically apply their knowledge of sound to the relationship which exists between letters and sounds. This must be taught.

The basic skill necessary to master letter-sound relationships is *auditory discrimination*. Auditory discrimination is the ability to distinguish the various speech sounds of the language. Children must be able to consciously distinguish one word from another and one sound within a word from another sound within a word. Once children can do this they must also learn that certain speech sounds are represented in writing by certain letters or combinations of letters. This latter step is essential in writing because it makes the connection between the visual symbol and the auditory one. As children acquire this skill they become increasingly independent in writing.

Teaching experience suggests that the following sequence of auditory discrimination exercises are beneficial in developing children's awareness of letter-sound relationships: (1) rhyming sounds, (2) beginning single consonant sounds, (3) ending single consonant sounds, (4) beginning consonant clusters and digraphs, (5) ending consonant clusters and digraphs, and (6) vowel sounds.

Words and Experience

Children have words and experiences at their command. Writing is a way to explore the meaning of experience. Words are the tools which children use to possess their own experience, to know themselves, to know the world around them.

In a metaphorical sense, teachers are the keepers of the keys to children's words and experience. They can lock them up for the duration of the school day or they can unlock children's words and experience and foster their use. They can do more than merely unlock the storehouse. They can, through the selection and direction of daily classroom activity, have a hand in stocking the storehouse of words and experience, and the subsequent use of them in writing.

The fundamental goal of teaching is to enrich and extend experience and, through it, to enrich and extend the thought structures and the command of words which are the tools of an educated mind. Ted Hughes (1, p. 124), an English poet and a person greatly interested in children's writing, has decribed something of what I have in mind but in words that I cannot match:

> Because it is occasionally possible, just for brief moments to find the words that will unlock the doors of all those many mansions inside the head and express something—perhaps not much, just something—of the crush of information that presses in on us from the way a crow flies over and the way a man walks and the look of a street and from what we did one day a dozen years ago. Words that will express something of the deep complexity that makes us precisely the way we are, from the momentary effect of the barometer to the force that created men distinct from trees. Something of the inaudible music that moves us along in our bodies from moment to moment like water in a river. Something of the spirit of the snowflake in the water of the river. Something of the duplicity and the relatively and the merely fleeting quality of all this. Something of the almighty importance of it and something of the utter meaninglessness. And when words can manage something of this, and manage it in a moment of time, and in that same moment make out of it all the vital signature of a human being—not of an atom, or of a geometrical diagram, or of a heap of lenses—but a human being, we call it poetry.[1]

SUMMARY

Getting children started on independent writing is easy only if one is prepared to make the commitment in time, energy, and self. Once the teachers have made a start, they must analyze the writing experience and the stories that result from it. On the basis of their findings, they determine what further steps must follow to improve both their performance and that of the children. They must be aware of the prerequisite abilities children must have before independent authorship is possible and must provide for them. This goal requires designing instruction so that children will reach that stage as soon as possible. Finally, they must be aware of their role as giver and receiver of words and experience. The teachers who are prepared to do all this will get children off to a good start in independent writing.

REFERENCES

1. Hughes, Ted. **Poetry in the Making: An Anthology of Poems and Programmes from Listening and Writing.** London: Faber and Faber, 1967. (Reprinted by permission of Faber and Faber, Ltd.)

Working on the Inner World: Therapy in Writing

Writing can be therapeutic. The expression *therapy in writing* is used in this book to mean that writing can serve to enhance the social and emotional adjustment and well-being of children. Therapy in writing does not happen automatically, nor does it occur in all circumstances. Writing need not be read by someone or reacted to in order to be therapeutic. But therapy is more likely to occur when a child's writing is properly received, intelligently analyzed, and sensitively responded to.

The term *inner world* refers to all those thoughts, feelings, and experiences that are part of our interior, private existence. We know something of the inner world of children from observing them at play, through analyzing their creative products, and from talking with them. In this chapter we are concerned with that which may be learned about the inner world of childhood through analysis of children's writings.

This chapter will consider four major themes: (1) how to receive children's writings, (2) how writing can be used to help children solve life's problems, (3) how writing can strengthen children's self-confidence and self-image, and (4) how writing can help children express the emotions that living generates.

The Art of Receiving Children's Writing

The effectiveness of children's writing is partially dependent on the reception this writing receives. The teacher whose behavior demonstrates to children that he or she can be trusted to receive and respect their gifts has discovered the

starting point for successful teaching of writing. Here are some ideas that will help you receive children's writing with the dignity, respect, and appreciation it deserves.

1. *Designate a specific place where children can deposit personal writing.* Mearns (1, p. 22) discovered the wisdom of this practice early in his teaching career:

   Some of the technique of approach I knew, but not much. Of one thing I was sure, however: place must be provided for the reception of material. One cannot say, "Give it to me." It requires a special kind of courage, which the creative life does not cultivate, to walk up to any person and present the things of one's private endeavor.

2. *Provide rest from constant creative activity and replenish the child's inner resources during the rest intervals.* Few things are more draining than constant creative activity unrelieved by periods of rest and refreshment.

3. *Be prepared to work with opportunities as they arise.* Children's writing is often spontaneous. One never knows when a serendipitous event will occur, but when it does, the teacher must be sufficiently resourceful to use it wisely.

One day, as I was writing this book, my nine year old daughter came into the office and asked, "Can I use the typewriter?" I was sorely tempted to say, "No, can't you see I'm busy?" Instead, I said, "What do you need it for, Amy?" She replied, "I have a poem to write." Well, I relinquished the typewriter immediately. When I returned a half hour later she had pecked out this poem on the typewriter:

> The Beechnuts
>
> Beechnuts, beechnuts,
> Flying away,
> Drift to the river
> And float away,
> Down the field,
> Past the cows,
> Past the sheep,
> And past the boughs.
> Hello sea!
>
>   Amy
>   Age 9

It is a lovely poem because it reflects her experience with the large beechnut trees in our yard with the River Ouse that flows nearby. This poem sparked a short burst of poetry writing. Perhaps this outburst occurred partly because she was pleased with the poem and partly because she knew that her poem pleased her father. After this initial short outburst of creative activity, Amy did not write again for three or four weeks. As good fortune would have it, I spontaneously did the right thing by relinquishing the typewriter. What I did was not much, but I did do the right thing at a critical moment. Teachers, likewise, must be prepared to react rightly and wisely when the critical moment arrives. Otherwise, the moment may pass, and the child, the teacher, and the world will be the poorer for it. Good teaching requires intuitive reflexes.

4. *Remember that all development proceeds by stages.* Piaget's research on cognitive development in children has established that mental development proceeds through four natural stages. These stages cannot be hurried, though they can be qualitatively enriched if the child is given appropriate experiences.

   The development of artistic personality requires a similar freedom. Children's writing abilities must be allowed to grow gradually through their natural stages of development. When this natural growth is severely interrupted by unnatural constraints, such as imposition of inappropriate standards or lack of appreciation and respect, something of the artistic personality dies. On the other hand, appropriate writing experiences can significantly influence the child's development. Writing development must not be rushed. Children must be paced through the natural stages of writing growth. Teachers must know something about the natural stages of development in written expression, therefore, and must be able to provide the environmental conditions under which written expression flourishes.

5. *Recognize that creative writing is not a mysterious, unknowable process.* Basically, effective teaching of writing requires intuitive teachers who trust and respect children. They must know something about literature, poetry, and the other art forms. It is important that this knowledge be combined with personal experience in the arts. These experiences need not be sophisticated or professional, but they must be sincere and genuine. Teachers who ask children to write poetry, for example, must have the courage to write poetry themselves or they will never understand what it is they are trying to teach. The teacher's creative products can be shared with children not only as models but for children's enjoyment and criticism as well.

How Writing Can Help Children Solve Personal Problems

Children often reveal personal problems in their writing. What motivates the choice of this medium is speculative. Perhaps it is because writing is private and intimate, and also provides an element of detachment, since the message is mediated by an impersonal set of symbols set down on paper. One may communicate effectively in writing without the necessity of the face-to-face confrontation that oral communication requires. The natural intimacy that writing provides makes it an ideal medium for communicating personal problems.

When asked to provide some examples of personal problems that were first communicated to them in writing, a small group of teachers listed dozens of examples. The teachers indicated that none of these examples had been revealed to them orally. Some examples are listed below to illustrate the range and type of problems typically disclosed.

1. A first grade child who regularly went without breakfast because there was no one to prepare it for him.
2. A seventh grade child who often missed school because a classmate was extorting his lunch money.
3. An eighth grade child who had written a great deal of poetry and wanted to share it with someone but was afraid it might be rejected.
5. A sixth grade child who was ashamed of her shabby clothing.
6. A fifth grade child who had great anxieties because he did not know who his father was.
7. A third grade child who was afraid that her father would harm her while he was drinking.

These examples represent but a sampling of problems that children share in their writing. It must be pointed out that stating a problem does not necessarily solve it. Sometimes, however, it does lead to a solution. Sometimes, simply having someone in whom to confide a problem provides release from anxiety, fear, or concern. The selections of children's writing below illustrate some specific instances where writing served children in solving some of life's problems.

Occasionally a child will state a problem in language so sincere and naked that one feels the pain and anguish of the writer. The poem below, taken from Jack Beckett's *The Keen Edge* (2, p. 133), illustrates this point:

> Ho God
> Help me to get
> Over things
> That worry
> Me so, Help me
> As I get older.
> I feel that I get
> Left out of things.
> Over children
> Have fathers
> But I have not
> They talk about
> The trips they take
> With there perents
> But I say
> I am happy

But deep down inside me
I feel hurt.
And it hurts more
And more all the time
Ho God please help me . . .

In this poem the writer pleads for someone to understand his pain and loneliness. In it he draws aside, momentarily, the curtain that veils his inner world. Writing the poem does not solve the actual problems. The problems will not now disappear. He is still lonely; he still has no father; he still hurts inside; he still feels left out. But in the subjective sense there is a potential gain. Articulating a problem is often enough impetus to start an interior solution. This is a gain. In this poem the writer has related his inner feelings to outward circumstances. He may now cope with his feelings more effectively. Also, there is now the possibility that he may enlist the forces of his outer world to assist in a solution. His teacher may be the one to begin this process.

Writing of this sort serves two important purposes. First, it communicates with the outer world. Second, the writer communicates with himself. Writing that integrates the inner world with the outward circumstances of life promotes mental health. In this sense, writing is therapeutic.

Ordinarily we do not think of second graders as having many of life's problems to worry about. The accounts below dispel that notion. Sometimes children's problems have life and death implications. The seven year old fatherless boy who wrote the following account was genuinely concerned about the safety of his four year old brother who was left at home, unattended, while his mother worked. He wrote this brief story:

> I am worry about my little Brothr becase my lettle Brothr be at home Bi hes self and I am saad Becas smbide can brake in my house.
>
> > Joe
> > Age 7

Joe's teacher contacted the school social worker who was able to help the mother make more suitable arrangements for the care of the little brother. Joe had never discussed his fear prior to writing this account. Why he chose to reveal his worry in written rather than oral form cannot be known. Perhaps the privacy of the written word had some effect. There is a certain anonymity possible in writing that is absent in direct oral conversation.

You will note two interesting characteristics of Joe's writing. First, he spells words phonetically as best he can. His phonetic logic is quite good. Second, his syntactic structures reveal the presence of a nonstandard dialect as shown in such phrases as, "I am worry," and "my lettle Brothr be at home."

Two questions naturally arise. Would Joe have communicated his problem in writing if the use of his natural language with its dialect characteristics had been unacceptable to his teacher? Probably not. If his native language had been rejected, his story could not have been written because it is the only language option he has. Would Joe have been able to communicate his message at all if his phonetic spelling approximations had not been encouraged? Probably not. Many children avoid writing because the words they want to use are not within their spelling abilities and the dictionary is still too difficult and tedious to manage. During the early stages of writing development, phonetic spelling is a logical and productive alternative. It does not interfere with meaning and it has other important benefits as well (see chapter 8).

The three stories below as well as Joe's story were written in response to the teacher's suggestion that the class might want to write about "Things I Often Worry About." All four accounts were written on the same occasion.

> I often worre about my friends moving away. I often worre about rain in the nite. I often worre about cars in the nite.
>
> > Marilyn
> > Age 7

> I often worry about my Gramma because she lives all alone and I go over to her house sometimes.
>
> > Tammy
> > Age 7

> I often worry about trying to do work in schol. Kids have trouble doing work. Kids get hurt in schol.
>
> > David
> > Age 8

When these stories are analyzed for content and symbolic meaning, some common childhood concerns become apparent. Three of the four stories reveal a concern about aloneness or loneliness. Marilyn's concern centers on the common childhood fear of darkness or night. David is troubled by school problems. When children's writings are read with the intent of understanding their content and symbolic meaning, teachers can respond to the needs the writings reveal. Unfortunately, analysis of children's writing is frequently limited to a search for mechanical and grammatical errors. This focus is too narrow to be productive. It unnecessarily and unnaturally limits the diagnostic and therapeutic uses to which children's writings can be put.

The teacher who collected the "I often worry" stories read them to gain insight into the problems of her children. She followed up her analysis in four significant ways:

1. She encouraged oral discussion of the most common concerns the writings revealed. These discussions were informal and often impromptu. Sometimes they were conducted with subgroups, other times with the whole class.
2. She located specific stories and poems that dealt with aloneness, fear of the unknown, and other potential problem areas revealed by her analy-

sis. The selected literature was read to the children. In some instances books were made available for those who were able to read.

3. She encouraged the children to draw, paint, or use other art media to depict the things that worried them.

4. She responded directly to indivdual needs where more personal intervention seemed warranted. The most dramatic result of her personal intervention was the solving of the crisis of Joe's little brother. More commonly her intervention took the form of a personal conversation or a specific act of kindness, praise, or approval.

Writing is not a panacea for solving childhood problems. But it does give the child an additional way of coping with problems. It also gives the teacher an additional way of knowing and understanding children's problems.

How Writing can Strengthen Children's Self-confidence and Self-image

One of the general functions of language is to serve as a vehicle for the emotional needs of the normally developing personality. Most commonly these needs are expressed through oral language. Writing is a way of extending the repertory of release mechanisms for personality expression. In writing, the product is permanent. Written language can be examined, compared, revised, extended, and revisited. Oral language has no such permanent quality. Once words are spoken, they cannot be retracted, revised, or even remembered for very long. While oral language serves the immediate need for emotional release, it cannot serve the long-range needs as well as writing can.

Literacy, in its highest sense, not only broadens the mind, but strengthens personality as well. Case histories drawn from the files of reading clinics amply substantiate this statement. When literacy is impaired, personality may be injured. A child who cannot read or write satisfactorily is often treated as a failure. He or she may react to this circumstance by behaving in unacceptable ways. Children who have difficulty achieving literacy may lose confidence in themselves and begin to think they are stupid or abnormal. Such children often seek help, either directly or indirectly, from teachers. The following story illustrates just such a case.

Something Concerning a Matter in School

I need some help in trying to do good in school if I can try and stop playing around like a little kid. Maybe I could get something done and get down to work because I don't want to fell and go back in stead of forward. If I do, my friends and my mother are going to tell me that I play too much, or I don't do enough of this or that. The reason I am talking about this is because I think it is a

problem for me to try to solve with a little help. I know a teacher
that is trying to help me and so far I am doing good as far as she is
concerned, but she said I could do better.

Keith
Age 14

Keith's school experience had been a history of difficulty with reading and
writing. He seldom wrote. He read poorly. Keith was failing in school and felt
the pressure of this failure from parents, teachers, and friends. His behavior in
and out of school had become increasingly erratic. In short, his self-confidence
and self-image were disintegrating. Finally, a teacher *discovered* him and
began to restore his shattered confidence by successfully tutoring him in reading and writing. The change in his attitude was dramatic. He wrote the account
recorded above for his English teacher just after being discovered.

From a literary standpoint his account is not remarkable. However, the
human element of this story is compelling. It represents a number of significant
personal revelations: (1) an explanation and apology for past behavior, (2) a
personal resolve to improve his behavior, and (3) a plea for understanding and
help.

The English teacher who received this composition did not offer the help
requested. Unthinkingly, he red-penciled the mechanical and grammatical
errors, gave the composition a grade of *C*, and wrote at the bottom, "All
teachers can help you individually after school." This response, whether intended or not, was a rejection of a gift of writing. Worse, it was also a rejection
of the giver. There was no recognition that grading and marking were irrelevant
to Keith's personal circumstances. There was no personal response to Keith's
cry for help except for the unhelpful comment that aid was obtainable from all
teachers.

Fortunately, this story had a happy ending. Usually, they do not. Children
like Keith often become school dropouts forever denied the opportunity to
achieve literacy and, through it, the potential they possess. Keith's self-confidence was gradually restored as he acquired the skills of reading and writing.
Cases like Keith's are common when successful literacy instruction has been
achieved after initial failure. More common, but less noticed, are those instances
in which literacy instruction has gone well. Children whose reading skills give
them access to literature and whose writing skills enable them to produce
poetry, stories, and other accounts are in a better position to explore the dimensions of their inner worlds and their relationships to the outer world.

The story below is an interesting one because it was written by a boy who
reads and writes exceptionally well. Nevertheless, he is extremely sensitive to
society's treatment of children who cannot read. In this story seven year old
Terrance has provided a scenario of the kind of therapeutic outlook society
ought to have toward the child who is having difficulty in school. Many of Terrance's friends could not read or write and one suspects that he knows what
actually happens to them and what ought to happen to them.

Can't you read?

Once upon a time in a school was a boy. He couldn't read or
jump. He could not add, Win he got eight years old he weat an a
farm. To pick coting and work "but . . . He Still couldn't read.
Well son you did a good job . . . Thank you: but I can't read! That
is ok you are a good worker. You may stay here or go home. Hurry!

Terrance
Age 7

Writing plays an important role in strengthening the self-image of children. The author recorded a conversation between a fourth grade boy and his
teacher. The conversation was about a story he had recently written. The conversation went like this:

Tommy approached his teacher who had just entered the room with a visitor (the author). "Miss Keense," he stammered shyly, "there's a story I want
to show you." After a brief pause Tommy added, without conviction, "You
might not like it." Throughout the reading Tommy watched Miss Keense's
face anxiously for clues to her reaction. So absorbed was he that he completely
ignored the visitor standing three feet away recording this conversation.
Tommy evidently discerned approval in Miss Keense's face, for suddenly a
bright smile lit up his face. Boldly, now, he asserted, "This next part is going
to be funny," and pointed to a passage in his story.

No one who saw this exchange could doubt that an important emotional
transaction had occurred between Tommy and his teacher. Miss Keense did
think his story was funny. Tommy was overwhelmed with pride in his authorship and the joy of sharing. The teacher's approval of his efforts delighted him.
Rushing off from the encounter he remarked with considerable cockiness, "I'm
going to write a better one."

The positive feelings released in children because of a successful writing
experience enhance their self-image. This self-image is further strengthened
when they find that their teacher, parents, and classmates approve of their efforts. Hughes Mearns was never more insightful than when he asserted, "It is
not enough to discern a native gift; it must be enticed out again and again. It
needs exercise in an atmosphere of approval. Above all it must be protected
against the annihilating effect of social condemnation" (1, p. 268).

How Writing Helps Children Express Their Emotions

Children experience the full range of emotions that are common among adults:
fear, anger, jealousy, hatred, joy, love, happiness, pride, and so on. Children express their feelings through oral language communication and act-
ing out. However, there are occasions when neither of these common outlets for

emotion is adequate. This fact alone clearly makes the point that the ability to write adds a significant dimension to an individual's repertory of release mechanisms for self-expression.

The stories and poems in this section illustrate some of the ways children express common emotional feelings in their writing.

Jennifer's story. Jennifer's story illustrates the importance of knowing the personal circumstances of the child. It also demonstrates that writing may serve a therapeutic function even when the teacher is unaware of the symbolic meaning of the child's writing. This story was written at school by my own daughter. The teacher was unaware that the situations described in the story were real rather than imaginary events.

Much of what children write appears to have only a surface meaning. Often what appear to be imaginary events are symbolic descriptions of children's personal circumstances. Jennifer's story appears to be an imaginary encounter of a child with an imaginary witch. In fact, from Jennifer's point of view, this story may indeed be an imaginary account. But it is also a symbolic representation of real events in her life.

Lisa and Griselda

Once upon a time there was a witch called Griselda   She was a nasty witch   She was always telling Lisa her servant to clean up her room   One day Griselda said go to the store and buy some eggs   Lisa was in a hurry and she dropped all the eggs   The witch was mad at her   One day the witch was going to her friends house and took Lisa with her   They stayed too long because the witch was talking to her friend it was getting dark and Lisa was getting afraid   Lisa did not know they were staying all night One day Griselda told Lisa to go to the store to buy some bread   There was a box of bread and she did not know how to get the bread out so she asked the man in the store   One day the witch took Lisa to a witches party   First the witch opened the presents   Then they played chasing games

Jennifer
Age 5

Lisa's adventures represent the combined real life experiences of Jennifer and her sister, Amy. All of Lisa's adventures had their real life counterparts in the month preceding the writing of this story. The witch in Jennifer's story is her parents and Griselda's behavior represents the actual behavior of Jennifer's parents. For example, Jennifer's sister, Amy, was the little girl who broke the eggs on the way home from the store. Griselda (Jennifer's mother) scolded Lisa (Amy) for being careless. Lisa, the servant, (Jennifer) is often told to clean her room by Griselda (either parent). Likewise, the other adventures of Lisa and Griselda can be traced to recent behaviors of Jennifer, her family, or her parents.

In Jennifer's story, the witch represents the bad parents who make demands, hold expectations, and discipline children. Jennifer writes, "They stayed too long," and "Lisa did not know they were staying all night," and "Lisa did not know how to get the bread out." Possibly these are references to a long time away from home and the familiar. Finally, the story ends with the comment, "Then they played chasing games." Here is a hint of a resolution in that there is fun for children too.

Throughout this story Jennifer is symbolically expressing her real-life anxieties, anger, frustrations, and resolution through displacement and the use of the witch archetype. Writing is a healthy and helpful way for her to vent her feelings. Children need emotional outlets. Writing gives the child another release mechanism to verbalize and reflect on life's problems and to vent excess emotion that otherwise might be repressed.

Teachers must realize that much of what children write has a symbolic meaning. Teachers will not always be able to identify and interpret the meaning of what children write, but if they know that much of what children write has a symbolic meaning, they will be better prepared to understand the therapeutic function of writing.

Mary's poem. Very young children may surprise us with the depth of their emotions. The following poem was written by a six year old girl:

> We Love
>
> We can love
> If white love
> Can't you love?
> Some want to love
> Some do not
>
> Mary
> Age 6

The poem reveals sadness, love, and puzzlement about a white world she already suspects is on the verge of rejecting her love, and by extension, her. In these few lines Mary indicts the white world for its racial hatred. Innocently, she wonders about the worst social disease known to man—prejudice. The poem shows how easily even young children express their deepest feelings in written form. This is not uncommon, as the next poem reveals.

Jennifer's poem. Adults are not accustomed to recognizing the profound thoughts of children. We are tempted to believe that the innocent minds of children are also shallow. Not so, as Jennifer's poem shows:

> I Wonder Why
>
> I wonder why there is not a black Santa Claus
> I wonder why Christmas only comes once a year

I wonder why I don't have a pair of new shoes
I wonder why it can't be a good Halloween
I wonder why someone stole our car
I wonder why the sky is full of pollution
I wonder why my grandmother is dead
I wonder why my daddy won't take us to dinner.

Jennifer
Age 6

Are you surprised that a six year old child worries about such weighty matters as prejudice, poverty, crime, pollution, justice, and death? The deep emotions stirring in Jennifer's mind are not unusual among young children. Jennifer has stated her feelings more profoundly in this poem than many children her age do. But it would be an underestimation of the emotional and mental capacity of children to believe that young children do not think and feel deeply. The full range of emotional experience common to adults is often felt by children as well. Writing gives children an opportunity to handle their emotions therapeutically.

Janet's story. When children express their emotions honestly, there is a profound effect on both the writer and the reader. The emotions revealed in children's writing is sometimes so moving that it brings tears to the reader's eyes. The following story has this effect on me:

I Have Friends in Heaven

"Look at this," mom said, pointing to an article in the newspaper. "The poor boy. Isn't it so very sad." She showed me the article. I read about one paragraph, and I couldn't bear to read another word. Staring out at me from the paper was a picture of a small boy, perhaps five years old. He was peering through the bars of a crib in the isolation ward of a hospital. His hair was bright red and his smiling little face was sprinkled with hundreds of freckles. David Gregory, a victim of a fatal disease, Luekemia, was playing with a toy airplane and grinning, possibly one of the last smiles he would ever show. In less than a month, David would celebrate his sixth birthday, maybe.

We called this little boy's parents and made arrangements to meet him. He came from a family of seven children, and his parents were very poor. So you can see that even though they wanted to, his mother and father couldn't get him all that David wanted and needed.

Almost every Sunday, we took him somewhere, usually the Zoo, which was his favorite place. We tried to show him a good time, but it ended up with him showing us a good time. We stopped at a store one day, and had him pick out something he wanted. He chose a farm set, and almost cried when he got it, because he was so happy.

I had been taking dance lessons ever since I was four, and was almost eight when I met David. We had a dance recital every

year in which I had a few solos. This year we invited David to attend. We got front row seats for him and his family, and after I had
performed, David came backstage and gave me a dozen beautiful,
red roses.

We exchanged letters and phone calls for about another
month or two. At Easter, David didn't forget me nor I him. It was
soon after Easter that we recieved a call from his mother telling us
that David had passed away, and inviting us to his funeral. Well,
of course we went, still in shock, even though we had expected it.
Ever since we had known David, we prayed every day.

On the sad day of the funeral, we said our good-byes to the
tiny child, whom we had come to love so much. In his hand he
held a baby rose from the spray I had sent.

This is a tragic story in many ways, but not entirely. David
showed me what real courage is. He also taught me that there is
joy and reward in giving. What began as pity changed to admira-
tion, for I got as much, or more from knowing David, than I gave to
him.

I truly have a friend in heaven.

Janet
Age 12

Janet's beautiful story and the many others I have collected over the
years, have convinced me that writing makes an enormous contribution to the
emotional well-being of those who write as well as those who read. Writing
fosters good mental health. Children can gain, through their writing, a release
from anger and tension as well as an opportunity to express joy, love, friendship, sorrow, and a host of other feelings. One need only look at the material
young children write to see how often conflict, worry, happiness, and other
strong emotions are revealed. There can be no doubt that writing can make a
significant contribution to the emotional well-being of children.

SUMMARY

This chapter has presented four major concepts: (1) how to receive children's
writing, (2) how writing can help children solve life's problems, (3) how writing
can strengthen children's self-confidence and self-image, and (4) how writing
can help children express the emotions that life generates.

Receiving children's writing is an art. Its successful implementation requires these five steps: (1) designating a private place for children to deposit
their writing, (2) providing rest from creative activity and replenishing
children's inner resources, (3) responding to writing opportunities spontaneously as they arise, (4) recognizing the developmental stages of writing growth,
and (5) knowing how to manage and motivate a writing program.

The samples of children's writing included in this chapter document the
fact that children often reveal personal problems in their writing. When
teachers respond to these problems sensitively they have an additional way of
coping with the daily challenges that teaching presents.

Successful writing experiences positively influence children's self-confidence and self-image. A well-managed writing program assures each child a continuous flow of reward and instructional criticism which enhances his or her awareness of his or her own developing abilities and attitudes.

Like adults, children experience a wide range of emotions. The personality constantly seeks outlets for these feelings. When children's emotions are not wisely channelled or dealt with, they can be damaging to the children, to classroom morale, and to academic achievement. Writing is an ideal medium for dealing with children's emotional experiences.

REFERENCES

1. Mearns, Hughe. **Creative Power: The Education of Youth in the Creative Arts.** New York: Dover Publications 1929, 1958. (Reprinted through the permission of the publisher.)
2. Beckett, Jack. **The Keen Edge.** London: Blackie, 1965.

6

The Role of Imitation
in Learning to Write

This chapter is concerned with the nature and purpose of imitation in teaching writing. It consists of three distinct parts. First, the nature and purpose of imitation are presented. It is suggested that there are three logical stages in imitative behavior in writing, including close imitation, loose imitation, and creative modeling. Second, reading to children is presented as an effective and pleasurable way to expose children to language models which may expand vocabulary, introduce useful syntactic and grammatical options, and increase children's conceptual and experiential understanding of prose and poetry. Third, writing by imitating language models is discussed as a teaching technique which has a beneficial influence on the quality and quantity of children's writing.

The Nature and Purpose of Imitation in Writing

Imitation has an honorable history but a bad reputation. Jack London, Winston Churchill, and Somerset Maugham, among others, owe a great debt to writers who preceded them. These three writers, and countless others as well, imitated the writing styles of others in the course of developing their own unique writing talents. There is no doubt that imitation in writing has a more honorable history than many writers are prepared to admit.

In spite of the honorable role imitation has played in the history of writing there remains a curious aversion to its open discussion and a prohibition on its practice. Writers and educators alike are fond of describing the mysterious dangers lurking for those who indulge in its iniquitous practice. The detractors of imitation are fond of claiming that imitation erodes personal integrity, saps creative energy, compromises originality, and diminishes individuality. These pronouncements have their roots in a misunderstanding of the role imitation plays in learning and an inordinately narrow definition of imitation.

When children imitate, they are usually unaware of having done so. Children assimilate what they see, hear, and read. Later, residual elements appear in their talk and in their writing. For example, a young child telling or writing a story may unconsciously use a specific word, phrase, or sentence recently heard or read. Whole plots and even entire stories may be thus imitated. Most children seem to assume that these imitated elements of writing are of their own invention. Such imitation sometimes tempts teachers to admonish children for stealing someone else's ideas. Such admonitions are inappropriate, for children are seldom aware of their own imitations. Even when they are aware, they rightly assume that imitation is appropriate behavior.

Imitation is an integral part of learning. For example, the more effective you are as a reader, the more likely you are to imitate the writing you have read. Anyone who reads thoughtfully is indebted to the authors he or she has read. The effective reader inevitably retains concepts and content and, in some instances, something of an author's writing style. Perhaps the reader will have assimilated someone's techniques of presentation, sentence structure, vocabulary, imagery, or metaphor. Many such "stylistic" items are intentionally and unintentionally stored in the memory of the keen reader and often are drawn upon when writing and speaking. This storage and retrieval may be practiced at a conscious or unconscious level. Nevertheless, it is practiced. This is a form of imitation, and to deny it is to deny that one learns from reading what others write.

There are three stages that children seem to go through in imitative behavior in writing. Each stage will be defined, discussed, and illustrated under the labels of close imitation, loose imitation, and creative modeling.

Close Imitation

Close imitation occurs when a child reproduces verbatim, or in summary from, a story, poem, or other account which he or she has heard or read. Close imitation usually happens without conscious awareness that someone else's work is being imitated. In close imitation, for example, a child may write a story which is a summary account of a familiar story. Close imitation is common in the story telling and writing of young children. It need not worry the teacher or parent. It must not be punished. It should simply be regarded as a transitional stage in story telling and writing which some children pass through.

The following story is an example of close imitation in writing. It is a summary of "Goldilocks and the Three Bears" retold as the author remembered it. This story was accepted by the teacher with praise because she recognized the stage of imitation that it represented.

The Three Bears

The three bears lived in the woods Thare was father bear and mother bear. and baby bear. Thare house was made out of wood. And thare was a girl named Golde lox. She went to the three bears house when the bears wer away from the house because they wer wateing for thare pareg to ceool.

Ted
Age 7

Loose Imitation

Loose imitation occurs when a child uses basic structures from a story, poem, or other source but adds certain unique contributions not contained in the original source. Sometimes children consciously use loose imitation to produce a specific effect. More commonly, children use familiar literary structures unconsciously because these structures are embedded in their memory. When literature and its various devices have become part of a child's thought structure, they are likely to be used in some form when the child writes or talks.

Loose imitation occurs commonly in children's writing. Indeed, some techniques for stimulating writing and story telling are based on a deliberate encouragement of loose imitation. Writing techniques based on the use of patterned writing, for example, are based on loose imitation (1).

The story "Groovylocks" is a deliberate use of loose imitation. The author used the plot and setting of "Goldilocks and the Three Bears" as the model for her own story. The story is an excellent example of the use of loose imitation which is one step beyond close imitation.

Groovylocks

Once upon a time there was a pad located smack-dab in the middle of the sticks, which had air conditioning, console stereo, and a color tv. In this pad lived Big Daddy, Big Mama and Big Baby, in that order. One bright sunshiney spring morn Big Daddy and Big Baby woke up to a tang and bagel breakfast. Big Daddy, slumping down in his big chair took a bite out of the steaming bagel. Big Daddy yelped "Don't you think this bagel is just a bit too hot to eat!" So then Big Mama and Big Baby tried theirs and agreed. Big Mama suggested that they take a walk to give the bagels a chance to cool.

Groovylocks, a girl wearing cutoffs and beads came walking down the street looking for a place to rest. She went up the walk and knocked on the door. No one answered. So she knocked again, the door creaked open a little bit. She called and when no one answered she walked right in. When she saw the Tang and bagels she exclaimed "Far out, finally I can get some good grub." She sat down in Big Daddy's chair and took a bite out of the bagel and yelled "Ouch, man this bagel is hot!" Then she went over to

Big Mama's bagel and took a bite out of the bagel but it was too cold so she then went over to Big Baby's and found it was just groovy and ate it all up.

Groovylocks got a little tired so she went into the living room. She sat down in Big Daddy's chair but it was too hard for her. Groovy then walked over to Big Mama's chair and sat down but it was far too soft. She spotted Big Baby's bean bag chair and said "Cool daddy, this is more my bag." After a while she almost dozed off so she got up and decided to look for a bed.

Groovylocks lazily walked up the stairs and into Big Daddy and Big Mama's room and lied down on the biggest bed but it was really hard so she tried the smaller of the two and found it was really too soft, just not her type! Groovylocks noticed that the other door was open that led into another room so she went in and saw a water bed, she tried it and said "Dig that H_2O."

She feel asleep within minutes without realizing she was so tired. A few minutes later they walked in the house. Big Daddy looked at the table and yelled "Somebody's been eatin' my bagel."

"Somebody's been eating my bagel too!" screamed Big Mama.

"Somebody's been eating mine too and it's all gone." sobbed Big Baby.

Big Daddy's voice from the living room said "Hey somebody's been sitting in my chair."

Big Mama and Big Baby went in to investigate. Big Mama screamed "Somebody's been sitting in my chair too." "Somebody's been sitting in my bean bag chair and the shape is all messed up." cried Big Baby.

"Something phoey's going on around here, let's have a look upstairs." suggested Big Mama. So they climbed the stairs and went into Big Daddy's and Big Mama's room only to find the beds messed.

They decided to have a look in Big Baby's room. They went in and saw Groovylocks lying on the bed asleep. At that moment Groovylocks woke up to the puzzled face of Big Daddy, the astonished face of Big Mama and the frightened face of Big Baby.

"What are you doing here?" asked Big Daddy as Groovylocks tried to ease her way toward the door and stairs.

"Well . . . um . . . I um . . . I've been walking for a few days you see man, my Ol' Lady and Ol' Man don't know what's happening so I'm running away to my aunt's," answered Groovy, "She's a real swinger!"

"Oh, you poor child why don't you stay with us a few days to rest up." said Big Mama sympathetically.

"OK, lady," answered Groovylocks, "thanks!"

In those few days they got to know each other pretty well. Then on the day she was to leave they asked Groovylocks to stay, but she said no that she couldn't because she wanted to go live with her swinging aunt, *GOLDILOCKS*.

Creative Modeling

The third stage a child may reach in imitative behavior in writing is the stage of creative modeling. In this stage the child may use some basic theme, plot, structure, or model common in literary works. However, the written product itself is unique. For example, a child may write a poem using a traditional verse form, but produce a poem that is an original contribution in itself. Or, a child may write a story using traditional literary devices to awaken interest, enhance characterization, establish mood, and so on. The examples below are of the creative modeling variety.

> Fog drifts in patches
> Seeking to blanket the earth
> With its wet grayness
> The wind wimpers its sadness
> Waiting to reclaim glory
>
> Jimmy
> Age 12

In this poem Jimmy has used the traditional Japanese poetic verse form called Tanka. This verse form uses thirty-one syllables in a five line composition structure of 5-7-5-7-7. The element of imitation is present since the verse form is not original. But, the poem is an original contribution representing the creative modeling stage. The author supplies his own ideas and words within a disciplined model to create his own unique poetry.

Autumn

The Autumn pays us a visit. It comes strongly like an army of ten million men. Each man of the ten million strikes a blow with his axe and each one kills a leaf. The birds zoom in like jet planes killing off the juicy red berries. The brilliant red apples fall and blow up the leaves bases. The army of leaves are finished they all lay on the ground like a corpse. The trees stand bare because of the battle. But the army of wind isn't satisfied they keep on striking killing off the petals on the last flowers. It just keeps on conquering the wing things. It knocks off the conkers so the little children can pick them up and the evil army faints seeing they have for once helped someone so they become silent for a moment. Only one moment, they can't waste any time they have to get on with their evil conquering. Then the leaves change colors on their carpet they become red and yellow and different golden colors as though they were turning into ghosts going to haunt the wind. The leaves call for reinforcements, the raindrops. The raindrops come and kill of the wind. The armys go away. The people pick the rosy red apples now because they daren't come out while

the battle was on. The harvest starts and the stubble is burnt reminding children to get their bonfires ready and to be buying their
rockets and bangers, airbomb repeaters and all the other fireworks. The children find the biggest potatoes and hide them so
their mums don't find them and use them. Then on bonfire night
they bring them out of their hiding places and roast them.

Paul
Age 10

In this account, a young English lad explains a common occurrence in nature through the brilliant use of the metaphor of war among the forces of nature.
The use of metaphor in this fashion is not an original literary device discovered
by Paul. Unquestionably, he has heard and read similar descriptions in literature and has chosen to use this literary model in his own writing. In this sense,
there is an element of imitation. But the element of creative modeling is clearly
present in that the author supplies his own unique descriptions to sustain and
heighten the effect of the metaphor.

Jimmy's poem and Paul's story were modeled on traditional literary forms
and represent the attainment of the stage of imitative behavior described as
creative modeling. This does not mean there are no weaknesses in their writing.
Still, making allowance for the age and experience of the writers, these selections illustrate originality and demonstrate the effective use of traditional
forms and structures common in literary works.

Literary critics maintain that Western literature contains only a few dozen
basic plots. If this is so then it can be seen that mature authors model or imitate
the plots invented by other writers. Yet, this common form of imitation does
not prevent us from regarding their writing as a worthy or even unique contribution to literature. Just so may children imitate a common literary structure, yet produce writing that can be regarded as an original and effective writing contribution.

Imitation and modeling in writing serves a useful purpose in teaching and
learning. Children may go through a close imitation stage where they produce
summary accounts of someone else's work which they have consciously or unconsciously memorized. There is no harm in this behavior. In fact, the children
most likely to do this are those who have had the greatest exposure to literary
models from their own reading or from being read to by parents and teachers.
Surely exposure to literature should serve this desirable end. The inevitable
consequence of such exposure is the attainment of a sense of literary form and
technique. The imitative behavior that appears in the writing of children who
have had an effective exposure to literature, then, is simply the harvesting of
what has been sown. Children who have been given literary models of good
writing and have had many opportunities to write will gradually move from
close imitation to loose imitation and finally to creative modeling. Of course,
some children do not appear to go through an identifiable sequence of stages in
their writing development. Nor do all children reach the creative modeling
stage during school years. Some reach this last stage subsequent to their school

experience. But the teacher who contributes to a child's writing growth any-where along the way is partly responsible for the end product.

Imitation is a natural and beneficial type of learning behavior among writers. Hemingway's writing style is said to have been influenced by Gertrude Stein, particularly during the early years in Paris. T.S.Eliot was profoundly influenced by Ezra Pound. It is evident when Ezra Pound began to read Chinese poetry for it showed up in his writing. All of these writers were "in-fluenced by" other writers. Do not be fooled by the term "influenced by." It is a euphemism for imitation and modeling. If writers of the caliber of Hemingway, Eliot, Pound, Churchill, London, Maugham, and others went through periods of imitation and modeling, why should teachers deny children the same opportunity? Children can profit from judicious encouragement of imitation and modeling as a means of motivating and improving their writing ability.

Imitation and modeling behavior is a legitimate and useful way of de-veloping and extending writing skill. There is no evidence that imitation and modeling behavior damages creative potential, nor does it stimulate unwar-ranted dependency on others. On the contrary, imitation and modeling have been part of the learning technique of writers for centuries. Furthermore, re-search has established that imitation and modeling plays a significant role in learning behavior of all types, including language learning.

Reading to Children as a Model for Writing

Children should read, or be read to, every day. Read poems and prose. Read fic-tion and nonfiction. Read adventure, fantasy, myths, fairy tales, legends, and folktales. Read about heroes and villains, gods and ghosts, cowboys and Indians, traders and trappers. The world of literature can be opened to children by reading to them.

Teachers cannot teach children to love books, but they can create an at-mosphere which will predispose children to appreciate the gift of literature. The enjoyment of books can be shared.

Why Reading to Children is Essential

Research and teaching experience have shown that reading to children is help-ful in teaching children to read. Teachers are less accustomed to thinking of reading to children as useful in learning to write. Yet, a moment's reflection will reveal the reasons that this is so. Reading to children contributes to writing ability in the following ways:

1. *Reading to children provides models for writing.* Children must inter-nalize a sense of story form, characterization, plot, mood, and so on in order to become effective writers. Listening to all types of literature provides necessary models. The personal testimony of great writers

The teacher is reading to her children. The sounds of language and literature must be anchored in the child's mind. Reading to children accomplishes
this by providing models for plot, theme, and other literary structures. Children who have been given good literary models inevitably reflect these models in
their writing.

such as Jack London, Somerset Maugham, and others is convincing in
this respect. Hence, the value of reading a wide variety of literature is
obvious.

2. *Reading to children sparks the imagination and provides images and
ideas for children to write about.* What is read today is likely to be written about tomorrow. If you want children to write ghost stories, read
ghost stories to them. All children are endowed with imagination and
the capacity to wonder. Reading to them is often the key to stimulating
an imagination that has been lulled asleep by the tedium and boredom
of daily classroom routine.

3. *Reading to children enriches the store of language available for writing,
and unconscious as well as conscious memorization of words, phrases,
images and syntax often results.* Depth and breadth of vocabulary are
enhanced. Part of a writer's stock in trade is his or her store of words
and the ability to string them together effectively. Listening to excell-
lent literature is a powerful way to affect a child's language.

4. *Reading to children develops the child's concepts, knowledge, and
thinking ability.* The firsthand experiences of a child are limited, even
under the most fortuitous of circumstances. Consequently, vicarious
experiences are essential in order to broaden the child's understanding
of the world. Literature is the greatest resource available to provide
such vicarious experiences.

5. *Reading to children illustrates specific concepts about writing which a teacher may want children to understand.* The teacher may wish, for example, to illustrate ways in which certain writers describe characters in their stories. Three or four selections can provide pertinent examples. The children may then imitate the models provided.
6. *Reading to children is an enjoyable activity.* It is the surest way to develop a love and appreciation for books. No child is immune to the sensuous pleasures of listening to an intriguing mystery, a gripping adventure, a compelling tragedy, or a sensitive poem. Such experiences leave an enduring residue in the mind and spirit of a child.
7. *Reading to children establishes a mutual bond and kindred spirit among the listeners.* The common experience of listening to a book or poem has a beneficial effect on class spirit.

How to Read to Children

In the preceding section, consideration was given to reasons why teachers should read to children. Understanding why this is important, however, is not enough. There remains the practical problem of how to go about it.

Reading to children requires thoughtful preparation and execution. It is not satisfactory to pick up any handy book and read it. The thoughtful teacher must give consideration to two major factors in reading to children. First, it is necessary to establish and maintain a climate of receptivity among the children. Second, it is necessary to read the selection effectively.

Several factors are involved in establishing a climate of receptivity.

1. *Make the reading—listening period a time for enjoyment and relaxation.* Informality should be encouraged. If children are more comfortable resting their heads on their desks, they should be allowed to do so. If cushions and rugs are available, children may wish to sit or lie on them. Textbooks and other working materials should be kept in desks or otherwise stored so they will not distract attention from the reading.
2. *Make the reading—listening time a special part of the daily schedule by setting aside a specific time for it.* The last twenty minutes of the day is a good choice because it sends the children home with a pleasant conclusion to the day's activities. The beginning of the day is also a good choice because it gets the children off to a good start. Teachers must decide for themselves what is best for their situation.
3. *Have the children establish a few simple behavior guidelines they are willing to observe.* The guidelines must not become so stringent that they interfere with the relaxed and pleasant atmosphere that must prevail. The guidelines may be as simple as no talking and walking about during the reading—listening time.
4. *Do not read longer than the time that children can sustain attention to the reading.* The time spent may vary depending on the mood of the

children and teacher, the passage being read, the amount of time available, the children's interest in the material, and other unpredictable factors.

5. *Never withdraw the reading—listening period as punishment for class or individual misbehavior.* It would never occur to a teacher to withdraw the day's work in math or reading as appropriate punishment for misbehavior. It makes no more sense to withdraw the reading—listening time, which is as important as math or any other subject.

If the five suggestions outlined are followed, the teacher will have little difficulty securing a climate of receptivity among his or her children for reading—listening experiences.

A second matter which is crucial in any discussion of how to read to children concerns the necessity of selecting appropriate materials and reading well whichever passage has been selected. Here are five guidelines that will help.

1. *Plan each day's reading selection in advance.* Normally, certain days should be reserved for the reading of a continuing story such as *The Boxcar Children* or *Charlotte's Web*. It is also useful to reserve at least one day a week for a special selection. This special time slot may be reserved for poetry, special surprises, or readings designed to mesh with other daily or weekly classroom activities.

2. *Select reading material best suited to the children to whom it will be read.* Keep in mind age and interest levels especially. The teacher's own judgment in these matters is most important. Many teachers choose to consult various sources in selecting appropriate books for children. Children's literature anthologies are often helpful in this respect.

3. *Interpret the mood, tone, and action of the passage being read.* Be dramatic. There is a little ham in most teachers, and this is the time to let some of it out. For example, the children will appreciate Mark Twain's *Huckleberry Finn* more if the teacher renders the dialect as it is written and lets his or her voice rise and fall with the natural emotions evoked by the story. Fear of making a fool of oneself often keeps teachers from entering into the drama of a story. Children, however, are a gentle and generous audience. They will appreciate and applaud a teacher's efforts to dramatize the literature read to them.

4. *Differentiate the time for reading to children from the directed-reading and directed-listening activities.* It is neither necessary nor desirable to make the reading—listening time a structured lesson. The primary objective is enjoyment. If this objective is accomplished, a host of other significant objectives will follow naturally.

5. *When reading a narrative that will be continued the next day, stop at a point that is likely to incite anticipation of the next episode.* Judicious use of this device can have a positive effect on attendance and sustain a high interest level in the selection being read.

What to Read to Children

Reading to children has many values. Chief among them are the obtainment of pleasure, the effect on writing, and the general gathering of knowledge and understanding. Each of these values is a powerful force that shapes children's minds and nurtures their spirits. Therefore, great care must be taken in selecting literature to be read to children.

A comprehensive program of reading to children must be carefully planned and balanced so that the best selection may result. Teachers may find the following guidelines helpful in selecting materials to read to children or for children to read independently.

1. *Provide both modern and traditional literature.* Classic literature links the present generation with its cultural heritage. The great themes of justice, equality, courage, and honesty are values commonly extolled in classic literature. Stories that stress adventure, fantsy, home, and family transcend time. These are concepts with which children can identify. At the same time, modern literature, with its contemporary language, settings, and situations, delights and enlightens the child. Both modern and classic literature have something to contribute to today's children. The literature children hear or read should be balanced between modern and traditional.

2. *Provide both fiction and nonfiction.* For the most part, selections read aloud should be fiction. Children delight in identifying with the characters fiction portrays. It gives them an opportunity to be someone else, to imagine, and to fantasize. To young children, fiction is quite real. On the other hand, children need to build a store of information about the past and present world from nonfiction works. As children gain knowledge, they are able to verify information and ideas through daily living and through other educational sources. The base of information thus obtained helps children to formulate new concepts and ideas, and expands their understanding of the physical world. Fiction, of course, does this too, but less directly and more aesthetically. Both types of reading are useful. The balance, however, should tip in the direction of fiction, since other curriculum experiences will provide the bulk of nonfiction resources for the child.

3. *Provide both prose and poetry.* Most of what is read by children is prose. Some children read poetry, but this is rare. Many children avoid reading poetry because they feel uncomfortable with it and have insufficient exposure to it. Reading poetry will help redress this imbalance and will provide the needed experience and exposure that develop understanding and appreciation. At the same time, children enjoy prose and should hear a wide variety of it. An appropriate balance must be maintained.

4. *Provide books which contain elements of surprise, suspense, action and universal characters with whom children can identify.* Children enjoy literature that tells of human struggle against the forces of nature and of the confrontation of evil with good. They like stories where the emotions revealed in the characters and tone of the book parallel those that children struggle with themselves: love, hate, anger, joy, grief, jealousy, envy gentleness, and tenderness.

Children's curiosity, enthusiasm, and emotional needs are a natural ally to the teacher who is attuned to children. The important thing about a book is the meaning it has for the children who read or hear it. The business of children is to assimilate, from each book, whatever they can. The business of the teacher is to select literature wisely, so that the children have something meaningful and worthwhile to assimilate. Therefore, the thoughtful teacher will study the various annotated bibliographies available on children's literature and choose those books best suited to fulfill the variety of needs that exist among children.

Appendix A contains a list of books prepared by Marie E. Taylor which is an excellent guide for selecting materials to read to children.

Writing by Imitating Language Models

In addition to independent reading and being read to, there is another method by which children can learn to imitate language models. This method is the use of patterned writing.

Many stories and poems are constructed with a distinct language pattern. Certain patterned stories, poems, and other types of writing are highly predictable, enjoyable, and sufficiently repetitious that children are naturally attracted to them. When children have heard a patterned story or poem several times they are often able to recall most of it. This listening experience serves to anchor the sounds of the story or poem in the child's ear, thus making it readily available for various types of language experiences such as choral reading and patterned writing.

Read the three patterned stories below to see if you can determine which story is the model upon which the other two are based

David Was Mad

David was mad.
MAD! MAD! ANGRY!
He was so angry that he kicked the
wall as hard as he could.
He felt hot - all RED inside.
Grandma knew that David was mad.
She knew because David wasn't smiling.
The cat knew that David was mad.
She knew because David was shouting.
Sister knew that David was mad.
She knew because David hit her.
The teacher knew that David was mad.
She knew because David wasn't working.
The children knew that David was mad.
They knew because David was arguing.
The children didn't like it, and they
began to argue. Then they began to

feel all hot and RED inside.
The children got angrier and angrier
and REDDER AND REDDER.
They shouted and pushed and kicked
and hit! It was a mess.
"This was an awful day," David said,
and he began to cry. He cried
and cried. "I got mad first and
then everybody else got mad."
"Yes, that's how it goes," Grandma said.
"Anger is like wet paint. It rubs off
on everybody who touches it."
Already David was feeling better. He was
beginning to feel all sort of blue
and squishy inside. His anger had
passed.

David Was Sad

David was sad.
SAD! SAD! UNHAPPY!
He was so sad he stayed in his room
for an hour.
He felt bad - all blue inside.
Grandpa knew that David was sad.
He knew because David wouldn't talk to
him.
The dog knew that David was sad.
He knew because David wouldn't pet him.
Brother knew that David was sad.
He knew because David didn't feel like
playing.
Mother knew that David was sad.
She knew because he wasn't smiling.
David's friends didn't like it.
Soon they began to feel all sad and BLUE
inside.
His friends got gloomier and gloomier
and BLUER AND BLUER.
They pouted and frowned and sulked around.
It was terrible.
"This was a gloomy day," David said.
"I felt sad first then everyone felt
sad," "Yes, that's how it goes,"
Grandpa said. "Sadness is like rain
falling down. It falls on everyone."
Already David was feeling better. He
was beginning to feel all yellow and
steady inside.
His sadness had gone away.

David Was Mean

David was mean.
MEAN! MEAN! BAD!
He was so mean that he kicked the cat.
He felt all black inside.
Mother and Father knew that David was mean.
They knew because David yelled at them.
Grandpa knew that David was mean.
He knew because David wouldn't get the paper for
him.
The teacher knew that David was mean.
She knew because David was hitting the kids.
Big brother knew that David was mean.
He knew because David tore up his room.
Little sister knew that David was mean.
She knew because David spit on her.
Everybody hated it. Everybody got meaner and
meaner.
They all began to get mean. They began to feel all
black inside. They were so mean they they began to
fight.
They fought and fought. Everyone has a terrible
time.
It was one of the horriblest days they ever had.
"This was a terrible day," David said. And he
began to cry. He cried and cried.
"Yes, that's how it is," Mother said,
"Meanness is like the wind. It blows on
everybody that's near."
Already David was feeling better. He was
beginning to feel all white and warm inside.
His meanness had passed.

The model story is *David Was Mad*. (2) It was written by Bill Martin, Jr., a well-known author of children's books. The story *David Was Sad* was written as a pattern story by a group of second and third grade youngsters from Webster Elementary School, Pontiac, Michigan. The story *David Was Mean* was written by Amy, a third grade youngster from the same school. These two patterned stories are excellent imitations of the original. Indeed, it is difficult to distinguish the patterned stories of youngsters from the original model written by an experienced writer.

This conscious technique for imitating language patterns in literature has numerous advantages which may strengthen the writing skills of children. The following benefits may be derived from this type of writing activity.

1. *Children receive direct, concrete exposure to writing models with discernible language patterns and constructions.* One can talk endlessly about patterns, constructions, and story forms but to write explicitly, to imitate and innovate upon these patterns, constructions, and forms

insures a greater likelihood that they will be learned. It is one of the most direct ways to apply writing principles to everyday writing activities.

2. *Motivation for continued writing is provided.* One of the most difficult chores a teacher faces is motivating children to write on a continuing basis. Patterned writing provides both the modus operandi and the materials for an upward spiral of challenge and accomplishment that keeps children on the writing track.

3. *Immediate, observable writing success occurs.* If children are to enjoy writing they must sense that their efforts have been rewarded. Patterned writing is sufficiently easy that even kindergarten and first grade children are able to use the technique successfully. *Brown Bear, Brown Bear* by Bill Martin, Jr., is an example of a patterned story that very young children are able to imitate successfully. On the other hand, more complex patterns can challenge even the most sophisticated writer.

4. *The end product of patterned writing is so pleasing to youngsters that pride of authorship is readily instilled.* This pride plays a significant role in future authorship.

In the beginning, patterned writing should be initiated with an entire class or a subgroup within the class. Once the precedures are understood individual children may wish to try it on their own. This should, of course, be encouraged. The following general guidelines are suggested for writing patterned stories and poems.

1. *Select a story or poem which will interest your children.* It should contain a pattern that is predictable, identifiable, and repetitious. Excellent poems and stories suitable for patterned writing are listed in Appendix C.

2. *Read the story or poem to the children in an enthusiastic and dramatic fashion.* This step is crucial since motivation must be established at this point. If this step fails to capture their interest, what follows is not likely to succeed.

3. *Anchor the sounds of the patterned selection in the children's ears by inviting them to chorus those patterned portions of the selection they will have already identified.*

4. *Conduct a brief oral sharing discussion about the selection.* Invite children to describe the images that the selection stimulates in their senses, the words or phrases that come most readily to their minds, and the part of the selection they enjoyed most. The teacher and children jointly identify the elements of the pattern that are to be imitated. In addition, the teacher may wish to point out specific words, images, patterns, and concepts not mentioned by children. It is an opportunity for the teacher to be didactic in a natural way. The teacher is cautioned against becoming overly technical at this point.

5. *Invite the children to write a story or poem (whichever is appropriate) patterned after the selection read.* Invite one of the children to offer a line or two to get started. If the children are hesitant and seem uncertain about how to proceed it is sometimes helpful for the teacher to contribute the first line or two. Record the lines that are offered on a large piece of paper on the blackboard so that the children can observe the story taking shape.

6. *Refine the first draft.* The teacher attempts to lead the children to see where they may have missed the pattern. It may be necessary to return to the original selection to find out where the pattern went amiss. There are occasions when an element has been suggested that departs from pattern but results in an improvement over the patterned selection. If the teacher or children judge that this has happened they may elect to retain the improvement.

7. *Illustrate the story or poem that has been written.* The teacher and children may jointly determine how they wish to prepare the finished material. Sometimes the teacher or children may appoint an illustrator or team of illustrators to prepare drawings to go with each line or page of the written product. Sometimes each child is given a mimeographed copy of the final product in booklet form and is encouraged to illustrate his or her own booklet. The first patterned story or poem should be given special treatment so that the best possible end products result. This will give the children a special feeling about their first attempt at writing a patterned book.

8. *Make the illustrated typed copy into a book.* All of the accoutrements of a *real* book should go into the production of this first patterned book. It should be bound, covered, titled, dedicated, and copyrighted. The name of the authors should appear on the appropriate page. The magnificence of having written their own book will be long remembered by children.

The teacher who intends to try patterned writing must recognize the tremendous impact it can have upon the writing program. At the same time it should not be naively thought that writing patterned books is an activity that can be accomplished in a spare hour. The activity requires thoughtful planning and swatches of time spread over several days. Once children have caught on to the use of patterned materials, however, they can begin to apply the concepts learned in many other writing situations. In addition to doing stories and poems, they may begin writing jokes, riddles, limericks, and other types of writing.

Of course, there are those who will worry that encouraging children to imitate will discourage creativity while encouraging unwarranted dependency upon others. Nothing could be further from the truth. Such a notion does injustice to the nature of childhood and suggests a lack of faith in children's individuality and integrity. Furthermore, it is clear that a great deal of learning occurs through the imitative process.

Each child has an individual personality. There is no way in which he or she can remain captive of another's style. No one can constantly imitate the style of another individual. The personality's demands for self-expression will win out. The fact that Churchill's writing style is reminiscent of Gibbon certainly doesn't lessen our enjoyment of Churchill's writing. Nor does it mean that his style is not uniquely his own. The style of Gibbon is so thoroughly accommodated into Churchill's own scheme of things that the similarities are virtually unrecognizable to anyone but an expert. This is the likely course of events for all those who model their writing styles on others.

Writing patterned stories, poems, and other types of literature is a form of imitative writing. It is a useful and effective way to teach children to write.

SUMMARY

Imitation and modeling behavior is a legitimate and effective technique for developing and extending writing skills. There is no evidence that imitation and modeling behavior will dampen the creative urge, nor will it stimulate unwarranted dependency on others. On the contrary, imitation and modeling have been part of the learning technique of writers for centuries. Furthermore, psychological research has established that imitation and modeling play a significant role in learning behavior of all types.

Reading to children facilitates writing growth because it: (1) provides models for writing, (2) sparks imagination, images, and ideas for writing, (3) enriches the store of language available for writing, (4) develops the child's concepts, knowledge, and thinking ability, (5) illustrates specific concepts about writing, (6) is an enjoyable activity in itself, and (7) establishes a spirit of cooperation among children which can motivate writing and other classroom activities.

A direct way of stimulating imitative behavior is through patterned writing. Patterned writing has the following advantages: (1) children receive direct, concrete exposure to writing models with discernible language patterns, (2) patterned writing motivates continued writing, (3) immediate writing success is possible for even the youngest writer, and (4) patterned writing helps to establish pride of authorship, which plays a significant role in future writing development.

REFERENCES

1. Cramer, Ronald L. and Cramer, Barbara B. "Writing by Imitating Language Models." **Language Arts** 52 (1975): 1011–1014, 1018.
2. Martin, Jr., Bill. **David Was Mad.** New York: Holt, Rinehart and Winston, 1971.

7

Evaluating Children's Writing

The first section of this chapter presents a discussion of the philosophy and objectives of marking. The second section discusses specific examples of children's writing. The third section consists of practice exercises for analyzing children's writing.

Marking

The objectives of marking are (1) to provide children with a feeling of accomplishment and satisfaction that comes through writing, (2) to provide specific criticism of an instructive nature that will foster future growth in writing ability, and (3) to assign grades in circumstances where grading is required or desirable. Each of these objectives requires some elaboration.

Satisfaction and Accomplishment

Praise that is genuine is a major source of satisfaction. When praise is properly given, it helps children achieve a sense of accomplishment from their writing. Praise must be discriminating. If it is excessive or undeserved it may overwhelm the child, leading to anxiety about equaling previous achievements. If praise is insufficient, children may lack incentive to strive for a better product. It is a rare piece of writing which is devoid of some item that may be genuinely appreciated. It may be a word, a phrase, a sentence, or an entire piece of writing that merits your praise. The approval reflected in your comments will serve as a benchmark against which children may judge the value of their work.

Instructional Criticism

Criticism is a postive term when properly understood. It is used here to refer to knowledgeable and thoughtful evaluation of children's writing. Criticism must not only have a positive tone but it must achieve positive results. Children's writings are a type of literature. Consequently, children's writing represents an artistic as well as an academic endeavor.

Children profit from criticism that promotes technical competence without destroying the joy of writing. Effective criticism helps children to recognize the progress they are making. Criticism may be communicated orally or in writing. Both types are useful and a proper balance between the two must be achieved. Oral criticism is called for in circumstances where the criticism (1) is of a delicate or private nature, (2) is lengthy and complex, (3) requires interaction with the writer, (4) relates to a serious weakness or fault, (5) extends praise or positive comments. Written criticism is most appropriate when the criticism (1) is brief, (2) concerns minor faults or weaknessess, (3) extends praise or other positive comments when there is not time to give them orally.

It is often difficult to decide which writings to mark. Personal writing based on imagination and fantasy and certain types of highly personal writing are difficult to mark. Many times they simply should not be marked. It is a delicate decision. Teachers must exercise their best judgment since strict guidelines cannot be drawn. Normally, the most appropriate writings for marking are research reports, factual accounts stemming from direct observation or scientific experiment, and writing that has been specifically assigned or designated for marking. Regardless of the type of writing, marking must always be sensitively handled to ensure maximum growth without sacrificing children's feelings.

The writing program can be structured so that marking decisions are simplified. Teachers can provide two separate notebooks for children's writing. One journal is reserved for personal writing that is read but not marked. A second journal is reserved for writing that can be marked. There are types of writing that do not fit either journal. These may include lengthy research reports, extremely personal writing, special assignments, and projects whose format precludes inclusion in a journal. Writing of this latter type must be judged case by case as to whether marking will serve an instructional purpose. Marking works best when it is unobtrusive, has some regularity, and is carefully performed.

Primary grade children must be given time to develop fluency in writing. For young children, enjoyment is paramount. Their writing is usually uninhibited and imaginary or personal in nature. Instructional criticism for primary age children must be delicately administered. It should center primarily, though not exclusively, on developing a feeling of satisfaction and accomplishment. Intermediate grade children, who write fluently, may begin to receive broader instructional criticism.

Instructional criticism must be carefully given. Every fault need not be pointed out. Such criticism implies deliberate fault-finding with little interest in what is good. Mechanical errors can be pointed out and appropriate instruction provided. Comments on the content and ideas of writing are especially neces-

These children are writing in their journals. The journal provides a permanent record throughtout the year of certain aspects of each child's writing progress.

sary. When children's ideas are good they must be told so. Children sense that content and ideas are more fundamental to good writing than are mechanics. When children know their ideas are good, they will learn the mechanics of writing more readily and be more inclined to continue writing because they recognize that they have the basic "stuff" to develop.

Instructional criticism ought to concentrate on teaching editing skills. Editing is the most effective means of learning mechanical skills. Children learn more about writing when they are able to improve their own work. A balance between teacher criticism and self-editing must be struck. Outside editors are helpful, but self-editing is more helpful.

Criticism implies pointing out both strength and weakness. It is the pointing out of weakness that is the most troublesome problem. Careful thought must be given to comments that point out weakness. Gentleness is always more effective than harshness.

Assigning Grades

Teachers are often required to assign grades, at least periodically. This especially true in intermediate grades and junior and senior high schools. The following remarks are directed toward teachers in this circumstance.

If grades are given, a set of criteria is needed. Traditionally, teachers have used two criteria: (1) accuracy of spelling, punctuation, and other mechanical skills, and (2) acceptability of grammatical usage. Sometimes, the quality of ideas is added as a third criterion.

The difficulty with the first two criteria is that they are incidental to good writing. Mechanical and grammatical skills are adjuncts to effective writing.

By themselves, they do not constitute good writing. Children may achieve both mechanical accuracy and grammatical excellence and still produce dull, insincere, and ineffective writing. Conversely, children may violate both mechanical and grammatical standards and still produce interesting, effective writing. The following two stories below illustrate this assertion.

The New Nest

When we went for our woak yesterday we found that the swans had finished their nest But two weeks ago it was raggy shaggy and ugly we wondered how ever she could lay her eggs in it. But when we went yesterday afternoon it was a beautiful nest like an eagles nest. the Miss Swan was asleep and the father swan was guarding the fort and if any enemies came he would stretch out his long neck and peck them with his beak. (1)

Boy
Age 6

Spring

I love Spring. I love Spring because the flowers bloom and the trees blossom. I love Spring because the birds sing. In Spring the leaves come out and everything turns green. The flowers are pretty in Spring. I love Spring.

Girl
Age 7

Chances are you chose "The New Nest" as the best of the two stories although it clearly contains the most mechanical errors. Despite this fact, most people familiar with good writing will judge "The New Nest" to be the better piece of writing. To arrive at this judgment, one must refer to some criteria either implicit or explicit. The following criteria are useful in making grading judgment as well as helpful in determining what constitutes effective children's writing: (1) quality of the ideas, (2) effective use of current language abilities, (3) sincerity, (4) extent of personal improvement over time, and (5) general writing skills including grammatical and mechanical skills.

1. *The most important single criterion of good children's writing is the qualtiy of the thinking that underlies the ideas.* Most children have something worth saying when they are given the freedom to say it in writing. Teachers can improve the quality of children's writing by spending instructional time enhancing the experiences that precede and follow writing. Children have a natural curiosity and an astounding ability to think creatively and critically. Grading can become a constraint that hinders writing. Consequently, grading decisions must be made with the utmost care.

2. *Expect children to use their available store of language to its maximum extent, but not beyond.* Hold each child to a standard that is fair and reasonable for him or her personally. Obviously, it is unreasonable to expect children to use grammar and vocabulary that are foreign to their dialect or current

language ability. Unfortunately, children are sometimes penalized for not possessing language skills their teachers arbitrarily believe should be possessed.

Good teaching creates conditions where children use the full range of their verbal abilities. Experiences develop concepts, and concepts extend language. New and extended experiences can expand vocabulary and develop new grammatical options. If something is missing from a child's language, the teacher can plan school experiences that will add the language that is missing. Children must incorporate new language elements into their oral language before it will show up in their written work. Sometimes language thought missing is simply not used in the school setting. Good teaching creates conditions where children can use the full range of their verbal abilities.

3. *Sincere writing expresses, in an open, candid manner, how you think and feel.* Sincere writing is truthful, honest, and based on genuine personal experience. Children seldom write insincerely unless the circumstances of teaching encourage or force insincerity. For example, children asked to write about, "What I Did Last Summer" (for the third year in a row) are forced by teaching circumstances to respond insincerely.

When children's natural emotions and language are not accepted, sincerity will disappear beneath a veneer of insincere patter. That is why we get stories like "Spring." The story does not represent genuine personal experience. The language lacks sparkle and direct experiential reference. A child forced by circumstances or assignment to write about spring without an immediate, personal experience of spring has little choice but to write insincerely. Children become facile at producing insincere writing when forced to do so by years of neglectful teaching. On the other hand, they respond readily to teaching that honors personal experience and accepts normal childhood emotion and language.

4. *Extent of improvement should be an element in the grading scheme, although it cannot be the entire scheme by itself.* Some proportion of a child's grade should be based on the amount of progress made during a given span of time, usually a semester or academic year. However, basing grades on this criterion alone can lead to glaring inequities. For example, if a grade were based entirely on personal progress, one might be forced to give the highest grade to the poorest writer in a given class. This could happen in a situation where a relatively weak writer made the most individual progress but remained the weakest writer among a group of good writers. On the other hand, one can imagine a reversed situation where the best writer in a given class receives the lowest grade because of the least progress made although he or she started and ended as the best writer in the class. Clearly, this kind of grading scheme will not do. But these situations only arise when grades are based entirely on personal progress. There is nothing inherently unfair about a grading scheme which includes extent of improvement as one element among several in a well balanced plan of grading.

5. *General writing effectiveness includes such writing characteristics as organization, interest, style, mechanics, and grammar.* Clarity is improved when a written account is organized either logically or chronologically; interest

keeps the reader mentally committed to the writer's product; style is that elusive quality which sets off one writer's product from another's; mechanics and grammar are the basic writing conventions (such as punctuation, legibility, format, standards of usage) that contribute so much to good writing.

The five criteria suggested above are in line with the general purposes of writing. While they are subjective, they are not narrow. Meaningful writing criteria are unavoidably imprecise and difficult to apply. Criteria that are easy to apply could hardly be adequate to the complexities of writing and its evaluation. Thoughtful teachers understand that there are no simple answers to complex questions.

The Analysis of Children's Writing

The analysis of children's writing has four purposes.

1. *Therapeutic.* To gain insight into children's inner world of thought and feeling in order to help teachers understand children's emotional and social experience. Such knowledge helps promote the general welfare of the child.

2. *Instructional.* To evaluate current levels of writing ability and provide children with information that will help them grow in writing ability and related academic artistic areas.

3. *Diagnostic.* To gain useful information which will help direct future instruction more precisely and knowledgeably.

4. *Marking.* To make judgments regarding children's relative progress in writing development. This information may be passed on to parents in the form of personal conferences or grades.

There are many questions that must be asked and answered in analyzing children's writing. To demonstrate what some of those questions and answers might be, we have outlined some case studies below. The analysis of these examples of children's writing does not purport to be *the* way to examine the meaning of children's writing. Rather, the intent is to show what some questions and answers *might* be. Teachers who are interested in such analysis may gain from these examples a recognition that it is important to develop their own analytical skills and to apply them to the writing their children produce.

Kathy's Story. Read the story carefully. You may find it difficult to understand in places, but much of what children write comes in this raw and unpolished state. In this respect Kathy's story represents a typical piece of writing. In other respects it is quite unusual.

The Princess and the L.S.D.

One grovey day a prince named Gotcha went out for a princess. He looked all over town.

When he came home he told his fokes that he couldn't find a gal good enough. So he took off his Madilian riped off his Moccasin and when he was in his jeans and swet shirt he went to eat.

All of a sudden it started to rain lightening and thunder. Then just as soon as the rain came there was a nick at the door. As soon as he opened the door in stepted a cool looking gal who claimed to be a princess. Well of course Gotcha believe her but his old lady was to go to find out for sure.

So Gotchas Mother asked her, her name she said "My name is Klara." Then she took a needle and shotit in her arm LSD was in it for only a real princess wouldn't react. The queen told her that it would make her feel better. Later the queen fixed a bed for her twenty feather matres.

Klara wanted to go to bed early to get a little more shut eye.

The next morning Klara was made because she forgot her midnight bourbon last night. But she figured as long as she was the only one up she could go have extra whiskey.

Two hours later the butlers got up this was at 7: 00 she talked to them until Gotcha got up then together they smoked their usual grass.

Then when the queen got up she could find no sign of the L.S.D. She knew she was a real princess she would arrange for a wedding ten minutes later they were married they went on a way out trip of heroin for there honeymoon.

Maybe if you go to Jackson State you'll see the needle that shot the princess May be if your lucky you'll see the prince and princess.

Kathy
Age 12

Having read the story, respond to each of the questions below as honestly as you can. Do not yield to the temptation of responding contrary to your personal beliefs and practices.

1. How sincere is Kathy's story?
2. What may be the symbolic meaning of Kathy's story?
3. What are the prospects that Kathy will become an effective writer? What evidence do you have for your opinion?
4. What ought to be done about the errors in Kathy's story?
5. How would you respond to this piece of writing if Kathy were your pupil?

Compare your answers to the answers given below. My answers, like yours, represent my beliefs and practices. Like your answers, they are based on my teaching experience and on some years of study of children's writing. Our answers may differ. In some instances, our differences may be minor, reflecting different experiences and perspectives derived from classroom teaching. In other instances, our differences may be major, reflecting fundamental differences in our way of looking at children's writing.

1. *How sincere is Kathy's story?* To answer this question I ask myself these questions: Did this piece of writing come from the heart? Does it seem to

represent the author's personal experience? If I answer *yes* how will I justify my response?

I believe this is a sincere piece of writing and that it represents a real experience with drugs. Kathy has chosen not to write a straightforward documentary account. Instead she chose the format of the fairy tale. One must examine, therefore, the probable symbolic meaning of this tale. Notice the language and the style with which she structures her story. The language is common and unaffected. There is no hint of melodrama or braggadocio. There is a hint of bitter experience as suggested in the last sentence where the Prince and Princess are *rewarded* with a term in a state prison in Michigan (Jackson State Prison, Jackson, Michigan).

2. *What may be the symbolic meaning of Kathy's story?* The story illustrates the extent to which young children are familiar with the drug culture. The fairy-tale format is used to describe, in a symbolic way, real events and experiences. This may be a conscious or unconscious intent, but it is there. The principal characters may represent friends, relative, or Kathy herself. Unlike the typical fairy tale, this story does not have a happy ending. Instead, the principal characters end up in a penitentiary. This ending may imply a need to punish, or it may represent fear of drugs and their consequences. There is a hint of a moral, namely, the use of drugs is foolish and may end badly. The incarceration of the principal characters of the story may represent the author's desire to punish herself for using drugs or a desire to punish friends or relatives involved with drugs.

It is likely that this story is a symbolic representation of real life events. Symbolic representation of life's experiences are more common in children's writing than we may realize. Whether such symbolism is conscious or unconscious is difficult to know. Whether we recognize or fail to recognize such symbolism is not necessarily critical. There are occasions, however, when it is useful, or at least interesting, to know.

3. *Is there any hope that Kathy will become an effective writer? What evidence do you have for your opinion?* Yes. The evidence is as follows:
   a) The author uses her knowledge of literature ("The Princess and the Pea") to structure her story, and she follows this structure reasonably well.
   b) The author uses the literary device of irony as illustrated in the final sentence, "Maybe if you're lucky you'll see the Prince and Princess."
   c) In spite of the ordinary language used throughout this story, there are a few hints of language power: (1) "riped off his moccasin(s)", (2) the invention of the name *Gotcha*, (3) the use of the word *react*, (4) the ring of the phrase, "you'll see the needle that shot the princess."

4. *What ought to be done about the errors in Kathy's story?* This question can only be answered fully when one knows the author's writing history. When this history is known, the teacher can develop a reasonable set of expectations for Kathy regarding standards of usage and other writing conventions.

The term *error* is a misunderstood concept in education. It is commonly used in a negative sense. Consequently, the term has limited usefulness in the analysis of children's writing. You will notice that Kathy spelled the word *folks* as *fokes*. In traditional analysis, this is just a plain old error with all of its negative connotations. But to consider it exclusively as simply an error takes no notice of the excellence of the approximation. In first draft writing, the spelling *fokes* represents an effective use of the author's phonetic skills. This fact should not be discounted.

If there were a reason to prepare another draft of this story, I would help Kathy edit her story to locate mechanical faults, to improve organization, and to rephrase sentences for greater clarity. In the heat of first draft writing, misspellings, repetitions, omissions, and awkward sentences inevitably occur. There should be no censure attached to this normal state of events.

Each child must be treated individually where standards of writing are concerned. One must take into account each child's language background, previous writing experience, and reading ability. For some children, wide reading and writing experience is sufficient to develop the needed technical skills of writing. Others require direct and extensive instruction on the conventions of writing. Each case presents a different problem and requires various solutions.

In Kathy's story there is an unevenness of adherence to certain writing standards. For example, the author sometimes uses punctuation and paragraphing appropriately, and in other instances, these matters are neglected. This suggests that Kathy knows more about writing conventions than she consistently applies. This may be due to haste, which is natural in first draft writing. Instruction in editing techniques will help her to improve her writing style.

Kathy's story contains such a poignant personal message that primary interest should be focused on the meaning of her story and on providing whatever help may be appropriate for Kathy. Perhaps she needs nothing more than an opportunity to write about her problem. On the other hand, she may wish to talk about the problem with someone. In any case, the receiver of her writing gifts must be ready to provide whatever help is needed.

5. *How would you respond to this piece of writing if Kathy were your pupil?* When a child voluntarily gives you a personal piece of writing, trust is implicit in the act. In fact, in the beginning it may be a test of your trustworthiness. I would, therefore, be pleased to have received this story. I would be cautious about reacting to it publicly because of its personal nature. I would not display it or read it aloud unless Kathy wanted this to be done. Certainly I would tell her how pleased I was to receive it and compliment her on the positive features of the story. I would attempt to discover whether Kathy wanted to discuss the story further, and would respect whatever decision she made. I would keep in mind that this story may be the beginning of the stirring of Kathy's creative urges. Trust must be established between us if the native gift is to be exercised further. Approval must be bestowed if the gift is to be advanced.

David's story. Children often write about death and disappearance. Their natural anxieties and curiosity about death and disappearance are normal and healthy. Typically, their concern centers on themselves, family, friends, and pets. Undoubtedly, writing about death helps the child draw nearer to the reality and acceptance of death as a harsh fact of life. David's story is about the death of his pet cat.

MY DED CAT

Ones I hade a cat.
He was white and yellow.
One night my father
Come fame my grandfathers house
Wenn father come home fame
my grandfathers house he said
Ruste is ded.

David
Age 7

There is no hint of David's reaction to the death of "Ruste," though one suspects it affected him deeply. The measured cadence of David's language is reminiscent of the last lines of Robert Frost's poem, *"Death of the Hired Man"*:

Warren returned—too soon, it seemed to her—
Slipped to her side, caught up her hand and waited.
"Warren?" she questioned.
                    "Dead," was all he answered (2).

The native language of childhood sometimes has the sound of poetry. Perhaps this is because children's language is naturally simple and their character naturally truthful.

Notice the uncomplicated sentence structure and common words that are characteristic of David's writing style. The adult, unlike the child, has to struggle with a sophisticated vocabulary and a complex syntax which can so easily obscure truth and destroy simplicity. David's story is elegant in its simplicity and profound in its sincerity. What great significance lies in the simple utterance, "Ruste is ded." The language of childhood is so profound that it is a constant challenge to our insight.

Susan's poem. Children play with language like kittens play with string. They love to hear the sounds that playful language conveys. The story below is a sophisticated example of language play. Susan's poem delights the ear and quickens the imagination:

Frogs and Kites

Frogs fly and kites jump.
No. I mean frogs jump and fly kites!
No, that's wrong.
But now I know what I mean.
Frogs flump and kites jy!

Susan
Age 8

Reading poetry and prose to children provides useful language models which anchor the sounds of language in the child's ear. The style of Susan's poem is reminiscent of Lewis Carroll's "Jabberwocky." Surely Susan has benefited from listening to poetry in the "Jabberwocky" genre.

Susan's poem has been carefully edited. The meaning is clear, the organization excellent, the mechanics perfect. There is a reason for the polished appearance of Susan's poem. She presented it in a beautifully illustrated booklet to Harry Hahn's Young Author's Conference at Oakland University. The public presentation of her work provided the stimulus for careful editing of the original draft. Even young authors can profit from the legitimate need to present their work in its best possible form to the public.

Larry's poem. If you were asked to write a poem about the sun's gravity, how well would you do? If you could do it at all, you would probably produce a ponderous, technical, boring poem. I doubt if one adult in a hundred could write a better one than Larry's:

> The sun has lots
> and lots of gravity
> ho boy does it
> man I tell you
> babby.
>
>   Larry
>   Age 6

This was one of Larry's earliest independently written poems. An analysis of Larry's poem reveals some interesting developments in his writing skills. Consider the content, spelling, punctuation, and capitalization in Larry's poem:

1. *The meaning of this poem is simple.* Larry does not attempt a scientific explanation of gravity because, like most of us, he probably does not have one. Wisely, he chooses to express what he has obviously experienced about gravity—a feeling of wonder and awe. Perhaps he has seen a movie, read or heard a book, looked at a picture, or listened to his teacher's explanation. Whatever the source of his inspiration, one senses that his imagination has been stimulated. When a child's imagination is excited, the language pours out in an uninhibited, delightful stream.

2. *Larry misspelled one word,* babby *for* baby. He is a good speller. Both his correct and incorrect spellings demonstrate this assertion. Better than 90 percent of the words he used were correctly spelled. His one misspelling shows a sophistication unexpected in a first grade child. The sound /b/ has two common spelling: *b* as in *boy* and *bb* as in *bubble*. Larry knows both spellings. Larry knows something that many first graders do not know. He will soon spell *baby* correctly. In the meantime, he is experimenting with the relationship between letters and sounds.

3. *Most adults would divide this poem into three separate sentences.* Larry chose to make it one continuous sentence and punctuated it accordingly. He knows the basic function of the period as his appropriate use of it demonstrates. Because he did not punctuate this poem the way most adults would is no cause for alarm. It would destroy the charm of his writing and interrupt the natural pace of writing growth. Technical competence is a natural outgrowth of writing fluency and expressive effectiveness.

4. *Larry knows two of the most common conventions of capitalization.* He capitalizes the first word in a sentence, "The sun. . . . " In Larry's mind his poem is one complete sentence; therefore, he sensibly refrains from putting in extraneous capitals. He capitalizes the word I, a common convention in English writing. Judging from what he knows already, it is a good bet that the other conventions of capitalization will be learned in due time.

Larry has learned a significant number of mechanical skills and applies them correctly in writing. Undoubtedly, he will learn other skills as he continues to write. His language is fresh, his sense of wonder is beguiling, and his imagination is vivid. This seedling of a writer will grow into the strong oak of a mature authorship if properly nurtured.

Terrance's stories. If you have taught for five years or more and have never found a diamond in the rough, your powers of observation may need to be sharpened. No teacher need be the living embodiment of the old adage, "He can't see the forest for the trees." Talented children abound everywhere. They may be black or white, rich or poor, big or little, talkative or quiet, bold or shy. Talented children are sometimes spotted early, sometimes late, and, sad to say, sometimes they are never identified at all. It is the responsibility of teachers to identify talented children and to direct and foster their development. It is particularly crucial that latent talent be identified. The failure to spot and encourage latently talented children is one of the most grievous omissions in teaching. On the other hand, to spot a diamond in the rough, and to commence polishing it, is one of the most rewarding experiences teaching can provide. Remember, the brilliance of the finest diamond is not apparent until it is properly cut and mounted. So, too, the finest talent may appear dull gray and rough in its early stages, but, polished and prepared, it will shine like the finest jewel.

The three stories below might be passed over by the unobservant teacher with the thought that the writer cannot spell, punctuate, or write coherently. Read the stories carefully. You may find them difficult to decipher, but much material of an exceptional nature may have a similarly ragged appearance:

Dade man's point

Once up time by a bech was a cave. With sea monsters
inside. The name was dade man's pont. Blurp, Slurp, Big Daddy,
Sweet momms. That's who lived in the cave.

Herd Headman

Once up time nere a Jell It was an man with an herd
head. pow! I'm going to rob a bank. I win! police lost. I'm
rich! I'm poor,

The Honted House

Once upon time nere the street. It was an house. It was
honted. On dear, eat all thir fod no more money, Come on
Mom, And Dide. Look! Thir a house. Help! momme, dide.
MOO! MOO! Pat, pat, pat, pat. Pow! pam! you dum dum
you ca't shoot a ghost. What! Just bat's! oh boy, spch! Thir
away, Now we may liv in it.

Terrance
Age 7

There are two questions you should attempt to answer before you read
further:

1. What evidence is there that Terrance has a latent talent for writing?
2. What steps would you take to insure that Terrance is given every opportunity to develop whatever writing potential he may have?

If you have been trained to analyze writing in the traditional manner, you
may be hard pressed to recognize the exceptional qualities in Terrance's early
writing. You may have found the two questions difficult to answer. Nevertheless, there are signs of talent in Terrance's work. He displays, in these beginning stages, many of the qualities of an extraordinary talent for writing. Here is
the evidence:

1. *Imagination is shown in the choice of topics such as* "Dead Man's
Point", "The Haunted House", *and* "Hard Headman." The manner in which
these stories are told suggests a flair for imaginative thought.

2. *There is power in Terrance's language.* Two examples are, "Blurp,
Slurp, Big Daddy and Sweet momms," and "you dum dum you can't shoot a
ghost." The unusual way in which he uses exclamatory words and condensed
conversation further reinforces this point.

3. *Each story contains the kernel of an intriguing tale.* For example, the
reader cannot help wondering who the Hard Headman is, and one's curiosity is
piqued by the situation in which the Hard Headman is apparently involved.
Curiosity is whetted by the titanic struggle that occurs before the haunted
house is rid of its ghostly inhabitants. And what went on at Dead Man's Point?
Who are Big Daddy and Sweet momms? It is apparent that these stories are
condensed scenarios limited in explanatory detail because Terrance's writing
skills are just beginning to emerge. When Terrance has fully developed his
writing repertoire, these condensed stories will become full-blown tales of extraordinary interest and power.

4. *Terrance's writing contains symbolic meanings that are much more penetrating than the surface story indicates.* For example, there are themes of conflict between the forces of good and evil, rich and poor, crime and punishment. What is the meaning of these conflicts? Without knowing the writer, we cannot be certain, but it appears these stories contain considerably more than meets the eye. Surely an internal struggle is being waged in the mind of this young writer.

5. *Terrance possesses a boundless enthusiasm for writing.* The words leap out at you. You sense that Terrance is trying to capture the raw emotions of life through the written word. Powerful emotions are symbolized in Terrance's use of punctuation, and terse, emphatic sentences such as Help! pow! MOO! bam! I'm rich!

6. *Terrance uses punctuation effectively though not always conventionally.* His punctuation efforts include the use of periods, commas, exclamation marks, and the apostrophe. Although he sprinkles punctuation marks with a-bandon, frequently they are appropriately placed. When compared against the norms for a beginning writer, his punctuation skills are effective not only for their suitability, but for the way he symbolizes feeling, meaning, and enthusiasm through punctuation. His punctuation marks are not always judiciously placed, but it is only a matter of time before he will have greater control over their use.

Terrance is a potentially powerful writer. He is already an exceptional writer when one considers his age and experience. It seems clear that Terrance has latent talent as a writer. His talent can be further developed. The following points outline briefly, though not fully, what must be done to further develop Terrance's latent talent as a writer:

1. *Provide every possible encouragement and inducement to assure that Terrance continues to write.* It is obvious that he likes to write. If that desire is not dissipated by injudicious teaching circumstances, his writing skills will continue to grow.

2. *Provide Terrance with a sense of satisfaction and accomplishment through discreet praise and recognition.* His teacher must know Terrance's personality thoroughly, so that her actions will be suited to his temperament. Some children have a greater need for recognition and praise than others. The teacher must know his intellectual and emotional character and direct her behavior accordingly.

3. *Provide instructional criticism cautiously at this stage.* Whatever is done should be done through personal conferences with Terrance. He must not be pressed to conform to adult standards of writing and usage, yet instruction of an informal nature may be given in Terrance's case. One excellent activity would be recording dictated oral accounts. These recorded accounts would contain the full richness of Terrance's oral language, and would provide a model of how his oral language looks when it is recorded by his teacher. His recorded language could

then serve as a benchmark against which he could compare his independent writing.

4. *Provide models for writing by reading literature that will enrich his repertoire of word choice, fire his imagination, and fill the storehouse for future writing.* He should also be provided with an abundance of materials which he can read on his own.

Terrance has writing talent. This can be inferred from an examination of his three stories shown above ("The Haunted House", "Dead Man's Point", and "Hard Headman"). Below are some stories written by Terrance a bit later. They appear in two versions, Terrance's original writing and a translated version.

Original Version	*Translated Version*
Can't you read!	Can't You Read
Once upon a time in a school was a boy. He couldn't read or jump. He could not add, Win he got eight years old he weat an a farm. To pick coting and work "but . . . He still couldn't read. Well son you did a good job . . . Thank you: but I can't read: That is ok you are a good worker. You may stay here or go home. Hurry!	Once upon a time in a school was a boy. He couldn't read or jump. He could not add. When he got eight years old he went on a farm to pick cotton and work—but he still couldn't read. "Well son, you did a good job.!" "Thank you but I can't read." "That is ok you are a good worker. You may stay here or go home." Hurry!
My Ark Story	My Art Story
Once upon a time in a ark school lived a boy He make good ark work. Miss dum-b-adump! Look! at this good ark work. Well I'm Miss dump-b-adump. And I say put it in the ark galary. Hey! "money Yes! it's for your good and best ark work. Mom! we're, rich! oh boy!	Once upon a time in an art school lived a boy. He made good art work. "Miss Dum-b-a-dump, look at this good art work." "Well, I'm Miss Dump-b-adump, and I say put it in the art gallery." "Hey, money" "Yes, it's for your good and best art work." "Mom, we're rich! Oh boy!"
The abc's	The abc's
Do you Kow, your abc's? Yes I do. A,B,Kj. Stop! that is not the way. Do you say it like this? a,b,c,d, e,f,g,h,i,j,k,l,m,n,o,p,q,r,s, t, u, v, w, x, y, z. Right!	Do you know your abc's? Yes I do, a,b,k,j, Stop! That is not the way. Do you say it like this? a,b, c,d,e,f,g,h,i,j,k,l,m,n,o,p,q, r,s,t,u,v,w,x,y,z Right!

Thuder is maick And
Lighting it too

Once up time in maick land. A funny thing happyen. Saturday liting stroock and people grew tall. Threes flew. Liting made people grow. Are we really tall?' Poor came rach, rach, came poor.

Thunder Is Magic and
Lightning Is Too

Once upon a time in magic land a funny thing happened. Saturday, light ning struck and people grew tall. Trees flew. Lightning made people grow. Are we really tall? Poor became rich. Rich became poor.

Have A Nice Day

Goodnight sleep tite. Have a dice darme. Darme nice dram's. Drame abote anything. Play nice gam's. Cont sheep cont 20, or more. Good night.

Have a nice day

Goodnight, sleep tight. Have nice dreams. Dream nice dreams. Dream about anything. Play nice games. Count sheep, count twenty or more. Goodnight.

My Sister

My sister name is An- gela. She is one year old. She runs around the house singing and dancing all day. She is sometimes bad but I like her alot.

My Sister

My sister's name is An- gela. She is one year old. She runs around the house singing and dancing all day. She is sometimes bad but I like her a lot.

The Clean and the Messy Pig

The Messy pig spilled food all over him. The clean pigs kicked him out the house. He went to get one sandwich and one grape. And they caught him. He ran away with a napsack. He came to a store. He thought it was a playground. The man said, "Will you like this suit"? Grunt! Grunt! "What is your name? Grunt! Grunt! He runned away. His finger- nail got caught in the suit. He passed a woman. She said, "My son, you in a hurry". She walked kind of slow. He ended back home. And the clean pigs said, "Woot-Whirl"! And they kept the messy pig forever.

The Clean and the Messy Pig

The Messy Pig spilled food all over him. The clean pigs kicked him out (of) the house (because) he went to get one sandwich and one grape and they caught him. He ran away with a knap- sack. He came to a store. He thought it was a playground. The man said, "Will (would) you like this suit?" (the pig says) "Grunt, grunt!" "Every- thing I say you say." "Grunt, grunt!" He runned (ran) a- way. His fingernail got caught in the suit. He passed a woman, she said, "My, son, you (you're) in a hurry." She walked kind of slow. He (the messy pig)

ended back home. And the
clean pigs said, "Woot-
Whirl" (wolf whistle of approval). And they kept the
Messy Pig forever.

Terrance
Age 7

You have read the stories that Terrance wrote a few months after he wrote "Hard Headman", "The Haunted House", and "Dead Man's Point." It is easier, at this point, to recognize the talent that was discernible, but less obvious, in Terrance's earlier writing. His later stories show improvement in both mechanics and organization. He incorporates more punctuation and uses it more conventionally, his stories are longer and more coherent, his sense of humor is obvious in the "abc" story, his tenderness is shown in his story about his sister, his wisdom shines through in the story about the messy pig and the clean pig, and his ambition is displayed in "Thunder is Magic and Lighting Is Too." The stories reveal the extraordinary panoply of emotion and thought that motivates Terrance. How skillfully he conveys his ideas and feelings! An alert, imaginative, and probing mind lies behind these stories.

Most of the characteristics revealed in the later stories were foreshadowed in the earlier ones. Teachers who have difficulty recognizing latent talent must work to improve their analytical skills; otherwise, they may inadvertently harm children. One need not actively repress talent to destroy it. The same result may be brought about by benign neglect. In teaching, the sin of omission may be just as devastating as the sin of commission.

Practice Exercises in the Analysis of Children's Writing

Below is a series of exercises designed to give you an opportunity to practice analyzing children's writings. Each exercise has several questions for you to respond to. Answer each question as completely as you can.

Exercise one.

What I Would Do If I Had One Hundred Dollars

by Mary, Age 11

If I had one hundred dollars, I would give it to my mother. The reason I would give it to her, because she would need it to pay a few bills. I no how hard it is for her. A woman like her working two jobs, and has to also help out with my grandmother, because she is very sick. That is what I would do if I had one hundred dollars. I wouldn't go and waste it up, like spend it on candy, buy me some new clothes, or save it up for college. I don't need any candy. I have plenty of clothes and what's the use in saving it up when you

need it right away. That's what I would do if I had one hundred
dollars.

1. Do you think this story describes a real or an imaginary experience? Why do you think so?
2. How does the language and organization of this story contribute to its effectiveness?
3. What would you say to Mary about this story if you were to have a private conversation with her?

Exercise two.

Christmas

by Dana, Age 9

Christmas is a time
For giving, for
Sharing
Christmas is thinking
Of others, not yourself
Of the birth of Christ
And the love inside us

1. What would you say to Dana about this poem?
2. What would you do with this poem after it had been written?
3. Do you think Dana has told the truth about how he feels about Christmas? Why do you think so?
4. Do you like this poem? Why?

Exercise three.

The Mistake

by Robert, Age 8 (A Dictated Story)

Me and Derrick walked around the corner. We looked at John
and Lonnie and they were fighting. John kicked Lonnie in the
mouth and Lonnie punched John in the mouth. Then me and Derrick held them apart and Mr. Yancey walked around the corner. He
thought that me and Derrick was holding them back so they could
kick each other in the stomach.

He took us into the office and got his paddle. Me and Derrick
were laughing and we didn't feel a thing. Lonnie started to cry before he got a whipping. John got five licks and then five more for
hollering at Mr. Yancey.

Then we told the truth and Mr. Yancey said he had made a
mistake. He said he would pay for our lunch or take us to Mac-
Donald's. We said MacDonald's.

1. Do you think the events described in this story actually happened? Give your reasons.
2. Assume that Mr. Yancey is the principal. If you were the teacher, would you show this story to Mr. Yancey. Why?
3. Compare the language and organization of this story with Mary's story in exercise one.

Exercise four.

Its the jigil (Jungle)	My Christmas Story
by Eric, Age 7	by Scott, Age 7
My dad brang us to the jigil We sal a lian. mi dad two (took) a pochir (picture) ov a lian	one day mray saw a aegll the aegll tid (told) mray she was going to haef a baby then she had the baby

1. Which story do you like best? Why?
2. In what way are these two stories alike? How are they different?
3. Analyze the misspellings in these stories. Tell how you would use this information to direct future instruction in reading and writing.

Exercise five.

Bird

by Paul, Age 10

You glide and swoop through the air performing endless feats of acrobatics. You are a graceful creature who has the whole world at your feet. Out of the forest you fly, your feathers, some smooth some fluffy hold your body in the air. You are the earths eye witness to the everyday events. You pearch on the wires like a human would wait at a railway station, waiting for the right time to take of for the south and the warmth. Ten, nine, eight, seven, six, five, four, three, two, one and a cloud of feathered creatures lifts into the sky like a cloud of locusts swarming to the crop of warmth. Over the sea, over the ocean your body flys. A ship sounds a warning as the cotton wool fog closes in. You see an ice berg the ship does not and the sea is the scene of death again. The fog clears and you see land a magnetic impulse tells you that this is your destination. You can feel the warmth of the friendliness of your new home.

1. Do you think this is a good piece of writing? Why?
2. How do you feel about this type of writing?
3. Discuss the quality of language used. In what way does it contribute to or detract from Paul's writing?
4. What instructional criticism would you give Paul to help him improve his writing?

Exercise six.

Autumn

by Paul, Age 10

The Autumn pays us a visit. It comes strongly like an army of ten million men. Each man of the ten million strikes a blow with his axe and each one kills a leaf. The birds zoom in like jet planes killing off the juicy red berries. The brilliant red apples fall and blow up the leaves bases. The army of leaves are finished they all lay on the ground like corpse. The trees stand bare because of the battle. But the army of wind isn't satisfied they keep on striking killing off the petals on the last flowers. It just keeps on conquering the wing things. It knocks of the conkers so the little children can pick them up and the evil army faints seeing they have for once helped someone so they become silent for a moment. But only one moment, they can't waste any time they have to get on with their evil conquering. Then the leaves change colour on their carpet they become red and yellow and different golden colours as though they were turning into ghosts going to haunt the wind. The leaves call for reinforcements, the raindrops. The raindrops come and kill of the wind. The armys go away. And the people pick the rosy red apples now because they daren't come out while the battle was on. The harvest starts and the stubble is burnt reminding children to get their bonfires ready and to be buying their rockets and bangers, airbomb repeaters and all the other fireworks. The children find the biggest potatoes and hide them so their mums don't find them and use them. Then on bonfire night they bring them out of their hiding places and roast them.

1. Is Paul a talented writer? Justify your answer.
2. Is Paul's use of metaphor effective? Explain your answer.
3. What would you say to Paul about his writing? What instructional criticism would you give him about this piece of writing?
4. What literature would you recommend to Paul to follow up his writing?

Exercise seven.

I Just Cant Stand Cigiret Smoke

by Eddie, Age 6

When my father runs out of cigirets and I see a pack I throw them away and he doesnt even no it becalls hes at the story bying another pack. When my father gos some place and takes me and the windows are closed my father smokes and I just hate it. I tell him to stop it but it doesnt do no use heal still do it.

1. What makes this an interesting piece of writing?
2. Do you think Eddie should feel proud of this story? Why?

3. What would you do to make Eddie feel good about having written this story?
4. How would you evaluate the status of Eddie's mechanical skills?

Exercise eight.

If I Were A Princess

by Louise, Age 6

If I were a princess I would have long golden hair. I would be rich enough to buy thousands of jewles. I would be the daughter of a king and queen. My name would be Maid Mateen. My dresses would go down to my toes. I would live in a beautiful castle high on a hill. There would be another castle on a high mountain. There in that castle would live a hamson prince. He would be the prince I would marry. Judy W. would be my sister. She would marry the princes brother. My age would be 19. My sisters age would be 18. I would get married when I am 20 years old. I would wear a golden crown to go with my golden hair.

1. Do you think this is a good piece of writing? Why?
2. In what way is this story similar to the story in exercise seven? How is it different?
3. What literature would you read to Louise or have her read as a follow-up to this type of writing?
4. What would you say to Louise in a personal conference about this story?
5. Are the ideas expressed in this story normal and healthy for a six year old child? Why?

SUMMARY

A fair marking system seeks to achieve three objectives: (1) to provide children with a feeling of accomplishment and satisfaction from writing, (2) to give children a sensitive and knowledgeable instructional criticism that will foster growth in writing, and (3) to assign grades using criteria which emphasize clarity of thought, language, sincerity, extent of improvement, and general writing standards.

The case studies of children's writing presented in this chapter reveal a remarkable range of intellectual and emotional content. The four purposes of analysis of children's writing are: (1) to gain therapeutic insight into children's thoughts and feelings, (2) to gain information that will enhance instruction in writing, (3) to discover diagnostic information that will direct future instruction more precisely, and (4) to make marking decisions regarding children's relative progress in writing development.

This chapter has presented a wide range of practical exercises which teachers may find useful in furthering their own understanding of children's writing.

REFERENCES

1. Clegg, Alec. **The Excitement of Writing.** New York: Schocken Books, 1972. Copyright 1964 by County Council of the West Riding of Yorkshire. (Reprinted by permission of Schocken Books, Inc., New York and Chatto and Windus Educational/Granada Publishing Ltd., England.)

2. Frost, Robert. From "The Death of the Hired Man," from **The Poetry of Robert Frost** edited by Edward Connery Lathem, Copyright 1930, 1939, © 1969 by Holt, Rinehart and Winston. Copyright © 1958 by Robert Frost. Copyright © 1967 by Lesley Frost Ballantine. (Reprinted by permission of Holt, Rinehart and Winston, Publishers.)

8

Writing and the Problem of Spelling

This chapter deals with three major points: (1) issues relevant to teaching spelling through writing, (2) methods for diagnosing spelling and word recognition skills through writing, and (3) guidelines for using personalized and commercial spelling programs.

Teaching Children to Spell Through Writing

The younger the child, the fresher and the more uninhibited the writing. Young children are seldom hindered by self-conscious feelings. They express their feelings and thoughts openly, bluntly, and with astonishing perceptiveness. This is their natural way. But if we are to know how well children can write, we must remove obstacles that stifle their thoughts. Among the most common obstacles is the demand for correct spelling before children have learned the complexities of the English spelling system.

Traditionally, American educators have used textbooks with lists of words selected by various criteria to teach spelling to children. The history of spelling books can be traced from Webster's famous blue-back speller to the profusion of spelling materials available today. But textbooks have not been entirely satisfactory. This is not surprising, since many spelling materials are divorced from writing. Textbooks tend to rely on spelling exercises and activities that emphasize either the teaching of linguistic rules, or the teaching of visual-tactile techniques, or a combination of the two. Linguistic rules and visual-tactile techniques alone are not sufficient to develop spelling competence. Spelling achieves functional meaning only through writing. The final test of good spellers is how well they spell words in compositions, not how well they spell words on tests or in spelling bees.

Accurate spelling requires the learning of a complicated set of linguistic rules and some learning of words by visual-tactile procedures. However, children are just beginning the long trek to spelling proficiency, and children in the primary grades are on the very threshold of spelling competence. Many years are required to master English spelling. How can children, who are just beginning to spell a few basic words, engage in meaningful writing when the spelling demands of independent writing are formidable? The answer is suprisingly simple, but its implications worry some teachers. My hope is to alleviate some of those worries by explaining how spelling competence is fostered through an active writing program.

To foster writing and spelling competence, teachers should encourage children to spell words as best they can. Teachers must be willing to tolerate misspellings. The teacher who overlooks misspellings at this stage enables children to achieve fluency in independent writing and opens the way for children to experiment with the relationships between letters and sounds.

Here is an account of how one teacher helped a first grade child to approximate the spelling of a word needed for writing. The child, Jenny, believed she could not spell the word she wanted to use:

Jenny:	Mrs. Nicholas, how do you spell *hospital?*
Mrs. Nicholas:	Spell it as best you can, Jenny.
Jenny:	I don't know how to spell it.
Mrs. Nicholas:	I know you don't know how to spell it, honey. I just want you to write as much of the word as you can.
Jenny:	I don't know any of it.
Mrs. Nicholas:	Yes, you do, Jenny. How do you think *hospital* starts? (*Mrs. Nicholas pronounced* hospital *distinctly with a slight emphasis on the first sound, but she deliberately avoided grossly distorting the pronunciation.*)
Jenny:	(*very tentatively*): h-s.
Mrs. Nicholas:	Good! Write the *hs*. What do you hear next in *hospital?* (*Again Mrs. Nicholas pronounced the word* hospital *distinctly, this time with a slight emphasis on the second part.*)
Jenny	(*still tentatively*): p-t.
Mrs. Nicholas:	Yes! Write the *pt*. Now, what's the last sound you hear in *hospital?* (*While pronouncing the word* hospital *for the last time Mrs. Nicholas emphasized the last part without exaggerating it unduly.*)
Jenny	(*with some assurance*): l.
Mrs. Nicholas:	Excellent, Jenny, *h-s-p-t-l* is a fine way to spell *hospital.* There is another way to spell *hospital,* but for now I want you to spell words you don't know just as we did this one.

Teaching spelling in this way has produced excellent results among children of all ages. The dialogue varies, but usually follows a similar pattern. Overcoming the spelling barrier in the manner demonstrated by Mrs. Nicholas achieves three important results. First, children are freed to express their thoughts and feelings in writing, because they may use any word in their speaking vocabulary. Second, children are able to practice, in a productive way, the word-recognition skills taught in the reading program. Third, children learn to spell better and faster when they are encouraged to test the rules that govern English spelling.

Children are well equipped to discover the historical and the linguistic rules that underlie English spelling. As Henderson said:

> They [children] are perfectly equipped to do it. They need only our confidence, encouragement and time. They need lots of activities and things of importance to do and feel and write about. They need the right to be wrong and an uninterrupted opportunity to try and test what will work for them at a pace that is right for them. They need schools that are interesting places to be and teachers of sense and sensitivity. Probably one of the most intriguing questions on earth is whether or not we can supply what is needed (1).

The problem of spelling and writing has concerned educators for decades. The concern has its origins in the unfounded belief that English spelling is highly irregular. Uncritical acceptance of this myth led to the belief that learning to spell requires memorization of the serial order of letters in words. While the spelling of a small percent of English words must be memorized, studies by Hanna (2) and Venesky (3, pp. 75-105), among others, have shown that English orthography is highly regular when all the important linguistic features that determine how words are spelled are considered. Nevertheless, the myth of irregularity in English persists and teachers continue in their reluctance to allow children to learn the rules of English spelling through experimentation in writing. Naturally, those who believe that English is irregular, or who refuse to acknowledge that there are rules to be discovered through writing, see little profit in spelling "as best you can." Fortunately, there is solid evidence from research and teaching practice to persuade reasonable people to reconsider their traditional reluctance.

Research conducted by Cramer (4,5) and by Stauffer and Hammond (6) has shown that first grade children whose language arts program emphasized writing and wide reading became superior spellers within six months. Furthermore, a follow-up study by Stauffer and Hammond (7) showed that these same children maintained their spelling superiority throughout their elementary school careers. In contrast, the same studies showed that children whose language arts program failed to emphasize writing and wide reading remained significantly poorer spellers throughout their elementary school careers.

The children who attained superior spelling achievement were encouraged to spell words "as best they could." For these children the phonological and the morphological knowledge they naturally possessed was applied every time they attempted to spell a word they did not know. Since they were rewarded for spelling as much of a word as they knew, they did not hesitate to write freely.

All spelling efforts, no matter how primitive, were treated as worthy. This freedom enabled the children to write any word in their speaking vocabularies almost from the beginning.

Research by Beers (8) and by Henderson and Beers (9) has shown that words misspelled in early writing are later spelled correctly. There was no tendency to remain at a primitive level of spelling competence. One first grade child's progress in learning, without formal spelling instruction, to spell the word *elephant* went like this:

TIME:	WORD:
October	lfnt
December	elfnt
February	elphnt
June	elephant

Many similar examples were reported in the various studies cited.

There is a similarity between learning to speak and learning to spell. The young child who is learning to speak first approximates the conventional pronunciation of *dad* with a more or less recognizable *da*. Parents are pleased with the progress of their child and immediately reward the approximation. When the response occurs again, it is further reinforced. Seldom do the parents tell the child that his pronunciation is wrong. Quite the opposite. Most parents marvel at how closely the mispronunciation approximates the conventional pronunciation. The young child who has many opportunities to explore and test his oral language learns the rules that govern that language. Children learn the rules that govern oral language precisely because they are allowed to pursue language exploration at their own self-governing pace in a highly stimulating oral language environment.

Teachers should accept children's early misspellings in the same spirit that parents accept the early mispronunciation in children's oral language. Sensible parents know that the child will not be saying *da* when he or she is five years old. They understand that eventually the child will say *dad*. Spelling growth operates on a similar principle. A child who starts out misspelling *elephant* does not need to continue to do so. In fact, it is extremely unlikely that the misspelling will continue, if children have abundant opportunity to write, read, and explore words. Surround the children with a rich oral and written language environment. Give children the freedom to explore their written language environment as active participants. Remember that making errors is not harmful—indeed, it is the common bond among successful experimenters. Nurture children with language activities that are interesting, enjoyable, and satisfying. If these conditions are met, children will learn the conventions of English orthography and become capable spellers.

Diagnosing Skills by Analyzing Children's Writing

Diagnosis seeks to examine weaknesses and strengths in order to gain information that will help direct future instruction. If the information gained from diagnosis is pertinent and accurate, as well as properly interpreted and applied, then diagnosis can achieve its purpose.

Children's writing is an excellent source of pertinent information about spelling and word recognition skills. Let's do an analysis of one child's writing to see how an analysis of misspellings might proceed and how information obtained might be used to direct future instruction. This analysis will be based on a limited sample, of course, although ordinarily such an analysis would cover several writing samples and supplemental information would be collected in any area where uncertainty prevailed.

The story "My Ded Cat" was written by a second grade child. The misspellings are analyzed to show they can give useful information about spelling and word recognition skills. The content of David's story is far more important than the misspellings. That aspect of David's story was discussed in chapter 7.

My Ded Cat

Ones I hade a cat.
He was white and yellow.
One night my father
Come fame my grandfathers house
Wenn father come home fame
my grandfathers house he said
Ruste is ded

David
Age 7

David misspelled six different words in his story: *ded* for *dead, ones* for *once, hade* for *had, fame* for *from, wenn* for *when,* and *Ruste* for *Rusty.*

On the other hand, David correctly spelled eighteen different words! *my, cat, I, a, he, was, white, and, yellow, one, night, father, come, grandfathers, house, home, said,* and *is.*

Several of the correctly spelled words can be regarded as superior spelling accomplishments for a second grade child. The words *father, grandfathers, white, night, house, said,* and *yellow* are in this category. One can look at David's spelling accomplishments and recognize his growing ability to correctly represent sounds with their appropriate letter and letter combinations. However, it is also instructive to examine David's misspellings for possible evidence of strength or weakness in spelling and word recognition skills. Following is an analysis for each misspelling.

1) *ded* for *dead.* The sound /e/ may be spelled *e* as in *bed* or *ea* as in *dead.* Apparently, at this time, David is unfamiliar with the *ea* option for the /e/ sound. Logically, David spells the sound /e/ with the short *e* spelling he knows. The letter *e* is the most common spelling for the /e/ sound.

2) *hade* for *had.* This misspelling appears to be an overgeneralization of the final *e* rule (sometimes called the silent *e* rule.) David showed that he has considerable awareness of this spelling rule. Notice he has correctly spelled the final *e* pattern in *home, come, white,* and *house.* If David is allowed to continue

to test the use of this spelling rule through his creative writings he will soon discover which words take the final *e* marker and which do not.

3) *wenn* for *when*. This misspelling shows knowledge of the second most common spelling for the /n/ sound (the double *n*). In this case David spelled the /n/ sound as in *tunnel*. Also, David misspelled the *wh* digraph although he gets the *wh* digraph right in *white*. A possible explanation for this misspelling is that the *when* is pronounced /wen/ in David's dialect rather than /hwen/. Some misspellings are aparently caused by dialect or pronunciation factors.

4) *Ruste* for *Rusty*. David sensibly spelled the last sound in *Rusty* with an *e* since it has the /ē/ sound. He has not yet learned that the final sound in words like *Mary*, *hurry*, and *carry* is often spelled with the letter *y*.

5) *fame* for *from*. At first glance this misspelling appears to be David's crudest mistake. However, this misspelling is not as unsophisticated as it might first appear. He has correctly spelled the first and last sounds of *from*. The final *e* in *fame* is probably another instance of over generalization of the final *e* rule. David's problems with *from* are the *r* in the *fr* blend and the vowel *o*. The omission of the *r* in the *fr* blend suggests unfamiliarity with the conventional spelling of this sound. The *o* in *from* is a schwa /ə/, although stressed. This vowel is spelled with the letter *e* in *taken*, the letter *a* in *about*, the letter *i* in *robin*, the letter *u* in *circus*, and the letter *o* in *wagon*. In other words, any vowel letter may spell the schwa sound in an unstressed syllable and sometimes in stressed syllables, as in from. Therefore, the letter *a* which David used was not an altogether random guess. Notice that he did use a vowel rather than a consonant to spell the schwa sound. His choice of the letter *a* to represent the vowel sound shows that he was aware of the need for a vowel letter in *from*.

6) *ones* for *once*. *Ones* and *once* may be homophones in David's speech. We know he can spell the word *one* ("One night my father . . . ") If *ones* and *once* are homophones in David's speech then this spelling logic is impeccable— he simply added the letter *s* to *one* to get *ones*. This misspelling shows good analogical reasoning and good sound discrimination. *Once* ends with the sound /s/ spelled *c*. David spelled the sound /s/ with the letter *s*—the most common spelling for this sound.

An analysis of David's misspellings as well as his correctly spelled words suggests the following tentative conclusions regarding David's word recognition and spelling strengths and weaknesses.

1) *David knows a large percentage of words by sight.* We know this because he correctly spelled 75 percent of the different words used in his story. This information suggests a solid reading vocabulary as well as substantial spelling strength. This conclusion is further strengthened by our knowledge that several of the words he has correctly spelled are words not normally in the spelling vocabulary of a second grade child.

2) *David has excellent auditory discrimination acuity and strong letter-sound association skills.* He applies his knowledge correctly in most instances, and makes appropriate guesses in all instances where he has misspelled words. His misspellings show an awareness that there is more than one way to spell a given sound.

3) *David is aware that certain consonant sounds have variant spellings.* This knowledge was revealed when he wrote *wenn* for *when*. Knowledge of consonant variability, and later vowel variability, is an important step toward spelling proficiency.

4) *David knows the final* e *rule, which is important for reading as well as for spelling.* Naturally, in testing this rule he misapplies it from time to time. Similar instances of overgeneralization are found in early oral language development. It is recognized in oral language as an important step forward in learning the rules of English syntax. It is a similarly important step in learning the rules of English spelling. Strength is shown in that David does try to apply this rule and frequently he does so correctly—as in *home, come, white,* and *house.*

5) *David has excellent control of the letter-sound associations for consonant spellings.* He rarely misspells single consonant sounds. When he does misspell consonant sounds the error is associated with blends (*fr* in *from*), digraphs (*wh* in *when*), or variant consonant spellings (*s* for *c* in *once*). In both the blend and the digraph he got the first letter correct but not the second. In *ones* he chose the most common option for the /s/ sound. Finally, his misspelling of the /n/ sound in *when* was caused by knowing too much rather than too little. We suspect that he knows both spellings for the /n/ sound since he uses *nn* in *wenn* and *n* in *grandfathers.*

6) *David is beginning to gain control of some difficult vowel spellings.* His attempt to spell the schwa vowel (*fame* for *from*), the final *e* spelling (*hade* for *had*), and the /e/ sound spelled *y* (*Ruste* for *Rusty*) may be regarded as steps toward learning these difficult spellings. They are not simply random errors. His guesses represented sophisticated exploration of letter-sound relationships. In all three instances his errors are logical steps in the right direction. Vowel spellings are the most variable and, consequently, take the longest time for children to master.

7) *David correctly spelled the blend* gr *in* grandfathers *but misspelled the* fr *blend in* from *and the* wh *digraph in* when. An educated guess would be that David is ready for some specific instruction on blends and digraphs. However, since there are not enough instances in this story of the use of blends and digraphs to make a sound judgment, further analysis is appropriate.

8) *David uses what he knows to solve what he does not know.* This is a significant learning strength and David uses it well. He also reasons well by analogy, as was illustrated in several cases. Analogous reasoning is an important thinking ability.

From the analysis we conclude that David is further advanced in spelling proficiency than many second grade children, and that his word recognition abilities are in advance of his spelling ability. In all likelihood he is capable of pronouncing words at a third grade level or higher. This is an educated guess based on the fact that word recognition ability often runs one-half to one grade level higher than the instructional spelling level. Given the opportunity to continue writing, David will likely develop into an excellent speller and capable reader. And, judging from the content of this story, he is on the way to becoming an excellent writer as well.

Systematic Spelling Instruction in Conjunction With Writing

Many teachers use commercial spelling materials but lack suitable criteria for evaluating these materials. Some teachers would prefer an alternative to commercial materials but are uncertain about how to develop and implement that alternative. This section will suggest guidelines for teachers in both circumstances. First, we will present an alternative to commercial spelling materials by outlining some principles and procedures for developing and implementing a personalized spelling program. Second, we will suggest suitable criteria for evaluating commercial spelling materials.

A Personalized Spelling Program

A personalized spelling program presumes that children learn at different rates and have different spelling needs. To accommodate different learning rates, the number of words assigned varies from child to child and from group to group. To accommodate the different spelling needs that children exhibit, the specific words assigned must vary from child to child or from group to group.

If a teacher chooses to use a personalized spelling program, it is helpful to understand some basic principles that underlie effective spelling instruction. The teacher must also have a set of procedures for implementing the program.

Basic Principles of Effective Spelling Instruction

The following list of basic spelling principles is not exhaustive. However, it is sufficiently complete to serve as a useful guide in developing a personalized spelling program.

1. *An excellent writing program is the key to a good spelling program.* Writing is the ultimate test of the effectiveness of spelling instruction. Writing creates the need to learn and to use word forms. Writing enables the teacher to determine what has been mastered and what has yet to be grasped. Writing is the most meaningful source for determining the extent to which lessons learned in spelling are being applied.

2. *Each child learns words at a rate suited to his or her ability and personal spelling needs.* Commercial spelling materials often take little note of the differences which exist among children with respect to learning rates and spelling needs. In a personalized spelling program these difficulties are avoided. The number of words assigned to each child or group is individually determined, hence, the learning rate is tailored to each child's pace. The specific words assigned are drawn from children's writing and other sources deemed relevant by the teacher, hence, specific spelling needs are recognized.

3. *Formal spelling instruction should not begin until a first grade reading level has been achieved.* The demands of spelling are such that writing words is more difficult than reading them. For this reason spelling achievement typically lags behind reading ability by one-half to one grade level. Once a child has achieved reading fluency formal spelling instruction should begin. In the

meantime, readiness for spelling is provided through auditory and visual discrimination activities, letter-sound association skills, and growth in sight vocabulary.

4. *Personalized spelling lists are an aid to writing.* As children learn new words they file them alphabetically. This file is used as an aid to writing. The file should be used with care, since constant reference to it may retard writing fluency. The alphabetical file is especially useful for second draft editing. Children should be encouraged to use it for this purpose.

Basic Procedures for a Personalized Spelling Program

A personalized spelling program may be organized in different ways. However, it is important that a systematic plan be followed. The procedures suggested below provide all the key elements needed for an effective personalized spelling program.

1. *Personalized spelling lists are prepared weekly for each child or group of children.* Words are selected from misspellings in writing, functional word needs identified by the teacher, and personal words chosen by the child.

2. *The teacher should be cautious when selecting spelling words from children's writing.* The child must not feel that writing is adding too great a burden to the spelling lessons. Excessive pressure can impede writing and do more harm than good. If children are encouraged to participate in the selection of a proportion of their spelling words, negative feelings are more easily controlled.

3. *The size of each child's weekly spelling list should vary according to his ability to learn and retain words.* The teacher should try different size lists with each child until a comfortable number of words has been discovered. The following chart may be helpful if it is used only as a starting point.

4. *Each child writes his or her weekly words on index cards and organizes them alphabetically in lists or in a notebook.*

TABLE 2
Number of Spelling Words Per Week

GRADE LEVEL	SLOW LEARNER	AVERAGE LEARNER	FAST LEARNER
1	2–4	4–8	8–12
2	2–6	7–12	13–18
3	2–6	7–12	13–18
4	4–8	9–16	17–22
5	4–8	9–16	17–22
6	6–10	11–20	21–26
7	8–12	13–24	25–30
8	8–12	13–24	25–30

5. *A method of study and practice should be suggested.* There are several possible methods for study and practice including that of allowing children to devise their own strategies. The following method is suitable for those who lack their own successful strategy.

Step 1: Say the word.

Step 2: Write the word twice while looking at the original copy.

Step 3: Write the word again without looking at the orginal copy. Check it against the original copy for accuracy. If the word was written correctly, go to Step 4. If the word was written incorrectly, go back to Step 2.

Step 4: Write the word once again without looking at the original copy. Check it against the original copy for accuracy. If the word is written correctly, go to the next word. If the word was written incorrectly, go back to Step 2.

6. *When a child is ready he or she takes a test on the weekly spelling lists.* Words that are missed are restudied, and the test is retaken later in the week. When a child achieves 90 to 100 percent accuracy on a weekly list, that list is considered learned. Tests are best administered using a buddy system. Children are paired and administer the spelling tests to each other. The teacher may give the tests but will find this a drain on his or her time.

7. *Review tests should be constructed periodically.* Once every four to six weeks is sufficient. Since it is impractical to review all words, select about one-fourth of the words at random for the review test. Writing is another source of review selection. Words that have appeared on earlier lists but are subsequently misspelled in writing should be selected for review.

Commercial Spelling Program

Commercial spelling materials differ in various ways but nearly all have four features in common. These similar features are (1) graded lists of spelling words, (2) exercises and activities for studying list words, (3) procedures for testing achievement on list words, and (4) systematic review of words previously taught. The purpose here is not to argue the merits of these features but rather to suggest guidelines for evaluating them. We shall also discuss a feature seldom included in commercial spelling materials but which is essential to an effective spelling program. This seldom included feature is (5) connecting writing with spelling.

Evaluating the Spelling Lists

Spelling lists are typically organized around such features as linguistic patterns, word frequency, and presumed word difficulty. Sometimes an attempt is made to use some combination of all three criteria.

Modern spelling lists are often selected to highlight a specific linguistic feature. When words are arranged by linguistic patterns specific spelling rules or generalizations may be learned. Linguistic patterns commonly include consonant, vowel, and structural features of words.

Certain words are useful to know how to spell because they are needed for specific school related activities and experiences. Other words are useful because they appear so often in oral and written language. Knowledge of a limited number of high frequency words enables children to spell correctly many of the words needed for writing.

The difficulty of a word is presumed to be related to meaning and orthographic complexity. Decisions about which words to include in a given spelling list cannot be entirely objective. Presumptions must be made about apparent difficulty. Consequently, spelling lists are constructed partly on the basis of linguistic patterns and frequency counts, and partly on the basis of subjective impressions about meaning and orthographic difficulty.

In evaluating the adequacy of spelling lists in commercial materials, teachers should seek to discover the extent to which the lists are based on the criteria stated above. Teachers must also decide if the spelling lists are suitable for the children who will be using them.

Evaluating Spelling Exercises

Spelling exercises should (1) focus on word meaning, (2) stress inductive learning of spelling generalizations, (3) incorporate word games and puzzles, and (4) be clearly written and illustrated.

Knowledge of word meaning is central to spelling success. If a spelling word is not firmly rooted in a child's meaning vocabulary, he or she will not use it in writing. If it is not used in writing it may be forgotten. Furthermore, many spelling generalizations are based on structural changes which affect meaning.

Exercises should be written so that featured spelling generalizations can be learned inductively. Inductive learning improves the chances of transfer of the generalization to other words where the same generalization applies.

Spelling exercises should be clearly written and functionally illustrated. Written material should be brief and simple. Arrangement of exercises should leave plenty of space for writing. Few things discourage a reluctant speller more than formidable, crowded pages. Crowded, print-laden pages overwhelm some children and defeat them before they begin.

Finally, spelling lessons are not among the most enjoyable of school subjects. For this reason an attempt should be made to provide exercises which incorporate word games, puzzles, and other activities that children seem to enjoy or at least find challenging.

Evaluating Pretest and Posttest Procedures

A pretest should be given to determine current spelling knowledge of all words in a particular lesson. This is necessary to avoid wasting time and effort studying words already known. Certain exercises or even whole lessons may be eliminated by carefully examining the results of a pretest. Posttests are useful for determining spelling growth or lack of it in a given lesson. For example, adjustment in level of materials or pace through materials is sometimes necessary. An examination of the results of posttesting enables the teacher to determine whether progress is satisfactory.

Evaluating Review Procedures

Commercial spelling materials should provide systematic review of words and spelling generalizations taught. It is particularly important to review spelling generalizations to determine whether children are learning the generalizations or simply learning words by rote. The best way to test spelling generalizations is to introduce new words not directly taught in the materials into the review lists. These new review words should require an application of the spelling generalizations taught. Few publishers are willing to put their materials on the line in this way. But, if spelling generalizations are worth teaching and are well taught they will withstand this test of their validity.

Review procedures should also test how well children have learned the words directly taught in the materials. Review lists need not be long to assess the effectiveness of the spelling lessons. For this reason, selective reviewing of old words is better than reviewing every word in preceeding lessons.

Evaluating the Connection Between Spelling and Writing

Commercial spelling materials should link spelling with writing. Activities which promote writing should be included in spelling materials. These activities should be included in spelling materials. These activities should include opportunities for practical and creative writing. Teachers' editions of commercial spelling materials should include suggestions which promote writing and explanations of the relationship of writing to spelling. The idea that writing makes spelling meaningful should be evident in both student and teacher materials.

SUMMARY

Spelling achieves functional meaning through real writing experiences; therefore, the teaching of spelling should be closely related to the teaching of writing. Spelling can be a formidable hindrance to independent writing for young children unless they are encouraged to spell words "as best they can." Research has shown that this approach produces superior spellers.

An examination of children's correct and incorrect spellings in written communication can provide useful diagnostic information about children's developing spelling and word recognition skills.

Children should receive systematic spelling instruction in connection with the writing program. Suggestions were given for developing a personalized spelling program and guidelines provided for evaluating commercial spelling materials.

REFERENCES

1. Henderson, Edmund. "Correct Spelling—An Inquiry." Paper presented at the First Annual Reading Conference, School of Education, Oakland University, Rochester, Michigan, 1973.

2. Hanna, P., Hanna, J., Hodges, R., and Rudorf, H. **Phoneme-Grapheme Correspondence as Cues to Spelling Improvement**. Washington, D.C.: United States Government Printing Office, 1966.

3. Venezky, Richard. "English Orthography: Its General Structure and Its Relation to Sound." **Reading Research Quarterly** 2 (1967).

4. Cramer, Ronald L. "An Investigation of the Spelling Achievement of Two Groups of First-Grade Classes on Phonologically Regular and Irregular Words and in Written Composition." Unpublished doctoral dissertation, Newark, Delaware, Reading Study Center, University of Delaware, 1968.

5. Cramer, Ronald L. "An Investigation of First-Grade Spelling Achievement." **Elementary English** 47 (1970): 230–37.

6. Stauffer, Russell, and Hammond, Dorsey. **Effectiveness of Language-Arts and Basic-Reader Approaches to First-Grade Reading Instruction**. Newark, Delaware: U.S.O.E. Project Number 2769, Reading Study Center, University of Delaware, 1968.

7. Stauffer, Russell, and Hammond, Dorsey. **Effectiveness of Language Arts and Basic-Reader Approaches to Reading Instruction: Six-Year Study**. Newark, Delaware: Reading Study Center, University of Delaware, 1973.

8. Beers, Jim. "First and Second-Grade Children's Developing Orthographic Concepts of Short and Long Vowels." Paper presented at the Southeast Regional International Reading Association Conference, Washington, D.C., November 1974.

9. Henderson, Edmund, and Beers, Jim. "A Study of Developing Orthographic Concepts among First-Grade Children." Unpublished manuscript. Charlottesville, Virginia: University of Virginia, 1975.

9

Teaching Editing Skills
to Children

Children must learn to edit their own writing. Editing skills are developed over a period of years through the internalization of a set of writing standards. Editing must be taught in a variety of interesting and motivating ways so that children will discover and internalize a personalized set of writing standards.

This chapter presents four factors relating to the teaching of editing skills to children: (1) imposing adult standards of writing on children, (2) helping children to become their own editors, (3) procedures and illustrations for teaching editing skills in an editing workshop, and (4) activities that will motivate and stimulate the teaching of editing skills.

Imposing Adult Standards of Writing on Children

Imposing adult writing standards on children has been a feature of writing instruction in American schools for over two hundred years. The history of children's writing instruction suggests that teachers have applied adult writing standards to children too early and too rigidly. This practice has prevented some children from reaching their full writing potential, slowed the writing growth of others, and destroyed the writing potential of still others. The misapplication of adult writing standards to children helps account for the writing illiteracy of many students, some of whom never learn to write with even minimal competency.

A fundamental link in the application of adult writing standards to children is the practice of "correctness" teaching. "Correctness" teaching holds

117

that there is a "proper" or "correct" set of language and writing standards that must be taught to all children. These writing and language standards are taught to children with little regard for children's writing capabilities. In fact, real writing has little or nothing to do with the teaching of these conventions, which are normally taught under the rubrics of "English." The "content" of this "Alice in Wonderland English" tends to emphasize other format mechanics of writing.

"Correctness" teaching does not produce good writers. On the contrary, it inhibits the development of writing skill. The reasons for the failure of "correctness" teaching are legion. Here are four of the most obvious.

1. *"Correctness" teaching is linguistically naive and pedagogically underproductive.* It implies that language is either correct or incorrect and that writing fails if it violates the standards of spelling and punctuation. Children's writing is not simply correct or incorrect in terms of its conformity to adult writing norms. Such simplistic ideas about children's writing conflict with the known facts of language and pedagogy. Furthermore, "correctness" teaching is pedagogically underproductive since it prevents children from entering into writing early, eagerly, and efficiently.

2. *The methods and materials associated with "correctness" teaching are insufficiently related to real writing experiences.* The most notorious of the devices for "teaching writing" is the textbook-workbook exercise where "rules for writing" are taught in a nonwriting context. Motivating, personalized methods and materials for fostering genuine writing experiences are available, but are not widely known or used by teachers. Consequently, the native writing potential of children remains largely unexploited.

3. *"Correctness" teaching values form over content.* As a result interesting ideas expressed in home-rooted language and unconventional form are undervalued, while undistinguished although "correct" writing is overvalued.

4. *The overemphasis on "correctness" has produced a core of teachers who are not well informed about children's writing or children's language.* Writing and language have concrete features. They can be examined, understood, and improved. However, when teachers overvalue the amenities of writing, the inevitable result is to neglect the substance of writing and, hence, to be poorly informed about its dimensions.

The misapplication of adult standards of writing to children can have a chilling effect on writing development. Writing, like talking, is a personal act. Writing talent can be damaged if mishandled during its delicate growing stages. For example, well-intentioned but inept criticism may stifle self-expression, rejection of childhood language may injure self-image, and rigid expectations may diminish writing fluency.

The major concern of editing is to teach the standards and conventions of writing. But these standards and conventions must be taught with due regard for the potential damage that insensitive application of them can do, and with full appreciation of the benefits that knowing them can provide. Of course, writing standards must gradually be learned but they must be learned in a context that stresses writing, not rules; that values content, not form; that honors childhood language, not rejects it.

Helping Children to Become Their Own Editors

To edit is to alter or refine a piece of writing until it conforms more closely to an accepted standard or specific purpose. Standards of writing refer to a body of generally accepted rules or guidelines for writing. They are sometimes called writing conventions. Standards of writing often refer to rules governing grammatical usage, syntax, punctuation, capitalization, spelling, and other format conventions.

One problem in the teaching of editing is the question of who should do it—the teacher or the child. There are times when both teacher and pupil should assume the role of editor. However, one of the goals of writing is to teach children how to edit their own writing. Even though some children may never become good editors, every child should have the opportunity to improve his or her writing through editing. The process of moving toward self-editorship is a significant one since it instills responsibility, independence, and an ear for good writing. Teaching self-editing techniques to children will make most of them better writers.

Teaching children to be their own editors is no easy chore. It is infinitely more difficult to teach children to edit their own writing than it is to edit for them. Teachers must accept the challenge, however, since self-editing offers the prospect of independence in writing, whereas excessive teacher editing encourages dependence. Of course, teachers may edit children's writing as necessity requires, but they must not waver from the ultimate goal of teaching children to be their own editors.

Following are some guidelines for teaching self-editing. These guidelines have been used by teachers who have had notable success in getting children to write freely and edit effectively.

1. *Use a wide variety of techniques and activities to stimulate self-editing behavior.* Editing activities should place children in various editing roles which require them to make judgments about their own writing and that of others.
2. *Model the type of editing behavior you wish to encourage among children.* The modeling of editing behavior takes place when you informally comment on children's writing and when you formally edit children's writing. Editing behavior consists both in knowing how to apply writing standards and in displaying behavioral traits useful in teaching children editing concepts. It is particularly important to display sensitivity, thoughtfulness, and accuracy in dealing with the personal writing of children.

3. *Use writing based on direct observation for self-editing experiences.* Reports of science experiments, nature observations, research reports, and other similar accounts are most appropriate. Children are sensitive about their writing, so care must be exercised while children become accustomed to editing and being edited.

4. *As a rule, avoid editing writing that is based on personal or imaginative experiences.* Imaginative and personal writing is privileged material. Editorial comments on personal and imaginative writing may miss the point entirely, intrude on private feelings and thoughts, or repress writing experimentation. Of course, when children seek editorial comment on personal writing, it should be given although caution is still advisable.

5. *Make no corrections or editorial comments beyond the understanding of the writer.* When you edit or teach editorial concepts, deal only with those matters within children's experience and understanding. For example, most first grade children understand some uses of periods and questions marks, although they seldom use them during the initial stages of writing. Therefore, editorial advice and discussion about periods and question marks are appropriate. However, few first grade children understand the mysteries of quotation marks. Therefore, quotation marks would not be an editorial concern for most first grade writers.

6. *Make editing comments and corrections in the presence of the writer when possible.* When you are editing children's writing or showing them how to edit, impress on them the importance you place in explaining the purpose and meaning of editorial corrections and suggestions. Editing in the presence of the child personalizes the teaching and makes the information more meaningful and useful. It also makes a dialogue between the editor and the writer possible.

7. *Show more concern for what is said than for how it is said.* Content over form is a cardinal rule of editing. The technical skills of writing are easily taught and readily learned when the teaching of writing is conducted in a professional manner. However, the ability to express good ideas is more difficult, perhaps impossible, to teach.

8. *Respect the native language of children.* Remember, children cannot write in a language that is substantially different from the one they speak. Dialect differences may account for some phonological, syntactical, and vocabulary differences among children. Attempts to help a child improve upon his or her initial writing efforts should be made, but certain amenities must be observed. Sometimes children cannot improve upon their original version. Coercing changes can result in artificial and stilted language that is scarcely an improvement over the original version. Revised writing must bear the clear imprint of the original author, otherwise the revision is a failure regardless of how much better it is than the original version.

9. *Identify common writing deficiencies by analyzing children's writings.* Plan teaching sessions for children who have a given deficiency in

common. For example, you may note that five children consistently place periods in random places long after they have achieved fluency in writing. A special editing session similar to the one described in the next section may then be conducted for the five children.

10. *Encourage children to listen to their writing before editing it.* This may be done by working with a partner, by reading the composition aloud, or by recording the composition and playing it back. Minor inconsistencies can be spotted immediately in this way. With experience, children will also learn to detect more serious writing flaws.

11. *Recognize the limits of editorial suggestion as it applies to individual children.* Above all, teachers must know their students. They must recognize what motivates them and be aware of their writing history. Writers wear their feelings on their sleeves. The personal feelings children have about their writing demand the utmost sensitivity to feelings of privacy and pride.

A major responsibility in teaching writing is to help children become their own editors. It is a challenging task. Successful teaching of editing requires diligent attention to detail without becoming pedantic, it requires planning and structure without becoming inflexible, and it requires that writing be an enjoyable and exciting enterprise without sacrificing discipline and responsibity.

The Editing Workshop

The purpose of the editing workshop is to practice editing written work. In the process of learning to edit written work, attention is inevitably drawn to standards and conventions of writing. The editing procedures suggested direct children's attention to specific elements of writing and use children's current knowledge of oral and written language to guide their editorial judgements.

General Guidelines for Editorial Workshops

The following guidelines for directing editing workshops are pertinent.

1. *Editing workshops should be conducted over a period of three to four years.* Time is needed to gradually build the editing skills needed for effective writing. Accordingly, a coordinated school-wide writing program is needed.

2. *Editing workshops should be conducted once or twice a week.* Typically, their duration ranges from twenty to forty minutes.

3. *Editing workshops should be initiated at the third or fourth grade level.* When they begin depends on children's writing ability. Children must be writing fluently, though not necessarily well, before editing workshops are useful. Editing workshops are not recommended for children with little previous writing experience, nor for first and second grade

children, as a rule. The early years of writing are best used to develop writing fluency.

4. *Editing workshops should be conducted on discovery learning principles and techniques.* The editorial judgments children make during an editing workshop flow from the abundance of previous oral and written language experiences they have had. Therefore, the success of editing workshops is partially dependent on the scope of the first and second grade language arts program. The reading and oral language program is of particular relevance.

5. *The materials used in editing workshops are those written by the participating children.* Each child should have some recently written but unedited material for each editing session. This material will be individually edited following the group editing session.

6. *Editing workshops are dependent on the capacity of the teacher to direct the process enthusiastically, efficiently, and thoughtfully.* There are two basic phases to an editing workshop. First, the teacher directs the group in the editing of a piece of written work. Second, the teacher monitors the children's individual editing of their personal writing. Both phases are crucial, and the teacher's role throughout is a subtle blend of intellectual agitator and friendly advisor.

7. *The materials needed for an editing workshop include an overhead projector, chalkboard, grease pencil or felt-tip pen, and a transparency overlay of a child's recent written account.*

Specific Procedures for Directing an Editing Workshop

The following procedures give specific directions for conducting an editing workshop.

1. *Direct a writing activity on the day preceding the editing workshop.* Have each child who is participating write an account in first draft form.

2. *Obtain permission from one child to make a transparency of his or her written account.* This transparency will provide the material for collective editing in the workshop session. If the paper is not sufficiently legible, recopy it exactly as it was written, leaving space between lines for comments and corrections.

3. *Project the written material on the screen.* Instruct the children to read the material, then say, "Tell me about anything that has been done well in this story." List their responses on the board.

4. *Ask the children to read the story again, then say, "Can anyone find something that needs to be changed?"* This instruction is neutral. It avoids using terms such as *wrong* and *error*.

5. *Make the changes suggested by children directly on the transparency.* Comment on each suggestion in a casual way. Be generous, but not insincere, with your praise for children's efforts.

6. *List the suggested changes on the board.* Children usually restrict their

initial observations to matters of punctuation, spelling, grammar, and syntactical items.

7. *Select, or have children select, one item from the list that the children will now apply to their own written work.* For example, if they have listed "punctuation at the end of each sentence" as an editing observation, say to them, "Read your written account carefully to see if you have put either a period, question mark, or exclamation mark at the end of each sentence."

8. *Circulate among the children offering help, advice, or praise as they edit their writing.* Students will often edit for more than the specified item. This behavior should be singled out for praise and recognition. Other children will copy this behavior and soon they will be doing a more thorough job than you had expected.

Follow-up Activities for Editing Workshops

There are a number of activities that naturally accompany or derive from editing workshops. The following items are pertinent in this respect.

1. *Gradually increase the number of editing chores assigned in one session.* The eventual goal is to have the general instruction, "edit your paper" taken on specific, performable meaning.

2. *After the children are familiar with workshop procedures, encourage them to work in teams of two or in small groups using workshop procedures.*

3. *Later, the workshop procedures described above should be used to edit for meaning, organization, sequence, clarity, paragraphing, and other substantive editing concerns.* Children initially tend to concentrate on the mechanics of writing. When this has gone on for some time, suggest a shift of emphasis by asking leading questions about meaning, organization, and so on.

4. *Develop an evaluation file for each child's writing.* Retain one copy of an edited and unedited piece of work in this file by selecting samples once every three or four weeks. This file can be used to report progress to parents, to demonstrate progress to children, and to fulfill the teacher's need for evaluation information.

Illustration and Case History for an Editing Workshop

So far we have considered some general guidelines for the editing workshop and outlined procedures and follow-up activities to accompany it. This section will explain how a typical editing workshop was actually conducted in a sixth grade classroom. Both the children and the teacher were familiar with the editing workshop procedures, having participated in several during the preceding weeks.

The story below was written by Nick on Monday. The other children also wrote on Monday. The teacher had planned the writing activity in advance.

When the writing activity was finished the teacher asked Nick for permission to use his story in the workshop planned for Tuesday. The editing workshop procedures outlined above were followed. For illustrative purposes the editing workshop described below covers more matters than would normally be covered in one workshop session. Here is Nick's story.

If I Were Rich

If I had a lot of money I would be rich I would not buy a car motrsikl house and all the candy I could eat.
My mom and dad woulnt have to work any more either they would have their own house and all they needed to live. I would give money to poor people to
I would not waste the money like some people. going to coledg is what I want to do with some of the money.
That is what I would do if I were rich.

Nick
Age 11

The story "If I Were Rich" was projected on a screen. The teacher instructed the children to "Read the story carefully, then tell me about anything in the story that you thought had been done well." The children made the following responses:

Each word in the title of the story is capitalized.
The word "I" is always capitalized.
There is a period after *eat.*
Paragraphs are indented.
Most sentences start with a capital letter.
Several sentences have a period after them.

The teacher wrote the responses on the board as they were suggested. An examination of the responses revealed that the children focused exclusively on the mechanical aspects of writing. This seems to be a common pattern. When the teacher judged that the examination of the mechanical aspects of the story had run its course she changed the focus of their attention by saying, "Let's look at what Nick has said in his story. What do you think about Nick's ideas?" This question started the children thinking about the meaning of Nick's story. The question elicited the following responses:

I like the things Nick wants to do with his money.
I think he has good ideas about sharing his money.
I thought the last sentence was good.
Sharing with his mother and dad was the right thing to do.
He does not want to waste the money foolishly.
Saving for college is a good thing to do.

Up to this point the teacher's comments and questions concentrated on the story as it was written. However, editing implies change and seeks to find ways to improve writing. The teacher must approach this objective with caution. Sensitivity is essential. The wording of the comments leading into initial editing behavior are crucial. The teacher's comments went like this: "You've done a good job looking at the things Nick has done well in his story. Now, let's look at it to see if there are some things we might want to change to make it even better." The teacher struck just the right note. Her remarks are brief and businesslike yet sensitive to the nuances of the situation. Her remarks elicited the following responses:

There should be a period after *rich* in the first sentence.

I don't think *motorcyle* and *college* are spelled right.

The word *going* should have a capital.

I think there should be commas after *car* and *motorcycle*.

I think there could be a period after *either. They* should be capitalized.

He used the wrong *to*. It should be *t-o-o* and it should have a period after it.

What is interesting, but not surprising, about these responses is the ease with which the children recognized writing deficiences. Teachers sometimes conclude that because children fail to use appropriate writing conventions they must not know the conventions. Often this is not true. It is a case of applying less than they know. What children commonly lack is a strategy for applying what they obviously know.

The teacher's final question was, "Is there one sentence in Nick's story which we could look at more closely and try to say the same thing another way?" One child suggested the last sentence in the third paragraph which says "going to coledg is what I want to do with some of the money." The following alternatives were suggested:

I want to go to college with the money.

I'll use some of the money to go to college.

A good way to use some of the money would be going to college.

Since I want to go to college, I'll use some of the money for that.

I want to go to college. I'll use some of the money for that.

The teacher recorded each suggestion as it was given without comment. When they had concluded she said, "Good. You've made some interesting suggestions and you've shown me that you can think of many different ways to get across the same idea. Good writers often do the same thing." The teacher's comment reinforced the importance of trying alternative ways of stating an idea without embarrassing Nick, and also associated what had been done with what good writers do. Note how brief and appropriate her remarks tend to be.

In this workshop session the teacher chose to focus on alternative ways of arranging a sentence. Over the course of time other writing concerns will be covered such as word choice, organization, sequence, paragraphing, and so on.

The editing workshop was nearly concluded. The teacher had one final instruction to give which introduced the second phase of the editing workshop. Her instructions were "Get out the story you wrote yesterday. Edit your writing for these two things: (1) make sure you end each sentence with the needed punctuation mark, either a period, question mark, or exclamation mark, (2) and be sure you capitalize the first word of each sentence."

In the beginning only one or two specific editing chores are assigned. Part of the difficulty children have in editing is that the generalized instruction "Edit your paper" is too broad a task. The instruction is too unfocused for most children to manage. That is why training in editing procedures is essential. Breaking the task down into smaller, specific tasks makes editing simpler. Gradually, as children develop greater understanding of the process, the teacher may assign editing tasks that require more and more responsibility. The editing workshop will help you teach editing skills in a systematic and structured way that does not interfere with children's enjoyment of writing.

Activities for Motivating and Stimulating Editing Behavior

The editing workshop is a systematic and structured procedure for teaching editing skills. However, if editing skills are to be learned, a variety of motivating activities for encouraging editing behavior must be used. The ideas listed below will add variety and scope to the teaching of editing skills.

1. *Have children dictate a story each has recently written into the tape recorder.* When the tape is played back, the children listen for one or two specific things they may wish to change. A checklist of what to listen for should be provided. A few examples of things to listen for are word selection, interesting beginning, strong conclusion, complete sentences, and discernible organization.
2. *Instruct the children to underline some words in their writing that might be changed to more interesting, precise, or vivid words.* Show the children how to use a thesaurus to aid them in their work. Care must be taken to avoid substituting words that destroy the intended meaning.
3. *Have the children underline all of the naming and action words in their writing.* Show them how these words may be modified to create more interesting images. For example, a sentence that says "The firetruck went to the burning house" might be modified to say, "The bright red firetruck roared toward the burning house."
4. *Have the children make a "sequence of events" chart from a recent writing.* Read the story from top to bottom. Make a decision as to whether the events appear in logical order. If the events are not sequenced properly, rewrite accordingly.
5. *Have the children write questions about the important ideas in their writing.* A partner is chosen to read the account and answer the questions. The writer and the partner discuss any problems that were encountered. The discussion should lead to decisions about rewriting.
6. *Pair the children.* Have them read their writing to each other. Encourage them to discuss the clarity of each other's written material. Then let them help edit each other's writing.

7. *A bulletin board display can be used to provide practice in editing sentences.* Use cutout letters to make sentences with no capitalization or punctuation. In an envelope tacked to the bottom of the bulletin board, have cutout capital letters, commas, periods, question marks, and so forth. Have the children edit the sentences using the letters and punctuation available. Here are some sample sentences:

I live in pontiac michigan
where is mrs brown's hat
abraham lincoln was our sixteenth president

8. *Two editing charts can be placed in a writing center to help children edit their writing.* One chart has some reminders about the mechanics of writing and the other chart contains reminders about content and meaning.

CONTENT CHART

Did I say what I wanted to say clearly?
Did I say it so that others will understand?
Did I arrange the paragraphs in a logical and interesting way?
Did I use the best possible words throughout my writing?
Did I use any unnecessary words?
Did my story have a good beginning, middle, and ending?
Did I make the people and events in my story real, interesting, and worth reading about?

MECHANICS CHART

Did I punctuate each sentence?
Did I use punctuation in other appropriate places?
Did I capitalize the first word of each sentence?
Did I capitalize other appropriate words?
Did I spell each word correctly or check my spelling for words I was unsure of?
Did I use proper form on titles, margins, indenting, and other matters?
Did I write in my best handwriting?

9. *Divide the class into small editing groups.* Each group has a designated leader. The group comes together at designated times following writing assignments. The group leader acts as an editing consultant and leader. The responsibility of the group is to edit all of the written work produced by members of the group.

10. *Pair a fifth and sixth grade class with a first or second grade class.* The older children act as editing consultants for the younger. Young children will often react more positively to another older child than to an adult. Care must be taken to instruct the older children both in the techniques of editing as well as in the techniques of working with younger children.

11. *Appoint specific children for certain editing jobs for periods of two to five days.* You can appoint a spelling editor, meaning editor, punctuation editor, and so on. Once you have taught a cadre of children to perform these roles well they can begin to train each other by serving an apprenticeship as assistant editor before taking over as an editor.

12. *If children have written a story or a play, it is sometimes helpful to have it acted out by others.* By watching, listening, or directing the play, children may discover that the story or play needs rewriting.

13. *Match your children up in pairs to work as editing partners.* Be sure to spend time preparing them for the role. When properly organized, the use of partners can be an excellent way to improve editing skills.

There are no magic solutions to the problem of teaching editing. The best that can be done is to develop editing activities that have an element of fun, variety, and challenge; work hard to involve children in these activities; write, write, and rewrite.

SUMMARY

Imposing adult standards of writing on children before they are ready to incorporate such standards into their writing is counterproductive.

Children must learn to be their own editors since this leads to independence and excellence in writing. Guidelines were suggested to direct teachers in the realization of this goal.

Editing workshops may serve as a systematic and structured means of developing editing skill. Procedures for conducting editing workshops were given. Finally, since editing skills are best learned through a variety of motivating and stimulating activities, a set of appropriate activities was presented.

10

Writing Poetry
With Children

Teachers have traditionally been skeptical about encouraging children to write poetry, though less so about requiring its memorization. Their skepticism is founded, one suspects, on a lack of useful personal experience with poetry. For it is personal experience that gives poetry lovers a special feeling about the sounds, images, and thoughts that poetry uniquely conveys. The lack of personal experience with poetry leaves teachers with a feeling of uncertainty regarding the value of encouraging children to write poetry.

This chapter is concerned with demonstrating the value of encouraging children to write poetry and in discussing issues relevant to the teaching of poetic writing. Major issues covered are (1) poetry and creative power, (2) poetry and language power, (3) imagery in poetry, (4) sharing poetry with children, and (5) types of poetic verse form.

Poetry and Creative Power

There is a secret resource of potential creative power in every child. This potential power to create must be freed if it is to be used. Insecurity, ignorance, and lack of opportunity prevent this potential power from expressing itself through literary and artistic channels. Teachers can, however, provide the environment which encourages creative activity.

The problem teachers face is learning how to bring out the creative tendencies that exist beneath the sometimes indifferent exterior of youth. There is no simple formula, but there is a place to start, a few first steps upon which

129

succeeding steps may depend. Here are some suggestions for teachers that may be helpful in directing children to use the creative power that is in them.

1. *Modify the customary criteria by which the worth of children's personal writing is commonly judged.* This means changing your traditional attitudes so that you decrease the importance of the mechanical aspects of writing and increase the importance of the meaning of writing. Mearns (1, p. 29) had this say say about the traditional attitudes toward the mechanics of writing: "They [teachers] must teach themselves not to see such things at all, to regard them, indeed, as comparatively unimportant."

2. *Diligently cultivate an openness of mind and spirit that shows itself in a receptivity to children's writings, their ways, and their ideas.* Openness does not mean a lack of conviction or a wishy-washy intellect. Openness is being receptive to people and ideas, sharing your humanity and your personal talents with others, and accepting their sharing with you.

3. *Lead children to develop a liking for the use of their creative talents.* Mearns (1, p. 29) has wisely counselled that creative activity "is not often a thing teachers themselves would prefer at first among the many offerings of their [children's] mind and hand." (1, p. 31)

4. *Develop a variety of ways to bestow approval and appreciation for the creative work children produce.* Above all, this approval must be sincere and must be limited to those products and behaviors that merit your approval. When your approval is sincerely given, children will respond by producing more of the good work that brought forth your initial approval.

5. *Be patient and courageous.* Patience is required to wait through the long periods of activity when little or nothing is produced to reward your faith in the creative ability of children. Courage is needed to respectfully receive the uninspired products that inevitably precede the good.

It is the business of teachers to improve the strengths their children demonstrate, to inspire and instruct each child to add to strengths already possessed, and to secure the best possible performance from each child. Good teachers must be capable of recognizing an effective poem, a sparkling line, or a wise thought when they occur. Good teachers seldom let a piece of work that can be improved go unchallenged, or allow any excellence, no matter how small, go unrewarded. There is no greater gift that teachers can bestow on children than the gift of literacy and an appreciation and love for its further development.

Poetry and Language Power

No other form of language usage can match poetry for diversity, beauty, power, and technical brilliance. As a vehicle for verbal expression, it is unrivaled. The purpose of this section is to discuss some of the language aspects of poetry.

Poetry's unique appeal and beauty are as much dependent upon the sounds of language as they are upon the sense of language. In this respect, music and poetry have much in common. It is sometimes said that poetry is the music of language. Like music, poetry must be heard to be fully appreciated. This section will consider some important facets of the sound of language in poetry.

Rhythm

Rhythm in poetry is the music of the words. Words and their sounds are arranged in poetry in such a way that they constitute an ordered, recurrent flow of sound and silence. Read the selections below aloud and note the difference in the flow of sound and silence as you read each selection.

> How Doth the Little Crocodile
> Improve his shining tail,
> And pour the waters of the Nile
> On every golden scale!
> How cheerfully he seems to grin,
> How neatly spreads his claws,
> And welcomes little fishes in,
> With gently smiling jaws! (2, p. 17)

> Charles Lutwidge Dodgson
> (Lewis Carroll)

> The Squirrel

> Whisky, frisky,
> Hippity hop,
> Up he goes
> To the tree top!
> Whirly, twirly,
> Round and round,
> Down he scampers
> To the ground.
> Furly, curly
> What a tail!
> Tall as a feather
> Broad as a sail!
> Where's his supper?
> In the shell,
> Snappity, crackity,
> Out it fell. (3, p. 473)

> Anonymous

The Daffodils

I wandered lonely as a cloud
That floats on high o'er vales and hills,
When all at once I saw a crowd,
A host of golden daffodils;
Beside the lake, beneath the trees,
Fluttering and dancing in the breeze.
Continuous as the stars that shine
And twinkle on the milky way,
They stretched in never-ending line
Along the margin of a bay;
Ten thousand saw I at a glance
Tossing their heads in sprightly dance.
The waves beside them danced, but they
Outdid the sparkling waves in glee—
A poet could not but be gay
In such a jocund company!
I gazed—and gazed—but little thought
What wealth to me the show had brought;
For oft, when on my couch I lie
In vacant or in pensive mood,
They flash upon that inward eye
Which is the bliss of solitude;
And then my heart with pleasure fills,
And dances with the daffodils. (4)

William Wordsworth

Onomatopoeia

This lovely sounding Greek word describes words that imitate their natural sounds. Words such as *buzz, growl, sizzle, hiss,* and *hum* are onomatopoeic. When they are pronounced they give the effect of the natural sound they represent. Onomatopoeia is a poetic device to enhance the sound or rhythm of a poem, an effect that is beautifully achieved in Rhoda Bacmeister's "Galoshes."

Galoshes

Susie's galoshes
Make splishes and sploshes
And splooshes and sloshes
As Susie steps slowly
Along in the slush.
They stamp and they tramp
On the ice and concrete,
They get stuck in the muck and the mud;
But Susie likes much bets to hear

The slippery slush
As it slooshes and sloshes
And splishes and sploshes
All around her galoshes! (5)

Rhoda Bacmeister

Children can be encouraged to invent words which imitate sounds such as:

zitt, the sound of a mosquito taking a bite, and *zott*, the sound of a mosquito being swatted.

A similar activity is to have children work in teams to prepare lists of words that have an onomatopoeic quality, as in the list below:

sizzle	purr	whine
pop	whoosh	screech
roar	ding-dong	jingle
bang	clang	growl
crack	bong	chug

Alliteration

Alliteration is the repetition of the initial sound of words in one or more closely following words. This device is used to good effect in the following poems.

Thaw

The snow is soft, and how it squashes:
"Galumph, galumph!" go my galoshes. (6)

Eunice Tietjens

Rabbits

Fuzzy, furry
Flipping, flapping, wiggling
Happy, gay, glad, funny
Bunnies

Craig
Age 9

Children can easily manipulate this technique, as Craig's poem shows, and will enjoy doing so. The following ideas are useful for helping children accomplish alliteration in their poems:

1. *Give the children several examples of alliterative phrases.* Then ask them to write some of their own, such as big bony bunnies, friendly freckled frogs, ghastly ghosts.
2. *Read the children poems which have effective examples of alliteration.* Have them listen and identify the phrases.

Repetition

Alliteration is a specific type of repetition limited to initial sounds of words. Naturally, repetition of words, phrases, and sentences is also used as a poetic device to achieve a desired effect or simply because the poet senses a necessity for repetition. The following poems illustrate the effective use children have made of repetition in their poems.

> Water lillies in the pond,
> The water ever so blue.
> Such a lovely color!
> Such a lovely hue!
>
> Susan
> Age 9

> I know what a lion does.
> It eats.
> It can scratch.
> It can smell.
> Maybe it can scare somebody.
> I know what a lion does.
>
> Steven
> Age 6

> The Fox
>
> Sleek, sly and sharp,
> The fox is on the run,
> The hens are wary,
> The moonlight strong,
> The fox is on the run,
> The hens shivering,
> The dogs trembling,
> It is midnight,
> The fox is getting nearer,
> It prowls around the hen hut,
> It creeps through the entrance,
> Then a scream, squawk, and shuffle,
> Then all goes quiet,
> The fox comes out
> With a hen in its mouth,
> And then goes off in the dark to
> devour its prey. (7, p. 85)
>
> Unknown
> Age 11

Rhyme

Rhyme is an important poetic device used primarily at middle and ending positions in a line of poetry. Undoubtedly the most universally recognized element in poetry, rhyme is a form of sound repetition which adds a pleasant rhythmic quality to poetry. There are various types of rhyming common in poetry. We shall discuss internal, near, and ending rhyme forms. Technically, alliteration is considered a type of beginning rhyme form, but we have considered that topic separately.

Near rhyme occurs when related sounds and words are repeated although the full elements of rhyme may be missing. For example, *toast* and *roast* are full rhyming words, whereas *toast* and *fist* are only near rhyming words.

Internal rhyme occurs when words are rhymed within the same line. It is extremely pleasing when it is well done, as in the first stanza of "The Remain," written by a seven year old English boy:

> The Remain
>
> On Wednesday a fire came,
> A big fire.
> On Wednesday a fire came,
> A jig fire.
> It came and went and saw
> and spent
> The value of the building

Ending rhyme is the most familiar rhyme form. Ending rhyme serves to relate one part of a poem to another. All rhyming schemes, whether near, internal, or ending, add to the pleasant sound of the poem but should do so without detracting from the intention of the entire poem. The first stanza of "The Remain" is an excellent example of the use of rhyme which adds to the pleasant quality of the sound of the poem without detracting from the meaning. The rhyme is natural and there is no straining to achieve rhyme for the sake of rhyme. Now read the second stanza of "The Remain" below. The second stanza is much less effective than the first because meaning has been sacrificed to rhyme.

> But now it is a ghost
> Because it took the most.
> It was a century old
> But now it is very cold.
> It will never work again
> And so it is a remain. (7, p. 45)

Of course, one must make an allowance for a seven year old child. Viewed from that perspective, the poem is a success and the first stanza is excellent. Nevertheless, the second stanza does illustrate a significant problem that must be faced when teaching rhyme. There is a danger that children may focus on rhyme to the detriment of meaning. When this happens, the natural beauty and rhythm of children's language are not reflected in their poetry.

The difficulty with teaching rhyme to children centers around the question of how and when it should be used. There is little doubt that of all the poetic devices, rhyming is most often misused. It is bad for children to get the notion that poetry must rhyme. Children's poetry should, above all, project sincere feelings cast in the natural tones of their native language. The premature introduction of rhyming may interfere with the natural use of language among young children. Consequently, it would seem sensible to allow children a significant period of time to write poetry unencumbered by the technical demands that rhyming presents. This delay in introducing children to rhyming will give children an opportunity to compose poetry in their natural language while providing an opportunity to increase their writing fluency. Further, they will be able to present their thoughts and feelings unhindered by the constraints that rhyming imposes on meaning.

The two poems below illustrate the points made above. In the poem "The Sky," we see a perfectly good idea ruined because the child felt obligated to rhyme the poem. Thus, we get an insincere piece of writing, which also lacks the pleasant sounds that rhyming should add to poetry. In the poem "Cobwebs on a Foggy Day," no attempt has been made to rhyme the poem. The poem is simply done in the natural language of the child. Both children who wrote these poems were ten years old. Both have something special to contribute. My guess is that the child who wrote "The Sky" would have written a much more sincere and lovely sounding poem if rhyme had not been attempted. Children must be shown when and how to use rhyme and when not to use it at all.

The Sky	Cobwebs on a Foggy Day
The sky is as blue	Wispy cobwebs strung the fences
As your baby blue eyes.	Loosely drooping everywhere,
The sky is a place	Like pearl beads.
That you dream of with sighs.	They fade away if you touch them.
The sky is a place	They hide in every crack;
To go when you're low.	They veil the trees
The sky is a beautiful place,	And carpet the grass.
You know!	Cold and grey
	They blanket the world,
	Patching up holes. (7, p. 36)

Rhyme is a delightful, important, poetic device. Furthermore, children should have opportunities to use it in their poetry. But it should not be stressed in early stages of poetic composition. When it is introduced or when children choose to use it on their own, they should be shown how it can both enhance and detract from the beauty of a poem.

Imagery in Poetry

Imagery in poetry is the creation of mental pictures through the imaginative, descriptive, and unique use of words. Imagery uses figurative language to achieve its unique, picture-like quality which distinguishes it from ordinary language. Simile and metaphor are most commonly used to give poetry its picture like quality.

A *simile* is a figure of speech which compares two unlike things. Words that often signal a simile are *as*, *like*, and *similar*.

A *metaphor* is a figure of speech in which a word or phrase which denotes one object or idea is used in place of another to suggest a likeness or analogy between them. Metaphors are often substituted for, or are analogous to, the actual object or idea. Here are some similes and metaphors written by children. Some of them are quite common, others are exceptionally fresh and interesting.

Simile

—his eyes seem to be shaped like a half moon
—the whole face wrinkled like a prune
—soft looking as a kitten's fur
—it falls down over the side with a great crash
    like a blast of dynamite

Metaphor

—twisted tongue of death
—the wasp of an essay kept stinging me
—rows of daffodils marching straight and tall
—the trees seemed to hold their breath
—the feathery fingers of the highest tree

Sharing Poetry With Children

Hearing, reading, and writing poetry are fine ways to help children know themselves and their world better. It is not so much a means of extending knowledge as deepening knowledge. Poets do not create new knowledge, but help us to see and understand old knowledge more clearly and wisely. Poetry builds on the foundation of previous experience and knowledge. Good experience with poetry, either as writer or listener, helps children to perceive and respond to poetry more vividly and intensely.

A young boy struggling with a highly emotional experience of personal loss wrote this simple poem:

> Too sorrowful to weep,
> Your mind concentrated wholly on that one thought,
> Just staring vacantly into space,
> Not even the rain pattering softly
> On the window pane disturbs you,
> As you think and ponder over the loss
> Of your beloved friend. (8, p. 90)

When I share this and other similar children's poetry with teachers and children, a bond develops between reader and listener that is extremely touching. We are bound together for a moment as one. The sharing of ordinary but profound emotion, whether it be sorrowful reflection or joyous elation, causes us to reflect together upon our common humanity. When teachers and children share such poetry, a spiritual kinship is established between them.

Writing poetry enables children to transmit to the outer world their internal experience. Writing poetry is a natural way for children to deal with the reality of their inner world and, at the same time, come to terms with the reality of their outer world. Much that children write reveals that a struggle is constantly being waged between these two worlds. Poetry is a natural link between the two. Writing poetry gives children an opportunity to symbolize their inner world in their poetry. Sharing poetry helps both teacher and children experience the human connection that exists between them.

Here are some guidelines that may be useful in sharing poetry with children.

1. *Establish a congenial classroom atmosphere where the writing and sharing of poetry can blossom.* The three most important elements in any classroom are the teacher, the children, and the physical and psychological environment. These three elements must function together if effective work is to be accomplished.

   Children must be taken seriously as poets and as people if anything worthwhile is to be achieved. Teachers must model for their children those desirable human traits they wish to reinforce and influence. This task demands an abiding, fundamental faith in children, their nature, and their ways. Teachers must respect children's mores without abandoning their own and must possess or acquire a working knowledge of children's abilities, background, aspirations, special talents, and peculiarities while remaining alert to the limitations and inadequacies by which this knowledge is necessarily constrained.

   Classrooms must reflect the character and personality of teachers and their students. If ever there was such a thing as a multipurpose room, the classroom is surely it. The classroom must be a place where quiet reflection is sometimes possible, yet talking and activity, including the natural noise this generates, are not forbidden. Creative writing of the most diverse sort may thrive in the midst of what would surely appear to the uninitiated to be a carnival atmosphere. On the other hand, equally good writing may be produced in a quiet, calm atmosphere. There are no special rules that will cover all circumstances. Flora Arnstein (1962) quotes a young girl who talks about her poetry writing under conditions of noise and quietness:

   > It's funny that sometimes when I'm most
   >   quiet and peaceful
   > It is hardest to write poems.
   > Sometimes when its noisy
   > And I am disturbed in my mind
   > Poems come quite easily. (9, p.5)

What constitutes the best classroom atmosphere defies description. Certainly, exciting teaching generates activity that, in turn, creates noise and bustle. What proportions this may be allowed to reach is a personal matter between teacher and children. Children and teachers differ in the amount of noise and activity they can tolerate. Most children and adults are able to operate effectively in an atmosphere of purposeful noise and activity. After all, this is the normal condition of all living and working circumstances. Still, there are times when an escape into reflective quiet is essential. A quiet time or place should, therefore, be planned for in all classrooms. But an objective analysis must reject, as artificial and deleterious to learning, a classroom atmosphere which is the product of an attitude that puts a premium on a tomb-like quietness as a precondition to effective instruction and learning. Such classrooms are unnatural, uncomfortable, and unhealthy for children. They do not promote learning or concentration. Rather, they promote boredom, antipathy toward school and learning, and mental escapism.

2. *Provide specific writing ideas and aids to motivate and direct the writing of poetry.* Teachers must go about this task in ways that suit their own styles and personalities. Sometimes it is helpful to consult resource materials to gain ideas. When this is done, it is best if teachers transform the ideas into their own, rather than following them verbatim. An idea that has not been transformed and made a part of your own teaching style will often not work as you had anticipated it would. Sometimes the problem is that the idea or resource consulted was not a good one. More often the problem is that any such idea or resource must be translated into your own terms in order for it to work most effectively. Chapter 12 contains many ideas for writing poetry. Transform some of these ideas into your own and make them work for you.

3. *Read appropriate selections of poetry to children.* It is especially helpful to read poems written by other children. Select poetry that matches the children's capacity to respond. The relevant factors in matching poetry to children include language, length, theme, interest, and relevance of poetry to children's knowledge and experience. This does not mean that selections should be limited to cute children's poems and Mother Goose rhymes. Sometimes relatively difficult selections can speak powerfully to children when the moment and topic coincide with children's needs and interests.

Poetry written by other children is particularly appealing to children. It seems to have the effect of demonstrating that writing poetry is natural and attainable. Furthermore, the topics and language are almost guaranteed to be suitable and interesting. Finally, poetry written by other children provides relevant models that will aid children in their own writing.

4. *The content of a poem is always more crucial than the form in which it is embodied.* After children have attained sufficient confidence, fluency,

and freedom in expressing their ideas in written form, greater attention can then be focused on teaching the necessary mechanical skills.

5. *Teach actively.* When children are composing in the classroom, the teacher must not withdraw to attend to other affairs. One notable exception is the time when the teacher is composing a poem along with the children. Normally the teacher should circulate among the students offering advice, encouragement, praise, and instruction while composition is occurring. The teacher's primary role during composition is that of a collaborator with children. For example, if a child is unable to get started, you may suggest a topic or offer to record a few lines of oral dictation to get the child going. You may listen to a child's poem and praise his or her efforts, or, conversely, suggest appropriate modification. Teachers must take an active role during composition if they are to succeed in getting the best from their children.

6. *Teach "happy."* Good teaching must have an element of excitement and enthusiasm. Happy teaching does not require you to dance and jump or act in a way that is unnatural to your personal style. Teach in the way that is natural to you, but whether you are quiet or effervescent, let there be some sparkle of joy and happiness in your teaching. Teachers who gain no joy or pleasure from teaching poetry will not get pleasurable and enthusiastic responses from children. Happiness, enthusiasm, and excitement in teaching stem from a conviction that what you are doing is important, worthwhile, and satisfying to you and to those you are teaching. Better not to teach at all if these characteristics must be feigned or if teaching is a dull and disenchanting chore.

7. *Use praise and criticism with discrimination.* When teaching writing of any sort, there are two major academic and psychological tools at your disposal—praise and instructional criticism. Neither can be wielded properly without intellectual and psychological insight. If praise and instructional criticism are used effectively, intellectual and social growth will assuredly follow. If they are used foolishly or insensitively, growth will be hindered, delayed, or even arrested.

   The highest praise should be reserved for work which illustrates the personal touch, bears the mark of original invention, or delights in a particular way. When work of this sort occurs, recognition must be forthcoming regardless of whether the poem meets the usual conventions of writing or not. In distributing praise or instructional criticism, the teacher must not neglect those whose work has not yet found its potential. There are many means of encouraging such youngsters and many appropriate comments you can give. The section in this book devoted to ways of valuing children's writing has many suggestions on this topic. (See chapter 1.)

Types of Poetic Verse Form

There are many predesigned verse forms to which children may be gradually introduced. A predesigned verse form is one which has an established structure.

There are many such forms including haiku, cinquain, tanka, senryu, couplet, triplet, quatrain, limerick, clerihew, diamante, concrete poetry, and others. It is helpful for children to be aware of different forms because (1) new forms present a challenge, add variety which may stimulate interest, and add vitality to children's repertory of poetic composition; (2) new forms provide a format for focusing on precision of language usage, using structures that are within many children's capabilities but outside their writing experience; (3) new forms often give pleasure and security to children who need the guidlines an established form can provide.

The following procedures should be considered when the teacher decides that the time is right to introduce a predesigned verse form.

1. *Help children discover the structure of the new form being introduced.* This may be done by allowing children to listen to, observe, and discuss the new form before beginning to write poetry using that particular form.
2. *Share examples of verse that you have personally written in the form being introduced.* This practice will familiarize you with the form, fortify your own resources for teaching, and help the children to identify more closely with the process of writing.
3. *Help the children to master the structural requirements of each form taught.* After the nuances of each form are understood, children may modify these forms to suit their own needs, interests, and abilities. The springboard to creativity is likely to have more bounce and orginality, however, if children are first fortified with a knowledge and understanding of the elements that constitute the form.

There are many predesigned verse forms which children are capable of using. Each form has its own unique structure enabling children to create different types of images, sounds, and visual effects. Children can discover and modify the characteristics of each form by hearing, seeing, and modeling the various forms described in this section.

Free Verse

Free or blank verse is unrhymed poetry unrestricted in length or rhythmic pattern. Writers are free to determine their own rhythm or meter, where they will end one line or stanza and begin another as well as the imagery and content of their poems. The poet alone determines when the poem is finished, without reference to an imposed structure. In strict terms, free verse is not a predesigned verse form. It is included here because of its importance in children's poetry.

The writing of free verse is natural to children. They may be encouraged to write free verse around the common stock of daily experience. The teacher may initiate the writing of free verse through discussion of a selected topic. Ideas and images supplied by the children may be recorded. These ideas and images may then be shaped into the form of a poem with or without the aid of the teacher, as necessity and previous experience may dictate. The poems below are typical of the sort of free verse young children are capable of writing.

Blackness in its darkest form
Creeps over all that dwell on earth,
And fills each separate being with a fear
Mysterious, overpowering and unfathomable.
The darkness hides away in deep oblivion
All things that daily give us confidence
In daylight unperturbed we walk in leafy woods,
At night fear secretes itself in us.
Mundane things become silent ghosts,
Haunting our fearful minds.
Every shadow, every rustic, is a spectre hidden
In depths of darkness.
Imagination plays his tricks and fear impedes our way.
But sleep locks out all thoughts of fear
And cheats him of his victims. (7, p. 13)

Unknown
Age 15

I wonder why my own father
Is killing me
For a brount offering
In place of a lamb,
I am the loved one
I am Isak
The son of Abraham,
I am not a lamb
Why must he put me
On a alter
And kill me. (8, p. 102)

Unknown

The Balloon

Bright leaves, Nature's pride and joy
Slender innocence,
Hanging like rain on the bough
Then, like a burst pipe expanding, lung-like
Aerobatic displays, bounding on air,
Hovering feats of twisting.
Then a child's heart is broken.
Nothing can replace it. (7, p. 55)

Unknown
Age 11

Free verse is the most natural form of poetry for a child. Anyone who has read much of what children write soon discovers that children who are completely unaware of poetry per se nevertheless write poetry. Generally it is in the form of free verse. Children should have a great deal of experience writing free verse before they are introduced to rhyming poetry.

Concrete Poetry

A poem is more than a poem when it is also a picture. Both visual and verbal, concrete poetry is sometimes referred to as picture poetry. The concrete images it can project and the variety of visual forms it can take make it an ideal form for children. Concrete poetry is to poetry what abstract art is to painting—despite the opposite nature of the terms used to describe these two forms of creative endeavor. With concrete poetry, the freedom from traditional linguistic structures and the puzzle-like nature it forms can assume add a zest to writing poetry that interests many children.

The most common type of concrete poetry is that in which the symbolism of the poem is recorded both pictorially and verbally. The following concrete poems illustrate the pictorial and verbal nature of the images created with concrete poetry.

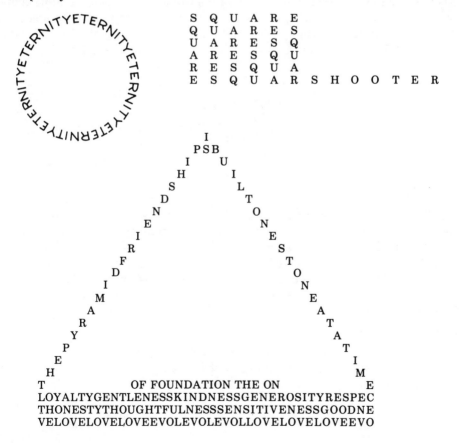

For those tempted to discount this form of expression as "not poetry," one might well remember that abstract art was once similarly regarded. While there are obvious limitations to what can be conveyed through this form of poetry, one need not discount its validity as a means of poetic expression.

Unrhymed Verse Forms

Rhyme and meter are associated with poetry as ice cream is with apple pie. This association is based on a lack of familiarity with forms that do not depend upon either of these linguistic devices. The Japanese forms of poetry called *haiku*, *senryu*, and *tanka*, and an American form called *cinquain* are illustrative of unrhymed, unmetered poetry.

Japanese poetry tends to emphasize the wonders and beauty of nature and the uniqueness of each individaul. It is strongly influenced by Buddhism; hence, it tends to stress the oneness of all creatures with the universe. The individual who understands one thing at one moment in time is better prepared to understand all moments and all things.

Haiku. In Japan, writing haiku (*hi-ku*) is a national pastime. Haiku is an unrhymed, three-line, seventeen syllable poetic composition form. The first line has five syllables; the second seven; and the third, five (5–7–5). Traditionally, there are three other criteria: they are free of opinion, they allude to a specific time of day or season, they encapsulate one precise moment. The following traditional Japanese haiku is among the more famous examples of excellent poetry:

> An old silent pond
> A frog jumps into the pond
> Splash! Silence again

> Basho

In introducing haiku, it would be wise to stress the traditional criteria. Capturing the essence of a moment within the framework of a definite linguistic structure can be an achievement that children will remember. Naturally, the child whose poem departs from the traditional criteria must be recognized for his or her efforts as well. Sometimes children modify the traditional form to suit a line that pleases them. Such modification is appropriate but children should at least be aware of the modifications and the reasons for them. Below are examples of haiku written by a ten year old boy:

> The Sun hides shyly
> Then coming out for a peek
> It darts back again. (10)

> Nick
> Age 10

Snow drifts helplessly
Not knowing which way to go
Then joining the rest (10)

Nick
Age 10

Senryu. When children attempt to write haiku, they may unintentionally produce a poem more properly called senryu. Senryu is a three-line Japanese poetic form. Unlike haiku, it is not restricted to seventeen syllables, does not require the capturing of one moment, and does not refer to a specific time or season. Senryu may be used before haiku is introduced and is especially easy for younger children. Here are some examples of senryu:

I have a big dog
As big as a pony
I ride him to school

Tony
Age 8

My dad is a doctor
He writes all the time
Is he a real doctor?

Laurie
Age 9

Fog is so strange
It swirls through the trees
And sleeps on the river

Harold
Age 10

Tanka. This ancient Japanese poetic form resembles an extended haiku. In this form, two lines of seven syllables are added to the basic haiku pattern of 5-7-5, giving the thirty-one syllable, five-line composition structure of 5-7-5-7-7. Tanka is not restricted by the necessity to capture one moment. On the contrary, tanka is a poetic form well suited to the recording of a continuing theme or a progression of ideas and events. Here are two examples of this type of poetry.

Icicles on the eves
Dripping slowly in the sun
Losing their life's blood
Waiting to be saved by night
Knowing their end is in sight

Pat
Age 13

Fog drifts in patches
Seeking to blanket the earth
With its wet greyness
The wind wimpers its sadness
Waiting to reclaim glory

Jimmy
Age 12

Cinquain. This is not a Japanese form, but its structure somewhat resembles haiku, senryu, and tanka. Cinquains are five-line poems that follow a syllabic pattern of 2–4–6–8–2. Following is a simplification frequently used with younger children in which the syllabic pattern is not adhered to but in which there is a set number of words for each of the five lines:

First line:	one word	seagull
Second line:	two words	speckled, motion
Third line:	three words	graceful wings dipping
Fourth line:	four words	distance in your heart
Fifth line:	one word	fisherman

Many children are capable of handling either form, although the modified version may prove easier for primary grade children. The following are some examples of cinquains by children.

Leaves
Different colors
Traveling, blowing, swooping
I enjoy their beauty
Acrobats (10)

Nick
Age 10

Mountains
White heaven
Purple in summer
Peaks reaching to God
Purity (10)

Angela
Age 12

People
Many kinds, many lands
Brothers under the skin
Some people need people, some don't
Do you? (10)

Solomon
Age 12

Diamante. The diamante (*dee ah mahn' tay*) is a seven-line contrast poem arranged in the shape of a diamond. This form along with others such as *septolet*, *quinzaine*, and *quintain*, was designed by Iris Tiedt. The contrasting feature of diamante and its interesting visual properties make it well suited to snagging the interest of children. It is particularly suitable for intermediate grade and older children. The poem is called a contrasting poem because it begins with a subject noun and ends with a noun which is the opposite of the subject noun. The diamante is arranged in this manner:

one word:	subject noun
two words:	adjectives
three words:	participles (ed, ing)
four words:	nouns related to the subject
three words:	participles (ed, ing)
two words:	adjectives
one word:	noun (opposite of subject)

War

death, sorrow

fighting, killing, hating

Nightmare of all nations

helping, healing, loving

life, joy

Peace

David

Age 13

Rhymed Verse Forms

There are many types of rhymed verse forms suitable for elementary school children. The sounds and rhythm that rhyme adds to poetry make it especially enjoyable to listen to. The types of poetic forms to be discussed in this section use various types of rhyme schemes. Keep in mind the warning given earlier about the problems associated with the teaching of rhyming poetry to children.

Couplet. The couplet is a two-line unity with each line in the same meter. It is the simplest kind of rhymed verse and is, therefore, normally the first type of rhymed poetry introduced to children. Here are some couplets written by children:

Life has it ups and downs

Life has its smiles and frowns.

Tim

Age 10

Christmas is a time for giving

Christmas is a way of living.

JoAnne

Age 9

The slithering snake goes on its way
Cold at night and warm by day

Matt
Age 11

Big cats stretch and yawn their jaws
Little dogs scratch and lick their paws.

Tom
Age 9

Beechnuts dropping from the trees
Branches bowing in the breeze.

Amy
Age 9

A good way to begin writing couplets is through group composition. After an appropriate topic has been selected and discussed, the teacher may begin by suggesting the writing of a poem. Teachers provide the first line of each two line-unit, making sure they end each line with a word the children can easily rhyme. Following is a poem written jointly by a teacher and her children:

Teacher: Trees huddling in the rain,
Children: People hurrying down the lane.
Teacher: Clouds rolling, lightning flashing,
Children: Rain gusting, thunder crashing.
Teacher: Pass these scenes before our eyes
Children: While the rainstorm slowly dies.

When group composition is tried, the teacher should keep these few matters in mind: (1) choose a topic and discuss it briefly. Encourage the children to talk about the topic and relate their experiences to it, (2) when composition begins, take several suggested lines before selecting the best one for the poem, (3) allow as many children as possible to contribute to the poem. It is possible to accept two or three lines from the children for each line supplied by the teacher, (4) help the children to feel the rhythm of each line by clapping or tapping. This may be the beginning of a feeling for meter in poetry, (5) when the first draft is finished, encourage the children to make needed improvements before a final copy of the poem is made.

Triplet. The triplet (or *tercet*) is a three-line rhymed verse form that may tell a brief story. The rhyme may be carried in two or all three lines. Triplets are an ideal verse form for humorous sketches of life. As with couplets, it is helpful to introduce this verse form through group composition.

For individual poetry have each child select a word or two that interests him or her. Help each child produce a list of other words that rhyme with the one selected. Then let him or her write a triplet around the concept or word selected.

The teacher may have a list of selected rhyming words available as a resource for the children. Here are some triplets that originated in this way:

> Our baby cow
> Knows how
> To eat his chow.
>
>> Pete
>> Age 9

> Children playing,
> Teachers praying,
> School is starting.
>
>> Kathy
>> Age 10

Quatrain. The quatrain is a four-line verse form. It is the most commonly used of all verse forms. This verse form provides numerous possible rhyme schemes. In the following quatrain the rhyme scheme is aabb, which means that the first line rhymes with the second (aa) and the third line rhymes with the fourth (bb).

> What is Red
>
> Red is a fire truck rushing by,
> Red is the sun in the evening sky.
> Red is my nose on a chilly day
> Red are the mittens I wear for play.
>
>> Amy
>> Age 8

There are other possible rhyme schemes as well: abab, abba, abcb. A quatrain may be combined with a couplet to produce a six-line poem and, of course, there may be any number of four-line stanzas. In the following poem, the first stanza has a rhyme scheme of abab. The next two stanzas rhyme only the second and fourth lines.

> The Quarrel
>
> I quarreled with my brother
> I forgot what about,
> But we fought one another
> By the old water spout!
> He squirted me
> I don't know why.
> So I squirted him,

Right square in the eye!
All was forgiven,
With nothing to say
Brothers and sisters
Are funny that way! (10)

Kathy
Age 9

Limerick. The limerick is a very old and popular verse form particularly suited to humorous and nonsense verse. The limerick normally uses a rhyme scheme of aabba in which the first, second, and fifth lines rhyme and the third and fourth lines rhyme. In effect, the limerick is a combination of a triplet and a couplet. Teaching this verse form is easy since children readily respond to the possibilities implicit in the humor and nonsense.

a) Start with the reading of a number of selected limericks. Children will soon recognize that limericks often begin, "There once was. . . . " The rhyming and rhythmic language of a limerick make it a natural device for poking fun at friends, enemies, and literary characters.
b) Provide children with possible first line topics accompanied by appropriate possible rhyming words as illustrated below:

a mad dad (*bad, cad, fad, had, lad, pad, sad, clad, glad*) a gnome from Rome (*dome, home, comb, foam, roam*) a young man named Ben (*ten, hen, pen, when, then, wren, den*)

c) Write some group limericks using several different starting lines. Encourage many different children to contribute.
d) Allow the children to begin composing individual limericks. Circulate among them, offering help as needed.
e) Share the limericks children have written by having them read aloud, displayed, or published.

Following are some limericks written by children:

A foolish young horse named Billy
Fell in love with a pretty young Filly
For forty-nine days
He lived in a haze
And now the Filly's got Billy

Rick
Age 12

A beautiful lady named Mary
Lived way out on the prarie
Fell in love with a man
To the preacher they ran
Now they're running a beautiful dairy

Mary
Age 11

Clerihew. Clerihew is a relatively new verse form consisting of two couplets of unequal length. They are usually humorous or satirical in nature and often take the form of a silly biographical sketch, as in the example below:

> Abraham Lincoln
> Started thinking
> I'll free the slaves
> From southern knaves

> Colin
> Age 13

SUMMARY

There is potential creative power in every child. This potential power may be dissipated through insecurity, ignorance, or lack of opportunity to exercise it in an atmosphere of freedom. Four suggestions for directing children to use their creative abilities are: (1) modify the traditional criteria by which the worth of children's writing is commonly judged, (2) cultivate an openness of mind and spirit, (3) develop a variety of ways to bestow approval and appreciation for the creative work children produce, and (4) be patient and courageous in your teaching behavior.

The language of poetry is unrivaled as a vehicle for verbal expression, yet few children have the opportunity to use their native language in poetic composition. Poetry's unique appeal and beauty are dependent on both sound and sense in language. Aspects of the sounds of language are rhythm, onomatopoeia, alliteration, repetition, and rhyme.

Imagery in poetry was described as the creation of mental pictures through the imaginative, descriptive, and unique use of words. Imagery uses figurative language to achieve a unique, picture-like quality that distinguishes it from ordinary language. Simile and metaphor are the most commonly used figurative language.

Seven guidelines for sharing poetry with children are: (1) establish a congenial classroom atmosphere where the sharing of poetry is possible, (2) provide specific writing ideas and aids to motivate and direct the writing of poetry, (3) read appropriate selections of poetry, (4) stress meaning over mechanical form, (5) be active in your teaching, (6) be happy in your work, and (7) use praise and instructional criticism discriminately.

Types of poetic verse forms discussed included free verse, concrete poetry, haiku, senryu, tanka, cinquain, diamante, couplet, triplet, quatrain, limerick, and clerihew.

REFERENCES

1. Mearns, Hughes. **Creative Power: The Education of Youth in the Creative Arts.** New York: Dover Publications, 1929, 1958. (Reprinted through the permission of the publisher.)

2. Dodgson, Charles L. **Alice's Adventures in Wonderland.** London: William Heinemann Ltd., 1907.

3. Hollowell, Lillian. **A Book of Children's Literature.** New York: Holt, Rinehart and Winston, Inc., 1966.

4. Wordsworth, William. **Poetical Works.** Boston: Heath, 1890.

5. Bacmeister, Rhoda. "Galoshes" from **Another Here and Now Story Book** by Lucy Sprague Mitchell. Copyright, 1940, by E. P. Dutton and Co., Inc.: renewal © 1968 by Lucy Sprague Mitchell. (Reprinted by permission of the publishers E. P. Dutton and Co., Inc.)

6. Tietjens, Eunice. "Thaw," **Child Life Magazine.** Rand McNally and Company, 1939, 1967.

7. Clegg, Alec. ed. **The Excitement of Writing.** New York: Schocken Books, Inc., 1964. Copyright 1964 by County Council of the West Riding of Yorkshire. (Reprinted by permission of Schocken Books, Inc., New York and Chatto and Windus Educational/Granada Publishing Litd., England.)

8. Beckett, Jack. **The Keen Edge.** London: Blackie, 1965.

9. Arnstein, Flora. **Poetry and the Child.** New York: Dover Publication, 1962.

10. Hahn, Harry. **The Seed.** Mimeographed. Rochester, Michigan: Oakland University.

11

Writing and the Language Art Skills

This chapter will concentrate on showing the positive influence writing can have on the development of academic skills. Specifically, writing can help children improve the skills of reading comprehension, word recognition, spelling, handwriting, the mechanics of written English, grammatical usage, oral language, and listening.

Writing and Reading Comprehension

Writing requires writers to focus on words and their meaning. The vocabulary building that results inevitably improves children's ability to understand what they read. Writers are constantly searching for a word that carries a precise nuance, for antonyms and synonyms, for connotative and denotative meanings. Writers consciously and unconsciously conduct this search when they read and when they write sentences. If teachers did nothing more than let children write, this search would go on unaided by explicit activities designed to encourage it.

Writing inevitably teaches writers about the influence of context on word meaning. But vocabulary development through writing need not be restricted to the incidental learning of word meanings through context. Children can systematically build a more powerful writing vocabulary by maintaining a journal of words, phrases, and sentences culled from their reading and listening environment. Children should be encouraged to use the journal to improve their writing. Winston Churchill, Jack London, and Somerset Maugham are examples of outstanding writers who maintained and used journals in this way.

Writing and Word Recognition

The skills required to read a word are the inverse of those required to write or spell a word. Consequently, an effective way to reinforce word recognition skills is through writing. Two basic skills of word recognition are auditory discrimination and letter-sound associations. These skills are most effectively practiced through writing.

Reading authorities consider auditory discrimination to be a foundational word recognition skill. Auditory discrimination is the ability to determine likenesses and differences in minute speech sounds at a conscious level of awareness. For example, auditory discrimination enables the reader to distinguish between such words as: *cat* and *fat*, *hat* and *had*, *pot* and *pit*. Reading teachers spend a great deal of time teaching auditory discrimination. Writing is the most practical way to reinforce the progress children are making in auditory discrimination ability.

Another basic skill of word recognition is that of associating letters with sounds. In reading, this skill helps the reader pronounce words, and, in writing, it helps the writer to spell words. The purpose of associating letters with sounds in beginning reading is to help children to read words that are not already part of their sight vocabulary. In reading, the letters are given and the child must supply the appropriate sounds. In writing, the child reverses the process by supplying letters to match sounds. Writing provides an ideal context in which the beginning reader can perfect letter-sound associations. A further advantage exists in that children's writings can be examined to determine which letter-sound associations are causing the child difficulty. Appropriate exercises may then be planned for word recognition lessons. In this way children's writing can become a fruitful diagnostic resource.

Following is an example of how auditory discrimination and letter-sound association may be practiced in writing.

> When children begin writing independently, they are likely to say, "But I don't know how to spell the word I want to use." When this happens the teacher should say, "Yes, I know you don't know how to spell some words, but I think you know enough to get started. What words are you having trouble with?" If the child says, "I don't know how to spell *house*," the teacher applies the word recognition skills that have been taught in the reading program by saying, "Listen to the word *house*. Say it to yourself. How do you think the word starts?" The child who has had auditory discrimination training is likely to respond, "It starts with *h*." The teacher should say, "Good, now listen to the next sound you hear in *house*." This time the child may say he or she hears an *s*. If so the teacher says, "Fine, you've spelled the word *house*, *h-s*. That's a good start. You've done just what I wanted you to do. Now try the same thing with the next word you don't know how to spell."

If this type of instruction is continued and children are rewarded for applying what they know, rather than penalized for what they have yet to learn, independent writing will be possible, spelling ability will be developed more rapidly, and word attack skills will be practiced in a meaningful context.

Writing and Spelling Competence

Spelling is an aid to writing and has no use apart from writing. Spelling competence should be developed within a writing framwork because writing improves spelling competence.

Research conducted by Cramer (1;2, pp. 240–47) and Stauffer and Hammond (3, 4,5,) established that children whose reading program stressed creative writing attained significantly superior spelling ability at the conclusion of their first, second, and third grade years. Furthermore, by the time the same children had completed sixth grade, they were still better spellers than children who had not written as extensively. The children in these research studies were taught to spell words "as best they could." The only behavior recognized as an unworthy effort was not trying to spell a word. Thus, the wealth of phonological knowledge the children had was put to use. Children were rewarded for spelling as much of a word as they were able, since the teacher regarded their spelling efforts, whether correct or not, as worthy. Children discovered that this freedom helped them to write any word in their speaking vocabulary. When children were freed from concern about the mechanics of writing, fluency and content improved along with spelling competence.

Spelling "as best you can" gives the child the freedom to experiment with written language and the opportunity to discover the relationships that exist between letters and sounds. Freedom to make discoveries about written language in a nonthreatening, nonpunitive atmosphere increases the likelihood that children will learn not only to write better but to spell better as well.

Application of this concept to writing is simply an extension of a concept that has worked well in initial language learning. Young children have always been free to make mispronunciations in their oral speech. For example, when a child says *I lub uh*, we regard this as a satisfactory approximation of *I love you*. We know that the young child is still learning the spoken language and will naturally make mispronunciations. Just so must the child who is learning to write be allowed to make misspellings. When a young child spells *heart* with the letters *hrt*, we should regard this as a satisfactory approximation, since he or she is still learning the written language system. Given the freedom to experiment with letter-sound relationships, children will gradually discover the conventional way to spell words, just as surely as the child who mispronounces words will gradually learn to speak as clearly as adults do.

Writing and Handwriting Ability

Learning handwriting is greatly aided when meaningful opportunities for practice are available. Learning to write legibly is enhanced when the teacher integrates the teaching of handwriting mechanics with written communication. Writing legibly is best motivated by making the child aware of the goal toward which handwriting is directed—independent authorship. Recording children's language enables them to observe the teacher as he or she prints their language and shows them the practical uses of handwriting ability. Much incidental learning of handwriting concepts may occur in this way.

Once children have had sufficient handwriting readiness and rudimentary instruction in letter formation, they should be encouraged to practice their handwriting skills by writing meaningful written messages. Children who have reached this stage, for example, might be asked to recopy a word or sentence they have dictated, a short message to take home to their parents, a message to another child, a story dictated individually or by a group, or a note to a teacher within the building. The natural motivation to produce a neat, readable copy is present in the context of each of these tasks. In each instance the product is a message which conveys meaning; in each instance it is possible for the children to observe the relationship between their handwriting skill and independent authorship.

Freedom to write does not mean freedom to be sloppy. Teachers have every right to expect children to write legibly. The pupils of one of the best teachers of writing I have ever known produced some of the best first grade penmanship I have ever seen. Teachers who stress writing have the best opportunity to develop children's handwriting abilities because their children have the most need to use handwriting skills. Meaningful practice has a beneficial effect on handwriting ability.

Writing and the Mechanics of Writing

The mechanical skills of writing include punctuation, capitalization, and format. Punctuation enables the writer to link and separate ideas, to indicate omissions and enclosures, and to emphasize certain ideas. Writers must learn to use the period, comma, question mark, exclamation point, colon, semicolon, dash, hyphen, parenthesis, quotation mark, bracket, apostrophe, and a few other specialized forms. Each type of punctuation has a number of common usages and a number of obscure and specialized ones. In addition, there are a few dozen common and uncommon uses of capitalization. Finally, there are numerous matters of format, such as titles, underlining, outlining, indenting, page arrangement, and margins. All of this adds up to hundreds of rules for applying mechanical skills. Even skilled writers sometimes apply the mechanical aspects of writing with indifferent success. This learning task for children, therefore, is one that requires time, repetition, and patience.

The mechanics of writing help clarify and emphasize the content of writing. Mechanics are important, but less important than the content of writing. Consequently, teaching the mechanics of writing must remain subordinate to teaching children to express their ideas and feelings with clarity and sincerity. Writing provides the most valid opportunity for learning the mechanics of writing. The mechanics of writing may be taught, but cannot be learned, from workbooks, as an aside in spelling books, or from that abominable purple flood of worksheets that litter so many American classrooms. Experience with real "flesh and blood" writing is the most functional way for children to learn the necessary mechanics of writing. Learning the mechanics of writing in nonwriting settings is too far removed from the real thing to provide meaningful practice, much less accomplish real learning of the mechanics of writing.

Teachers should introduce the rudiments of punctuation, capitalization, and format concurrently with the beginning of reading instruction. Only incidental references to the names and functions of major concepts such as periods, question marks, commas, quotation marks, and common capitals need be made. There are many occasions when a brief discussion of such concepts is appropriate. The teacher who has initiated reading instruction by recording children's language has a natural opportunity to do this. When children's language is recorded, they inevitably ask questions about the meaning of the punctuation and capitalization signals they see recorded. Answering these questions helps children understand the relationship between speech and its written counterpart. Thus, an important link is established between oral language and written discourse. Many children spontaneously incorporate punctuation into their independent writing as a result of the recording experience provided in the reading program. This informal approach is sufficient to familiarize children with a wide range of mechanical skills required in writing.

Eventually a more systematic approach to the teaching of mechanics should be started. The mechanics of writing can be systematically taught through editing. The teaching of editing skills is a necessary element of a complete writing program, since editing is one of the writer's most indispensable skills. Growth in writing ability is likely to be stunted if ways are not found to develop editing ability. No program of writing that anticipates continuous writing growth can afford to ignore it.

Children should begin to learn editing techniques at different times. When they begin depends on how far advanced they are in writing. Only children who write fluently are appropriate candidates for learning editing techniques. Children who are still struggling to put down a few meager sentences should develop fluency in writing before editing is introduced. Many children will not begin serious editing efforts until they are in third or fourth grade. Much depends on when children begin writing, how rapidly they progress, how frequently they write, and how fluently they express themselves in writing.

When children are ready to begin serious editing work, the teacher should organize as many kinds of editing activities as possible. The editing activities outlined in chapter 9 are suggestive of the types of activities that should be provided.

Writing and Grammatical Usage

Few people feel neutral about grammar. To children it is an excruciating bore and often an enigma wrapped in a riddle as well. To some adults it serves as a barometer by which they measure education, culture, and refinement.

Others believe grammar represents a vestige from teaching concepts long since passé. Fortunately, a more balanced view is consistent with linguistic information and educational goals.

There does exist a widespread, uniformed bias against certain forms of speech. For example, those who speak a "prestige" dialect may shudder to hear the emphatic declaration, "I ain't going to do nothing." Having long since been inoculated with the grammatical needle, they believe that two negatives make a positive. Therefore, "I ain't going to do nothing," by their lights, really means, "I am going to do something." This is nonsense, of course. No sensible person would interpret an emphatic "I ain't going to do nothing" to mean anything other than an emphatic negative statement. Double negatives are considered *bad* English today because Bishop Robert Lowth said so back in 1762 in a book entitled *A Short Introduction to English Grammar.* Lowth's misapplication of mathematical logic to English grammar has triumphed completely in elite standard English. Hundreds of other examples of *bad* English remain in the speech of the common person and on the taboo list of English teachers to this day. This situation is unfortunate since there is no such simple dichotomy as *correct* and *incorrect* English, *good* or *bad* grammatical usage, *right* or *wrong* language. This is a linguistic fact of life. To deny it is no more valid than to deny the Copernican concept that the earth rotates daily on its axis and that the planets revolve in orbits around the sun. To continue to maintain this language fairy tale adversely affects teaching and learning.

A brief glance at the history of language will suffice to illustrate the fictions that have grown up around the concept of *correct* and *incorrect* grammar. People are accustomed to regarding *bad* English as a degenerated form of *good* English. Thus, *he don't* is *bad*; *he doesn't* is *good*. But language historians have shown that *he don't* was part of cultivated English usage one hundred years before *he doesn't* ever appeared. Today, their usage is reversed. *He don't* is considered bad English and *he doesn't* is considered *good* English. There are literally hundreds of other similar examples. Standards of usage are simply matters of arbitrary choice, not absolutes that can be sensibly labeled *correct* or *incorrect, good* or *bad, right* or *wrong.*

A proper understanding of language usage leads us to conclude that there are three principles which govern grammatical usage. They may be summarized as follows:

1. *Usage standards are relative.* What is considered good usage at one time may be stigmatized as bad usage at a later time and vice versa. What is considered correct by one group of people may be considered incorrect by another group of people. When groups are in conflict, usually the educated or more influential group wins the argument since they tend to control access to powerful media, write textbooks and dictionaries, and dominate prestigious cultural institutions.

2. *Correct usage is based primarily on tradition and taste, although this is seldom admitted.* For some people, correct usage supercedes common usage and sometimes common sense as well, as in the case of double

negatives. Those who control correct usage standards always label their language *good* and the language of those groups in conflict *bad* since it is psychologically and sometimes economically useful to do so.

3. *Common usage standards are often labeled incorrect.* This description is scientifically inaccurate since no language facts exist to substantiate such a claim. It would be more accurate to label common usage standards as unfashionable among certain educated and influential groups who speak, or believe they speak, the prestigious dialect.

Usage differences arise out of a milieu of cultural, geographical, ethnic, and individual factors that exists among groups of people. Usage differences are linked with dialect, and dialect accounts for much of the controversy that exists over grammatical usage. Americans speak a number of different dialects of English. Dialects vary in three major ways: pronunciation, vocabulary, and syntax.

Pronunciation varies according to geographical region, ethnic background, and cultural and individual peculiarities. For example, the word *park* is pronounced differently in Boston than in Detroit. Some people pronounce *Mary, merry,* and *marry* alike, others pronounce two of them alike, and still others say each word differently. For some people, *bin, bean,* and *Ben* are homonymns for *been*; for others, this is not the case.

Among different dialect groups, different words are often used to describe the same object or function. For example, some folks drink *soda*, others drink *pop*, and still others have a *soft drink*. In some dialects, a child would be told to *quiet down*; in other dialects the expression would be *quieten down*. There are numerous vocabulary differences among different dialect groups. However, these differences are seldom substantial enough to seriously hinder communication.

Different dialect groups sometimes form sentences in different ways. These differences involve tense, plural formation, use of negatives, and other syntactical elements. For example, in some dialects a person describing an ill friend might say "He is sick," whereas in another dialect the same description might be "He sick." Syntactical differences occur relatively infrequently among American-English dialects and, of course, in all dialect matters, there is much more in common than there are differences. Usage differences of a syntactical nature are most likely to be singled out as *grammatical errors* and *bad English*. Dialect does create language difference. However, it would be linguistically inaccurate to say that one structure is correct and the other incorrect. For example, from a grammatical point of view the two sentences "I brung my lunch to school," and "I brought my lunch to school," are equally valid. The word *brung* signals past tense in some dialects, whereas in another dialect *brought* signals past tense. Since both of these grammatical structures perform their function of signaling past tense equally well, both must be *grammatically correct*.

Teachers have traditionally believed that one of their functions is to teach children how to use *good* English *correctly* and to teach children that *incorrect*

English is *bad. Incorrect*, or *bad*, English is often associated with dialects and so-called nonstandard English. This unfortunate and linguistically naive notion has gone unchallenged by many educators and some linguists. Current linguistic understandings have settled the question: everyone speaks a dialect of some sort. One dialect is neither inferior nor superior to another.

Once we dispense with *correct* and *incorrect*, what is there left to teach about grammatical usage? At first blush, one might logically conclude that there is nothing to teach since all language and dialects are valid unto themselves. But there are certain standards of usage which may be useful to teach. They are useful because they provide children with alternative language options. Children have a right to know the dialect of the educated and influential class. Knowing this dialect may be economically useful. Furthermore, being bidialectal may prove culturally and aesthetically satisfying as well. Learning alternative grammatical options has much the same educational validity as learning a foreign language. Thus, the argument for continuing to teach certain forms of grammatical usage is wholly a pragmatic one. It has nothing to do with concepts of *correct* or *incorrect, good* and *bad, right* and *wrong.*

In teaching grammatical usage, there are some things that must be avoided. For example, some textbooks insist that *this* and *these* refer to nearby things and *that* and *those* to things further away. Such distinctions are questionable in terms of their validity and are certainly so pendantic as to be impossibly obscure to children. Grammatical usage standards of this sort have no place in teaching. Wise teachers must critically examine available materials that deal with usage options. From this material they may determine which usage standards are appropriate for their children. It is helpful, therefore, for teachers to have some language training, so that decisions can be made on a knowledgeable basis.

Children write much as they talk. Therefore, if new usage options are to be learned, they must become part of children's oral language. The child must internalize the sounds of the new language usage options and use them in oral speech. When this is accomplished, an opportunity to use the new language options in writing should follow.

Changing language habits is difficult. Teachers must not expect changes to occur rapidly or easily. The changes that occur will be few initially and they will develop slowly. School can have only a limited impact on the speech habits of children. Other societal influences must occur simultaneously with schooling if the speech habits of a lifetime are to be modified.

A final caution is in order. Teachers must never keep children from writing because their usage habits are different from the norms of the school. Children should not be kept from using their native language when they write or talk. They should be proud of their language heritage and appreciative of the language heritage of others. This attitude helps create a setting where it becomes desirable to add new language without feeling that current language is inferior.

Writing and Oral Language Development

There is general agreement among language specialists that most children have a basic command of the grammatical structure of their language before they come to school. While there may be gaps, basic language competency is already well established. A teacher's job is to enrich, extend, and elaborate the basic structures.

Writing can foster the growth of oral language if the context in which writing is taught is structured to encourage oral language as a natural activity which accompanies writing. Writing activities should be preceded, when feasible, by oral language activities. It is seldom wise to simply assign writing chores to children without first providing an oral language experience. The prewriting discussion gives children a chance to reflect on the topic, to consider the problems they may encounter, and to exchange ideas they may have about their writing. This sort of discussion not only enriches oral language, but provides ideas and words that will improve the writing that follows.

Writing activities should be followed by an opportunity for children to share their writing. A writing program that neglects to devise ways to talk about products and outcomes will soon falter. The constant work of the teacher is to find ways in which children can discuss their writing with others and share the projects that stem from their writing. As teachers discover better ways to accomplish this objective, they improve both the oral language competencies of their children and their ability to communicate effectively in oral and written language.

Writing and Listening

A complete writing program provides many natural opportunities for listening. These opportunities must be built into the writing program or it will not flourish. Listening opportunities can be provided for in a writing program in many different ways.

Reading to Children

Children should be given a myriad of chances to listen to a planned sequence of literary selections read orally by the teacher. Story form, sentence structure, vocabulary, and other elements of language are learned through listening. The sounds of language and literature should surround the child. Opportunities to listen have a facilitating effect on a child's writing and listening skills.

Prewriting Stimulus Conversations

An effective writing program allows children to talk about experiences and ideas prior to writing. While this need not always be done, it must be done frequently. When stimulus conversations are held, a natural context exists to stress the importance of listening as well as talking. The sharing of ideas, concerns, and opinions on such occasions gives children a reason to listen and to think about the concepts that are discussed. The group dynamics of a shared experience provide an important listening experience.

Sharing Written Products

When children write, they need an appreciative audience. One way to get children to listen attentively is to provide a forum where they may read their writings to each other. Various formats for this activity may be devised depending on the objective in mind. Teachers must determine the specific listening behaviors they wish to foster in this forum.

Listening to Recorded Material

There is an abundance of recorded material available for children to hear. Listening materials may be obtained commercially or recorded by children. Such materials may serve as input for writing experiences while, at the same time, providing an opportunity to listen.

A writing program, by virtue of its necessary connection with all facets of the language arts, can have a positive effect on the listening habits and skills of children. Clearly, the extent and significance of the interrelationships between writing and listening depend on the teacher's willingness to integrate writing and listening in a deliberate and meaningful way. The opportunity is naturally present in the set of circumstances described. If teachers understand this, and plan instruction to take advantage of the opportunity to relate writing and listening, much can be done to improve the listening-writing skills of children.

SUMMARY

Writing has a beneficial influence on the development of a broad range of academic skills within the traditional language arts area. An effective writing program inevitably improves children's ability to read with better understanding, to attack unknown words with greater assurance, to spell more accurately, to practice handwriting in a more meaningful context, to use the mechanics of English with improved precision, to adopt grammatical usage options more readily, to talk with increased assurance, and to listen more acutely. The natural interrelationships and interdependence of the skills of literacy reinforce one another when the total language arts program is designed to function as one entity rather than as separate skills functioning within their own narrow confines. If this description makes writing sound like a prescription for academic anemia, so be it. In many significant respects, it is just that. Writing skill is at the apex of the skills of literacy. As such, writing deserves recognition as a potential contributor to academic growth and development.

REFERENCES

1. Cramer, Ronald L. **An Investigation of the Spelling Achievement of Two Groups of First-grade Classes on Phonologically Regular and Irregular Words and in Written Composition.** Unpublished doctoral dissertation, University of Delaware, Newark, Delaware, 1968.

2. Cramer, Ronald L., "An Investigation of First-grade Spelling Achievement." **Elementary English** (February, 1970): 240–247.

3. Stauffer, Russell and Hammond, Dorsey. **Effectiveness of Language-arts and Basic-reader Approaches to First-grade Reading Instruction.** U.S.O.E. Project number 2769, University of Delaware, Newark, Delaware, 1968.

4. Stauffer, Russell, and Hammond, Dorsey. **Effectiveness of Language-Arts and Basic-reader Approaches to Reading Instruction—Extended Into Third Grade.** University of Delaware, Newark, Delaware, 1970.

5. Stauffer, Russell and Hammond, Dorsey. **Effectiveness of Language Arts and Basic Reader Approaches to Reading Instruction—Extended Into Sixth Grade.** University of Delaware, Newark, Delaware, 1973.

12

Ideas for Writing

The ideas in this chapter were contributed by practicing teachers who were especially interested in children's writing. Each idea was tried and proved useful in the classroom. Therefore, it can be said that all of the ideas in this chapter have practical validity.

Using Ideas for Writing

There are two types of ideas in this chapter. The first set of ideas consists of 172 briefly stated ideas organized into sixteen different categories. Each of these ideas was designed to provide the basic concept of a writing idea and some information about how to implement the idea. The ideas are for the benefit of teachers, although older children who read well could use some of these ideas independently.

The second set of ideas in this chapter consists of ten fully developed lesson plans for writing. Each lesson plan includes an objective, materials needed to implement the idea, procedures for carrying it out, and suggestions for follow-up. The lesson plans are designed exclusively for the teacher's use.

Making an Idea Work for You

A teaching suggestion is little more than a springboard for the thoughtful and creative teacher. These ideas must be supplemented with your own stock of information and teaching expertise. You must implement these ideas within the framework of your own teaching style, educational philosophy, and the circumstances peculiar to your own teaching situation. To make an idea work for you, keep these two suggestions in mind:

1. *Use only those ideas that seem appropriate for your children.* You must consider such matters as age, previous writing experience, and background of experience. If you are uncertain whether a given idea is appropriate, it is best to give it a try. Your uncertainty must not interfere with your enthusiasm, preparation, and presentation of the idea. If it does, you will communicate your uncertainty to the children and insure your own failure.

2. *Present your writing idea with genuine enthusiasm and careful preparation.* If you cannot muster enthusiasm for an idea, you had best not use it. Enthusiasm is contagious, but so is its counterpart, boredom. When possible, give advance thought as to how you will present the idea. This usually requires advance preparation of materials, examples, and whatever else is necessary for the successful implementation of the idea.

When an Idea Fails

Good teachers fail more often than is commonly recognized. The difference between good and poor teachers is often the extent to which good teachers have learned from their failures. There is a peculiarly masochistic tendency to regard failure as a wholly negative event. Indeed, failure sometimes is negative, but often this is because we have not examined the failure to extract its meaning and relevance to past and future events. While there may be many reasons for not achieving success with a writing idea, here are two of the most common:

1. *Failure to understand the idea you are trying to implement.* Often failure to understand the idea is that you have not taken the time to think the idea through or you have no clear expectation of what should result. Sometimes failure occurs because the writing objective is entirely outside your personal experience. For example, you cannot expect to teach children to write good haiku if you have never written haiku yourself. You will feel uncomfortable in describing it, have difficulty recognizing what to praise or criticize, and be unaware of the ease or difficulty of the task you have asked your children to perform. The best way to understand a writing idea is to think it through, prepare carefully for the implementation of the idea, and do a bit of the writing yourself to see how it goes. This last step is particularly helpful since it will not only familiarize you with what you are teaching but will also provide you with examples to read to your children when you introduce the idea to them.

2. *When the writing project has been completed, make an informal assessment of the degree of success or failure met.* It is crucial to examine what happens when an idea does not work. The easy way out is to as-

sume that the idea was not a good one. Sometimes this assumption is true, but usually it is not. A particularly helpful procedure is to have several colleagues try the idea in their classrooms at the same time you are trying it. Later, you can compare notes. Often you will find that an idea failed for you but worked well for another teacher. Try to discover why this happened. Avoid accepting easy answers to rationalize failure. A positive, inquiring attitude will serve you well and contribute enormously to your teaching success.

172 BRIEF IDEAS FOR WRITING

Beginning Writing

1. Before show-and-tell or sharing time, encourage children to write two or three sentences about what they are going to share. This activity may help the child to organize thoughts for more effective presentation but should be used only occasionally.
2. Allow children who have difficulty getting ideas on paper to dictate stories on tape to be transcribed later. If someone is available to take dictation directly, this would also be helpful and probably more effective.
3. Read "What is Big" from *Sounds of Numbers* by Bill Martin, Jr., Holt, Rinehart and Winston. Talk about things that are bigger and smaller than the children. Pass out diagonally cut paper. Children who wish to draw themselves as the biggest object begin at the large end of the paper. Example: a boy, a sled, a pan, a tomato, a bug. Children who wish to draw themselves small begin at the small end of the paper. Example: a girl, a stove, a car, a tree, a house. Have the children write the name of each object above it.
4. Ask the children to sit quietly and listen for sounds. Have them list the next ten sounds they hear.
5. Choose a color. Cut out pictures from magazines which illustrate your color. Make a collage with the pictures. List other objects that are usually the same color.
6. Cut out pictures from magazines and make a collage with a theme, such as happy, angry, excited, sad, lazy, brave, sleepy, cold, and hungry. Label the collage with the one word that describes it.
7. Make as large a list as you can of wet things, things with handles, rough things, smooth things, ugly things, beautiful things, things found in a desk drawer, smelly things, noisy things, or things you can do with a brick.
8. Make a word mobile using color words, foods, wild animals, tame animals, desserts, names of cars, football players, baseball players, basketball players, hockey players, movie stars, pop singers, cars, presidents.

9. Work in teams to make a rhyming dictionary. Each team is responsible for several specific phonograms (-*ick*, -*og*, -*and*, -*ed*, -*ug*, and so forth). Be sure that all the important rhymes are included. Collate the work of the different teams, mimeograph the lists, and make the lists into booklets. Each child should have his or her own copy. Rhyming dictionaries are available from commercial companies, and one should be available in the classroom. It is not a substitute for this activity, however.

10. Staple thirteen pages of paper together with a cover. Beginning with the letter *A*, label each page with a letter of the alphabet. As children learn new words from their writing activities, the teacher can help them write the word in their dictionaries.

Writing Techniques

11. Think about the images and associations evoked by certain words. Write the images and associations in a word, phrase, or sentence. Later you may wish to develop and elaborate your initial reactions. Poems and stories may eventually be developed from some of your best efforts. Here are some words to work with: terror, red, food, movies, school, home, mother, father, brother, sister, friend, storm, wind, animals, trees.

12. Group children into teams of three. Ask them to list words to use instead of certain other words. The teacher or children may supply the "instead of" words. It is especially helpful to do this activity with overused words appearing in compositions. Here are some words to consider: said, happy, good, bad, fast, ask.

13. Work in teams developing word families. Word families may be useful in certain types of writing such as limericks. Example: *quake*, lake, make, snake, fake, shake; *out*, shout, snout, bout, clout, doubt. Remember, if the lists are to be used for rhyming, endings may be spelled differently as long as they sound the same.

> A girl from Detroit ate a snake
> Her stomach oh how it did quake
> Her teeth flew out
> She gave a shout
> Her friends now know they were fake.

14. Over a period of time acquaint children with the function of describing words (adjectives). One activity is to distribute magazines and have children cut out and paste describing words into a collage or in some organized way. This procedure may be repeated with other types of words such as naming words (nouns), doing words (verbs),

and so on. These collected sets of words may then be stapled together into a booklet for reference purposes while editing.

15. Choose an interesting photograph of a person. Ask the children to write one sentence to answer each of the following questions. What do you see? Describe something about the person. What may have happened just before the picture was taken? What may have happened just after this picture was taken?

16. Read a well-known children's story such as "Little Red Riding Hood" or Cinderella." Summarize the essential facts of the story in as few sentences as you can.

17. Practice packing more information into one sentence. Begin with two or more separate sentences and combine them into one. It is best to start with simple sentences and then work on more complex ones. Here is an example:

Four simple sentences: Mary had a new dress.
It was blue.
She was going to Susie's party.
She decided to wear the new dress.

Combined sentence: Mary had a new blue dress which she decided to wear to Susie's party.
or
Mary decided to wear her new blue dress to Susie's party.

18. Choose the opening sentence of a short story or play and discuss all the information the reader is given in that one sentence. When the activity is completed, children should practice writing their own opening sentences. Here is an example from Chekhov's *The Lady with the Dog:* "It was reported that a new face had been seen on the quay, a lady with a little dog." Information given: setting is a port, seaside resort, or fishing village; gossip circulated about the new person in town; somebody finds this new person newsworthy; the new person has a dog.

19. A good title is usually brief and striking in its effect on the reader. It often sums up the essence of the picture or story or gives a clue to content or intent. Try inventing some titles that meet these criteria. Display several large pictures in front of the class. After study and discussion of the pictures, encourage the children to write titles for each picture. In some cases single words will be best and in other instances phrases may be appropriate. For children who have difficulty with this activity, try getting them to write brief sentences about each picture. Then work on reducing the sentence to a word or phrase.

20. Read a story where several endings are plausible. Sometimes this activity requires modifying the original ending or omitting it. Have the children suggest possible alternative endings and their consequences. Then ask them to write their own endings to the story. Jack London,

Edgar Allan Poe, and O. Henry have written many short stories that are particularly useful for this type of activity.

21. Many things happen in the classroom that are worth writing about. When an interesting event occurs, discuss the sequence of events that preceded the event and what occurred afterward. List these on the board. Then have the class construct a story about the incident.

22. Have the children listen to conversations of their friends, parents, or of people in public places. Practice reproducing these conversations as accurately as possible as a writing activity.

23. Draw a cartoon or cut one out of a newspaper, leaving off the caption. Write your own captions or humorous lines to go with the cartoon. Work with a partner and have him or her write captions or humorous lines without seeing yours. Then exchange captions and discuss the differences.

24. Write a description of a scene which creates a specific mood. For example:

As we entered the room an oppressive smell assailed our nostrils. The scent was pungent, slightly sweet and faintly unpleasant and seemed to be a mixture of decaying flowers and room freshener. The room itself had a light and airy appearance but strangely lacked cheerfulness and warmth. Clearly someone had made a strenuous effort to turn an unpleasant atmosphere into an inviting one, but the effort had failed.

25. Write a description of the physical appearance of a person which gives some clues to mood. For example:

John strode in, holding himself rigidly erect. Each step seemed carefully and deliberately rehearsed. As he moved from one place to another, he seemed to focus his eyes in the direction of his destination and then, almost as if he were controlled by a machine, he marched toward the door, never veering from his chosen path.

26. Observe someone you know well and write a fictional account of some aspect of that person's life. You may wish to take some notes before beginning the account.

27. Observe a stranger and write a fictional account about that person's life. Here are some common events that you might consider:
    a) An elderly person waiting nervously on a park bench.
    b) A man visiting a museum by himself.
    c) A young person in apparent deep thought walking down the street.
    d) A middle-aged woman waiting for the bus or walking to work.

28. Be an artist. Paint a verbal picture of something you see every day. Remember the reader must visualize the picture you paint with words. Here are some scenes you could paint with words:
    a) A tree outside your classroom window.

b) The traffic in front of your home or school.

c) The sidewalk in front of your house (note the irregular cracks, grass growing in places, the smooth or rough surface, and so on).

d) People shopping in a crowded store.

29. Show a movie to the class without the sound. Have the children write their version of what the movie was about. Have several children read their accounts to the class. Then run the movie again with the sound.

30. Introduce the children to the uses of simile and metaphor. For younger children the terms need not be used. Find examples of good metaphor and simile from poems, stories, and children's writing. Share these with the children. Find examples of overused simile and metaphor (pretty as a picture, straight as an arrow). Get a set of particularly interesting pictures and encourage the children to use metaphor and simile in their descriptions of these pictures. Sometimes it is helpful to have them first use all of the clichés and trite expressions they can think of to describe the pictures, before you encourage them to invent their own original descriptions.

31. Read "Skyscrapers, A Summer Morning" and "The Little Rose Tree" by Rachel Field from *Time for Poetry*, Scott, Foresman and Company. Explain personification as giving lifelike qualities to objects that are not alive. Study the poems to see what human qualities the poet gives to inanimate objects. Have the children select an object and write about it as if it were a living thing.

32. Use a nursery rhyme to write a short-short story. For Example:

> Once upon a time, a little girl named Mary had a pet lamb. One day when she got to school she discovered, to her surprise, that the lamb had followed her. All the other children laughed because they had never seen a lamb in school before.

33. Take a riddle walk. Notice things and listen to sounds along the way. When you return to the class, write riddles about things you saw or heard on the riddle walk. Write the riddles on cutout footprints. Place the footprints on the wall around the room so others may take a riddle walk at their convenience.

Encouraging Creative Thinking

34. Write a "magic power" poem. Imagine you have a third eye that is invisible. This eye can see things that your regular eyes cannot see. Write about what this eye sees.

35. Pretend you are invisible. However, your clothing is not invisible and everything you touch becomes invisible. Write an account describing how this situation would affect your life.

36. Make a list of things you would like to do before you die. Think seri-

ously about it and be sincere. A man once made a list of one hundred things he wanted to do, and by the time he was forty years old he had done all but five of them. Look in travel magazines and consult reference books to help you visualize some possibilities.

37. Here are some questions that might give you an idea for writing:
    a) What is the quietest sound you know?
    b) What is the noisiest racket you've ever heard?
    c) If you could meet a special person who is not alive today whom would you choose?
    d) What would you say in a note that was going to be put in a bottle and cast into the sea?
    e) If you could choose ten things to put in a time capsule that would not be opened for 1,000 years, what items would you select?
    f) If you were stranded on a deserted island, what ten things would you want to have along with you?

38. Pretend you are a famous chef and have just invented a new recipe. Give it a title, list the ingredients, and explain how to prepare and serve it.

39. Pretend you are a famous inventor. If you could invent anything you wished, what would you invent? Describe your invention fully and tell why you invented it.

40. Here are some "what if . . . " situations. Choose one of them and write about it. If you prefer, you can make up your own "what if . . . ".
    a) What if you were principal of your school?
    b) What if the president of the United States asked you to colonize the moon?
    c) What if there were no automobiles?
    d) What if you had one hundred dollars to spend?
    e) What if . . . ?

41. Invent a machine that does a particular task very well. Describe the machine in detail. Include such things as size, color, materials, sounds, movements, and the reason it is useful. A diagram or drawing of the machine should be included. Here are some ideas for machines that need to be invented:
    a) A machine that cleans up messes you have made in your room.
    b) A machine that makes ice cream cones so cheaply they can be sold for a penny.
    c) A pair of workable wings so people can fly.

42. Suppose that we did not have any way of telling time. How would your life be different? Would you prefer life with or without clocks? Why?

43. Pretend you belong to a "Liar's Club." There is a contest with prizes to be awarded for the "biggest whopper" of the year. Here are some topics around which you may build a championship "whopper": sports, hobbies, heroic deeds, pets.

Feelings and Values

44. Look for pictures of faces that show different emotions. Identify the emotion and describe why you think the person feels the way he or she does. Various emotions to look for include sadness, joy, excitement, fright, love, hate, envy, jealousy, grief, anger.

45. Write a short account of a time when you felt an emotion very strongly. You may have been angry, happy, disappointed, or excited.

46. Pretend you are on a life raft and are the only survivor of a shipwreck. Tell how you would survive and the different feelings you might have at different times during your ordeal at sea.

47. Think of all the words that you associate with a word like *loneliness.* Write these words in a box in the corner of a paper. Try to use these words in a story or a poem.

48. Write a story or poem based on a keen disappointment such as:
    a) a school disappointment
    b) a present you hoped for but did not get
    c) a game you wanted to win but lost
    d) a broken promise
    e) a trip you did not get to take
    f) a friend who let you down

49. First thing in the morning write a paragraph about how you feel and why you think you feel that way. Near the end of the day do the same thing again. The following day compare the two paragraphs. What explanations can you think of to explain the differences or similarities?

50. Do some hard and honest thinking about either of these two questions. What is the happiest situation you can imagine? What is the worst situation you can imagine?

51. Cut different colors of paper into leaflike shapes. Write how you feel about these questions. What does this color mean to you? What do you associate with this color? A good book to read before doing this activity is *Hailstones and Halibut Bones* by Mary O'Neill, published by Doubleday.

52. Old memories are sometimes triggered by certain sights, sounds, and smells. What memories are triggered for you by these experiences? Fourth of July, the beach in August, a family picnic, a circus, a ball game, a stuffed toy. Think of experiences you have had that trigger old memories and write about them.

53. Start a diary in which you record personal things that are important to you.

54. If you could be the person you would like to be, would you be different? Perhaps you would prefer to be just as you are. Write about either of these possibilities.

55. Have you ever wished you could change the world? When things do not go the way we had hoped, we often wish we could. Imagine that you have the power to make things the way you would like them to

be. What things would you change? What things would remain as they are? How would all of this affect you?

56. Most people do not know what they want to do when they get older. But that does not keep us from dreaming about what might be. Write about your dreams of the future.

57. There is a saying that goes like this: "Don't criticize your neighbor until you have walked a mile in his shoes." It is hard to know how other people feel. Imagine what it would be like if you were someone else. Write a story or poem entitled:
    a) If I Were a Father
    b) If I Were my Friend
    c) If I Were a Mother
    d) If I Were a Teacher
    e) If I Were a Rich Man's Child
    f) If I Were a Migrant Worker
    g) If I Were Handicapped

58. Write some sayings that you think are good advice for parents, teenagers, children, teachers, politicians, doctors, and so forth. Design a poster and illustrate your saying. Here is an example:
    For a parent: Children should be *heard* and *seen* not *herd* and *scene.*

    For a teenager: Cigarettes are good for your *hearth* but not your *heart.*

59. Think of an idea on which you disagree with your parents, such as the time you must go to bed, eating (or not eating) a particular food, the length of your hair, and so on. Write five arguments which support your side of the question and five arguments of your parent's side.

60. Write a persuasive paragraph for or against any topic about which you feel strongly. Here are a few suggestions:
    a) Schools should be run twelve months a year.
    b) Parents should spank their children regularly.
    c) Watching too much television is bad for you.

61. Imagine you can change anything in your school, provided you make a good case for doing so. What would you change? What reasons would you give for the changes you would like to make?

62. When you watch the news on TV or read the newspapers, it sometimes seems that certain things need to be changed or improved in our country. If you could make five changes in the country, what would they be? Why?

Poetry

63. Read poetry to children. From this activity other ideas may occur to you. For example, as you read you may occasionally stop and ask

them to supply the next line. Everything in poetry starts from listening to it and enjoying the experience.

64. Write a class poem. Start with a theme to give the poem unity. Everyone contributes one line. When the contributions have been collected, the teacher may work with a small group to arrange the contributions to best advantage into a class poem.

65. Write an "I wish . . . " poem. Let your imagination carry you into the magic land of dreams and fantasy. Here is an "I wish . . . " poem:

I wish
> I had a mansion in the sky
> And a chariot pulled by winged horses
> Driven by angels.

66. Write a poem telling what *quiet* means to you. You may choose a different theme if you prefer. Here is a *quiet* poem:

Quiet
> is my breath on a frosty morning
> and the dew settling softly on the morning
> grass
> is my father reading the evening paper
> and my cat purring in my lap.

67. Here are some ideas for writing a poem like the *quiet* poem:

> Loud is . . .
> Sweet is . . .
> Soft is . . .
> Green is . . .
> Love is . . .
> Hate is . . .
> War is . . .
> Peace is . . .
> Old is . . .

68. Poetry is all around us. On the way home you may notice a leaf falling gracefully to the ground or a shadow creeping slowly across the lawn. Writing what you see and how it makes you feel is poetry.

69. Read a poem with a recurring pattern or theme. When the children are familiar with the pattern and rhythm, invite them to write their own verses. Here are some good books for patterned poetry writing:

Catcha Little Fox by Fortunata. Lucky Books
Round Is a Pancake by Joan Sullivan. Holt, Rinehart, and Winston.
Brown Bear, Brown Bear by Bill Martin, Jr. Holt, Rinehart, and Winston.
Why? . . . Because by Jo Ann Stover. McKay.
Some Things Are Scary by Florence Heide. Scholastic Book Service.

70. Have several children bring their pets to school. Talk about pets and allow everyone a chance to touch and talk to the pets. Invite the children to write a poem on what it would be like to be a pet.

71. Write a color poem. Close your eyes and imagine all sorts of colors. Write a poem using a different color in every line or the same color in every line.

72. Trace the outline of a bare foot on construction paper. Cut it out and write a verse praising feet and toes. The foot can be decorated and a trail of "footprints" can be hung around the room.

73. Doodles can stimulate creative thinking. Make an interesting doodle. Imagine what it might be. Write a two or four line poem about your doodle.

74. Write a poem about a snowy day. Pretend you are a snowflake falling through the air. You have magic powers. Wherever you land, you can do good or evil. Write a poem about what you would do if you were a magic snowflake. Try the same thing with a raindrop on a rainy day.

75. Write your favorite word on a piece of paper. Then read the poem "My Favorite Word" by Lucia and James L. Hymes, Jr., from *Poems Children Will Sit Still For*, published by Citation Press. Write a poem or paragraph about your favorite word.

76. Read the poem "Galoshes" by Rhoda Bacmeister from *Poems Children Will Sit Still For*. Many of the words in this poem sound like the thing they are describing: "splishes, sploshes, slooshes and sloshes." There is a special name for this kind of "sound" word. See if you can find out what it is. Write a poem using some words which sound like the thing they are describing.

77. Think of an idea for a poem. Then make a list of rhyming words that would be useful for your idea. Try writing a couplet. Here is one:

> As I was walking in the park
> I thought I heard an otter bark.

78. Think of an idea for a poem. Make a list of rhyming words for your poem. Try writing a triplet. Here is one where the idea was to write about trees:

> Trees are lovely in the day
> But nighttime brings a ghostly sway
> That steals the loveliness away.

79. A limerick is a kind of nonsense poem. It has a special rhythm and rhyme. In a limerick, lines one, two and five rhyme. Lines three and four rhyme and are shorter than the other three lines. First think of an idea for your poem. Make a list of rhyming words that fit your idea and write a limerick like this:

> A cheerful old bear at the zoo
> Could always find something to do

> When it bored him to go
> On a walk to and fro
> He reversed it and walked fro and to

80. When people die, they sometimes have an *epitaph* written on their gravestone. Often epitaphs are serious, but sometimes they are humorous. In Boot Hill, a graveyard for outlaws and cowboys, one epitaph reads simply "He Called Bill Jones A Liar." Try writing an epitaph for the following people: a cowboy who died in a gunfight, an old lady who loved animals, a soldier killed in war, a faithful country doctor, a famous singer, a corrupt politician, a police officer killed on duty.

81. Read the following poem. Notice the pattern, then try to write something similar with a different theme.

> a fish died
> because
>   it couldn't breathe
> because
>   its gills were clogged with silt
> because
>   mud ran into the river
> because
>   there was a forest fire
> because
> someone was careless with fire
>   so please be careful with fire
> because

82. Write a poem about the way things are, but ought not to be. A poem like this says things one way but means them another way. Sometimes this is called irony or satire. Here is a poem that says things one way but means them another:

> Lovely, acrid, billowing factory smoke
> Obscures the ugliness of distant snowcapped mountains
> Trucks rumble quietly over the thruways depositing
> lovely black soot
> On corroded picturesque city buildings
> Children chatter happily on their way to school
> Coughing, laughing, rubbing their eyes in delight
> As the city gasps gaily to life.

83. Write acrostic poems where the first letter in each line can be read vertically to form a word. Here is an acrostic poem:

> T̲he snow falls quietly
> O̲bscuring the bare fields
> I̲t glides gently in the air
> L̲ike dandelions gone to seed

The vertical word is *toil*, which means *to work*.

84. Write a cinquain using this formula:
    Line 1—a noun
    Line 2—two adjectives that describe the noun
    Line 3—three verbs which relate to the noun
    Line 4—a short statement about the noun
    Line 5—a restatement of the noun or a synonym for it
    For example: Trees
                    Shady, bare
                    Branching, blooming, growing
                    They eat kites
                    Trees

85. Write a cinquain using this formula:
    Line 1—2 syllables I have
    Line 2—4 syllables Three kinds of friends
    Line 3—6 syllables Those worthy of friendship
    Line 4—8 syllables Those unworthy of my friendship
    Line 5—2 syllables And Friends

86. Write a diamond (diamante) poem. Use this formula:
    Line 1—a noun
    Line 2—two adjectives that describe the noun
    Line 3—three verbs ending in *-ing* or *-ed* which relate to the noun
    Line 4—four nouns, the first two being opposites of the second two
    Line 5—three verbs ending in *-ing* or *-ed* which indicate a change
    Line 6—two adjectives relating to the second two nouns in line 4
    Line 7—a noun that is opposite of the noun in line 1

87. Write a haiku poem. Haiku poetry tries to capture a momentary impression in three lines. Use this formula:
    Line 1—5 syllables The lonely wolf howls
    Line 2—7 syllables Like a ghostly night shadow
    Line 3—5 syllables Seeking its lost mate

88. Write a tanka poem. Tanka is an extension of haiku but does not require the capturing of a momentary impression. Use this formula:
    Line 1—5 syllables The wind blows gently
    Line 2—7 syllables Across the field and meadows
    Line 3—5 syllables Covering the earth
    Line 4—7 syllables With leaves then dawns its sterner
    Line 5—7 syllables Winter personality

89. Write a clerihew poem. Clerihew poetry has four lines consisting of two couplets. The first line of the poem is usually the name of some well-known person, alive, dead or fictional.
    For example: Charlie Brown
                    Is always down.
                    When Lucy drops by
                    He's sure to sigh.

90. Write a concrete or picture poem. Concrete poetry expresses an idea in both verbal and pictorial forms. It is fun, easy to do, and you will like the things you can do with it.

jj
jinj
jinglj
jinglebj
jinglebelj
jinglebelljj
jinglebelljinj
jinglebelljinglj
jinglebelljinglebj
jinglebelljinglebelj
jinglebelljinglebelljj
jinglebelljinglebelljinj
jinglebell jinglebell jinglj
wewishyouamerrychristmaswe

Story Writing

91. Write a rebus story by drawing a picture in place of some of the words. Here is a rebus story:

   The little 🧍 lived in a small 🏠 in

   the 🌳 . She lived with her 👩

   and her 👨 .

92. Write a story about an adventure in an attic, a cave, a tree house, a fort, a closet, the woods, the desert, an alley, a basement, an abandoned house.

93. Choose a familiar character from a book or TV show. Decide on a title and write a story about your character. Here are some ideas for a title for your story:
   a) The Day Tom Sawyer Painted My Fence
   b) Christopher Columbus Tells How He Goofed
   c) How Flipper Saved My Life
   d) My Gunfight with Pecos Bill

94. Paste pictures on poster board. Write words that fit with each picture. Write a story or a poem for each picture.

95. Read a story which requires the solving of a code as part of the plot, such as *Tony's Treasure Hunt* by Holly and John Peterson, Franklin Watts Inc. Write a story which has a code as part of the plot. *The First Book of Codes and Ciphers* by Sam and Beryl Epstein, Franklin Watts Inc., will teach you how to write codes.

96. Here are some story starters you might like to try:
   a) If I had three wishes, I would wish for. . . .

    b) I saw something funny today.

    c) I'd like to be a clown when I grow up.

    d) It was the middle of the night and everyone was asleep. It was then I decided. . . .

    e) All the way home I kept wondering how I was going to explain this to my parents. Then I had an idea.

    f) The old crippled tiger crept slowly through the tall grass.

    g) It was the saddest thing I ever saw.

    h) I wish I could. . . .

    j) It rained and rained and rained.

    k) I just can't open this door. I wonder. . . .

    l) I thought she was the meanest person in the world.

    m) Bob stood rooted to the ground. His legs refused to listen to his head.

97. Here are some questions that may help you get started on a story:

    a) What would the world be like if everyone was the same color?

    b) Can you imagine having two heads?

    c) Would you rather live in a tree, or a cave?

    d) What would it be like to live on the moon?

    e) What would you do if you were suddenly put down in the middle of a jungle?

    f) How would you feel if you were a shoe?

    g) What would you say to visitors from Mars?

    h) If you were a bird, where would you fly to?

    i) Would you rather be a blanket or a potato chip?

    j) Can you imagine having four feet?

    k) What would life be like if you were eight feet tall?

    l) What is the first thing you would do if you woke up and found you were an adult?

98. Here are some sentences to start your story with:

    a) All during the long night. . . .

    b) I was stopped dead in my tracks by those fierce, blazing eyes. . . .

    c) Few people are calm when they have only ten minutes to live.

    d) I watched in fascinated horror as. . . .

    e) I shall never forget that long, endless night. . . .

99. You are on a spaceship traveling to another galaxy. You were born on the ship and now are ten years old. Describe a day in your life from the time you get up until the time you go to bed. Remember to include such things as the clothing you wear, the food you eat, the education you receive, and how you entertain yourself.

100. You discover a tiny woman with her arm caught on a branch of the apple tree in your backyard. You set her free and she says she will do anything you want with that apple tree. You tell her that you want every apple you pick from it to turn into solid gold. She says, "I will do as you say, but first I must tell you the rules for making the apples turn into gold."

     a) What are the rules the tiny woman gives to you?

     b) What do you think you would do with your gold?

     c) What problems do you think your gold might cause you?

101. Suppose you were able to invite any famous person in the world to spend the weekend with you. Whom would you invite? What would you talk about? What would you do? Why did you choose this particular person?

102. Think of some of the "bad guys" in well-known fairy tales and children's stories such as the wolf in "Little Red Riding Hood," the giant in "Jack and the Beanstalk," and the troll in "The Three Billy Goats Gruff." Write a story telling how it was from the point of view of the "bad guy."

103. Compile a book about yourself. Make a page for each of these topics:

     a) All about me in fifty words or less

     b) My friends and enemies

     c) My favorite records and TV programs

     d) What I do when I'm not in school

     e) Favorite sports, hobbies and recreation

     f) Things I like and dislike

     g) What's really important to me

     h) What I'd like to do some day

Books to Motivate Writing

104. Read *Have You Seen My Brother* by Elizabeth Guilfoile, published by Follett. Many young children have been lost, and this book will encourage them to express their feelings and emotions about this experience.

105. Children who must wear glasses, hearing aids, braces, and so forth are often bothered by this necessity. Other children sometimes make the problem even more difficult. A book to help develop compassion, understanding, and awareness of this problem is *About Glasses for Gladys* by Mary Ericsson, published by Children's Press. This activity may be developed around a unit on health and can become part of a writing project.

106. Read *Happiness Is a Sad Song* or *Happiness Is a Warm Puppy* by Charles Schulz, Scholastic Book Services. "Happiness is . . ." poems can be developed from either of these books.

107. Read a book such as *Snowbound with Betsy* by Carolyn Haywood or *The Night the Lights Went Out* by Don Freeman, Viking Press. Discuss the things the family found themselves without when they did not have electricity. Suggest the writing of a story with a setting where modern conveniences are not present.

108. Read several stories from the Encyclopedia Brown series by Donald J. Sobol. Discuss the manner in which the detective stories are set up. Have the children try to write their own detective stories modeled

on the Encyclopedia Brown formula. Be sure to remind them to give clues but not to reveal the solution to their mystery.

Letter Writing

109. Contact a school in a nearby community. Make arrangements with a teacher of the same grade level to set up pen pals between the two classes. Work on good letter writing procedures. Try to arrange a meeting of the two groups at a future date. A more difficult to arrange, but interesting variation, is to set up a similar arrangment in another state or country.

110. Contact your state Employment Security Commission to obtain job briefs. Have each child choose an occupation which interests him or her and write a formal letter of application. The application should include qualifications, reasons for choosing a particular job, and why the children feel they would be successful. Another activity is to ask a classmate to write a letter of recommendation to accompany the job application.

111. Set up a postal system in your room. Have a box for each child to receive mail. Encourage the children to write letters to each other.

112. The visual image of a letter form should be clear in children's minds before they write letters. The following activities may help children to develop correct letter writing styles:
    a) Cut letter forms into puzzles that can reconstructed.
    b) Keep a file of different types of letter styles.

Television

113. Discuss TV commercials and what makes them catchy. Examples are the famous "Coke Song" and the line "I can't believe I ate the whole thing." Have each child choose a product or invent a product and write a commercial to sell that product.

114. Watch one of your favorite TV programs. Try rewriting the story, but change some of the important events in the story and write a new ending. You may wish to keep the characters the same.

115. Pretend you are a sports announcer. Research the facts and write an exciting broadcast featuring highlights of your favorite team's best game. Read your bradcast to the class.

116. Write a telelvision commercial to describe your favorite toy or game. Make a "storyboard," which is a series of pictures to describe what the actors in the commercial are doing. Under each picture indicate what they are saying.

117. Write a review of a television program or a movie. To get the idea, read a few reviews in your local newspaper. Here are some questions you may want to consider:

a) What kind of program was it? (comedy, drama, cartoon)
b) Who were the main characters?
c) Was it an interesting plot?
d) What did you like or dislike?

Holidays

118. Use magazine pictures with captions written by the children to form New Year's resolutions. Divide 24 by 31 inch paper in half. One half is to contain pictures and captions under the title "I resolve to . . ." and the other half is to contain pictures and captions under the title "I resolve not to."
119. Around Halloween time much attention is focused on witches. Pretend you went to a witch's restaurant for dinner. What kind of food would be available? Make a menu for such a restaurant. Include salads, drinks, main courses, desserts, appetizers.
120. Use traditional Christmas carol tunes and write new words which apply to different seasons. You might have Pumpkin carols, Turkey carols, Fourth of July carols, Valentine's carols, and so on.
121. Write an original message on homemade Christmas cards. The message may be a poem or prose. Arrange for illustration of the cards and send them to someone.
122. Make holiday dictionaries. Decide on an appropriate shape for the pages. For example, for Halloween you may want a page shaped like a ghost. Think of as many words as you can that pertain to a given holiday. Work in teams to illustrate and spell the words. Then write a sentence using each word. Put finished pages together into a booklet for use on special occasions.

Music

123. Play an expressive piece of music such as "The Dance of the Flowers" or "Swan Lake" by Peter Tchaikovsky. Do not reveal the title to the children. Have them write a story about what the music suggests to them.
124. Listen to some of your favorite popular or folk songs. Write new lyrics to the old tunes. "Row, Row, Row Your Boat" is an example of a tune that everyone knows, and new lyrics can readily be written for this song.
125. Play a record which stimulates a definite mood: calm, excited, scared, and so on. Discuss some examples of the types of moods music can suggest. A mood of calmness could be an early morning setting, the lull after a storm, or a lazy summer afternoon. Have the children write poetry or song lyrics to fit some of the moods the music suggests.

126. Music can motivate creative thinking. The sounds of the various instruments and the rhythm and moods of the music can motivate children to express their feelings and emotions in writing. Have them write stories or poems telling how specific types of music make them feel.
127. Cover a table with a large piece of butcher paper. Play various kinds of music. Have the children write words that come to mind as they listen.

Book Reports

128. After reading a book make a poster advertising the book. Write a catchy phrase or jingle that will attract others to the book.
129. Write a diary as you read a book. The diary may be written from the point of view of one of the characters in the book.
130. Make a book jacket illustrating one of your favorite books. Fold the paper to fit your book and then design the cover. Write the blurb inside the flap, giving clues to the story line, and developing interest in the story.
131. Choose a book that has been given the Newbery Award. Read it carefully, considering some of the qualities that you think make a good story. Write a paper telling why you believe this story deserved the award. Some suggested titles are *A Wrinkle in Time* and *Caddie Woodlawn*. If you did not like the book, tell why you think it did not deserve the award.

Social Studies

132. Read the story "Benny's Flag," about an Alaskan boy who designed the flag of Alaska. Think about what a flag stands for. Design your own flag and explain the meaning of it.
133. Pretend that you were asked to plan your family's summer vacation. List the places you would like to see. Use road maps to plot the route. You may wish to write letters requesting information.
134. Put yourself in the place of the people who made history. Choose an event in history that interests you. Research the event carefully. Write a radio or television script entitled "You Were There."
135. Read a book written about life as it was over one hundred years ago, such as *Huckleberry Finn, Johnny Tremain,* or *Caddie Woodlawn.* As you read the book, think about living conditions in those times. Write a report comparing life then and now. Think about whether you would rather have lived then or now and tell why.
136. Imagine you are going to meet a boy or girl your own age from another country. What questions would you ask about living conditions, customs, home life, and school? What would you tell your friend about your own life in America?

Science

137. Keep a journal of a science experiment. Make an entry every day noting specific details. Possible suggestions are planting seeds and growing plants, temperature and weather reports, and hatching eggs and raising chickens. When your experiment is finished, display your work on the science table. Write a final report. Include these things:
    a) materials used
    b) what you were trying to find out
    c) how you carried out the experiment
    d) what happened
    e) what you thought of the experiment

138. Do a study on ecology and pollution. Keep track of all the waste which you are responsible for making in one day or one week. Read about *biodegradability*. Try to discover what kind of waste will decompose. Write about your ideas on how to dispose of waste materials. Think of ways that we could waste less.

139. Show a health and nutrition film such as *Eat for Health* by Encyclopaedia Britannica Films. Try to discover what types of food you should eat each day. Plan a menu which includes three meals a day for a week.

140. Display pictures of the four seasons. Read the poems "Four Seasons" (author unknown) and "So Long as There's Weather" by Tamara Kitt from *Poems Children Will Sit Still For,* Citation Press. Have the children write about their favorite season telling why it is their favorite.

Practical Writing

141. Create a ficticious company name, address, and telephone number. Pretend that you are the personnel director for the firm and that a job opening has come to your attention. You are to interview applicants for the job. Design an application form for this job. Have several classmates fill out the form and interview several for the job.

142. Take a survey of the students in your school about possible changes in playground rules. Write a report about your survey. Publish it in the school paper and send a copy to the principal.

143. Advertisements use different kinds of propaganda techniques. Look for examples of different kinds of propaganda in magazine advertisements. Write and illustrate your own advertisements using some of the different techniques. Some propaganda techniques are:
    a) testimonial—endorsement by a well-known person
    b) card stacking—listing all the outstanding features
    c) transfer—endorsement by some respected group or person (similar to testimonial)
    d) band wagon—everybody is doing it so you should do it too

e) reverse band wagon or snob appeal—be an individual; do not follow the crowd

f) plain folks—endorsement by common, everyday people

g) glittering generalities—using words and sentences that make emotional or extravagant claims

144. Be a reporter. Interview leaders and members of the safety patrol, service squad, Boy Scouts, Girl Scouts, or some other group. Write a report on your interviews.

145. Write a commentary for a filmstrip. Block out the words that are already on an old filmstrip or use a filmstrip without dialogue. You can also make your own filmstrip and write the dialogue for it.

146. Study various sets of instructions for assembling such things as toys, fixtures, small kits for models. Then try to improve on the manufacturer's instructions.

147. Write a set of directions telling what must be done to survive an earthquake, tornado, or other natural disaster.

148. Write about your favorite game. Tell how it is played with exact directions so that anyone could play it after reading your directions.

149. Invent a new game. Make the game board and other elements for the game. Write the directions for playing the game. Try playing the game with friends to see if they understand your directions. Make needed changes in the directions as your friends indicate. When your game is complete, make an extra copy for the game area in your room.

Editing

150. Dictate into a tape recorder a story you have written. Listen to see if the following things are present:

a) Is the meaning clear?

b) Is the story well organized, that is, does each part seem to be in the right place?

c) Are there places where you could change some words or whole sentences to improve the story?

d) Is the story interesting enough for someone else to want to listen to it?

While you are listening to your story, take notes about things that should be changed. Make these changes after you have listened to your story several times.

151. Here are some questions you should ask yourself when you write a story that has people in it:

a) Have you told how each character in your story got into the story?

b) Have you described your characters well enough so that your readers can feel that they know them?

c) Have you explained something about why your characters act the way they do?

152. Read your story and underline all of the naming words (nouns). Have you used the best possible naming word in each case? When you use words to describe the naming words (adjectives), have you chosen interesting and colorful describing words? Make sure your naming words (nouns) and describing words (adjectives) make your story as meaningful and interesting as possible.

153. Check your paragraphs. Make a list of the main ideas in your writing. Underline the sentence that introduces each main idea on your list. Check to see if each main idea is in a separate paragraph.

154. Read your story, then write some questions about the most important things in your story. Ask a partner to read your story, then see if your partner can answer your questions. If your partner has trouble answering your questions, you can do two things. Ask someone else to read it to see if the same thing happens again, or rewrite your story to be sure that it is written clearly and is well organized.

155. If you have written a story or a play, it is sometimes helpful to have it acted out by others while you watch. If you listen carefully, you may discover that the story or play needs some rewriting to improve it.

156. Two editing charts can be placed in the writing center to help children edit their own materials. One chart has some reminders about the mechanics of writing, and the other chart contains reminders about content and meaning.

Content

a) Did I say what I wanted to say?
b) Did I say it clearly so that others will understand?
c) Did I arrange the paragraphs in a logical and interesting way?
d) Did I use the best possible words throughout my writing?
e) Did my story have a good beginning, middle, and ending?
f) Did I make the people in my story seem real, interesting, and worth reading about?

Mechanics

a) Did I capitalize the beginning of each sentence and other special words?
b) Did I punctuate each sentence?
c) Did I spell words correctly or check on those I was unsure about?
d) Did I use proper form on margins, indenting, titles, and other matters?

157. Make arrangements with a class of fifth or sixth grade children to work with your younger children. On specified occasions they may serve as editors. Young children will often react more positively to another older child than to an adult. When this activity is done, care must be taken to instruct the older children in the techniques of editing as well as in the techiques of working gently with the younger authors.

158. Match your children in pairs to work as editing partners. Be sure to spend time preparing them for the proper execution of this role. When properly administered, the use of partners can be an excellent way to improve editing skills.

159. Appoint specific children to certain editing responsibilities for periods of two or five days. You can appoint a spelling editor, a meaning editor, a punctuation editor, and a format editor. Once you have taught a cadre of children to perform these functions, they can begin to train each other by serving an apprenticeship as assistant editor before taking over as an editor.

160. Conduct editing workshops periodically. Obtain permission from a child to use his or her work for the editing session. Make a transparency of the work and project it on an overhead projector. Ask the children to locate specific items that need to be changed. When the workshop is over, ask the children to edit a recent piece of writing to correct one or two specific items in their writing. This procedure is an extremely useful one but must be directed with great care. The procedure is explained in detail in chapter 9.

Ideas for Advanced or Older Children

161. Sometimes people have a tendency to let others worry about the problems in our society. However, in a free society, issues like pollution are the responsibility of the individual as well as the government. Write a paper which tells what your responsibility is in safeguarding the environment and what action you can take.

162. You are the president of a large corporation that is being criticized by a citizen's group. The citizens believe your factories are polluting the environment. You feel, as president, that you must defend your company's policies. You realize that it is impossible to justify the pollution, so you base your defense on the problems of costs, the importance of business, and the heavy taxes your corporation pays. Write a speech that gives your side of the issue and presents both factual and emotional reasons for your company's policies.

163. As a member of a family, your actions and attitudes are influenced and shaped by your parents in many ways. Usually family instruction is not formal, but you are learning in that atmosphere all the time. Write about how you feel your thinking and your attitudes are influenced by your parents and your family. How would you bring up your children so they would not resent the learning that occurs in a family unit? What values and ideas would you want to pass on to your children? How will you do this?

164. Some people judge others by the jobs they hold. Such people might respect a doctor and disrespect a janitor even though they know nothing about the character, honesty, and competency of either. Write about this type of discrimination. Why do you think it occurs so commonly? What can be done about changing these attitudes?

165. You have just sat down in class when the teacher announces a "free period." What do you think you would choose to do?

166. Justice is often portrayed as a woman wearing a blindfold and carrying scales. How do you suppose this symbol originated? What is its meaning? Can you design a better symbol? Write an explanation in language so simple a young child could understand it.

167. You have just been given enough money to establish and operate a commune for one year. The money can be used for no other purpose. You decide to take the money and establish the commune. You want to develop the best possible commune. What kind of people would you select? What rules would you establish to govern the commune? What will be the philosophy of the group? What type of commune will you operate? If you are opposed to the idea of a commune, write an explanation of your views. Tell why you oppose the idea.

168. For two weeks, collect and organize every news story, article, cartoon, editorial comment, advertisement, and other information you can on the subject of youth or young people. Write a report summarizing what you have discovered about the way young people are represented in society.

169. Select a magazine published especially for young people. Consider all the information and write a report on it. Does the magazine depict young people accurately and fairly? Is the magazine directed at a specific group of young people? Are there ways you would suggest to improve the publication?

170. Sometimes young people feel they are more *adult* in their attitudes and behavior than many *adults*. Write about what it really means to be an adult.

171. You are waiting for a train at a subway station when a stranger approaches and asks, "Why have you been following me?" At first you assume he is talking to someone else but he persists. You deny his accusation but he continues to question you. He becomes angry and begins to shout. What would you say? How would you feel? Write a story based on the conversation that would follow between the two of you.

172. You are walking down a city street and see a man suddenly fall to the pavement. No one else is around and he calls to you for help. What would you do? Write a story based on how you think you would act.

TEN LESSON PLANS FOR WRITING

1.

Title: Secret Pal Letters

Objective: To practice letter writing within a meaningful and enjoyable framework.

Materials: Envelopes, stationery, and stamps. The stamps are optional depending on whether you mail the letters or rely on internal delivery.

Procedures: 1) Place each child's name in a container and have each child draw the name of the person who will be a "secret pal" for the next three days.
2) The children are to write letters to their secret pals revealing some information about themselves but not so much that their identities will be readily guessed. Letters should be signed "Your Secret Pal."
3) Have the children secretly address their letters and either mail them through the postal system or arrange for internal delivery in a way that will heighten expectancy and interest.
4) After the letters are written, the children are to make or purchase an inexpensive gift for their "secret pals". Arrangements must be made for these gifts to be distributed without revealing the identity of the givers.
5) On the day that the "secret pals" are to be disclosed, the children write a short paragraph guessing who their secret pals are and giving the clues and reasons that lead them to their conclusions. These statements should be read in class and the secret pals revealed.

Follow-up: 1) Have the children write a thank you letter to their secret pals for the gifts.
2) Make arrangements with another class and establish pen pal correspondence between the children from the two classes.

2.

Title: I Could Have Been . . . But . . .

Objective: To develop appreciation for the humorous use of language. To use language to create puns.

Materials: Overhead projector and a set of puns written for the occasion.

Procedures: 1) Prepare a transparency with examples of puns such as:
  a) *I could have been* a dressmaker *but* it did not seem right.
  b) *I could have been* a hockey player *but* I did not know Howe. (Gordie Howe is a star hockey player).
  c) *I could have been* a butcher *but* I could not hack it.
  d) *I could have been* a doctor *but* I did not have the patience.
2) Place the puns on the transparency so that the "I could have been . . . " part of the sentence can be exposed without revealing the " . . . but . . . " half.
  Example: I could have been a dressmaker
  but it did not seem right
3) Give several examples where the full pun is shown. Then, expose only the "I could have been . . . " half and encourage the children to supply the " . . . but . . . " half.

4) Elicit their ideas about how a pun works. Lead them to the conclusion that punning is using words in such a way as to suggest a different meaning or application than would be expected in the context in which the word or pun is used.

5) Invite children to write their own puns. Supply several "I could have been . . . " leads on the board to get them started. Have them work in pairs for their first attempt at pun writing.

Follow-up: Obtain a copy of a book on puns. Read some other types of puns that do not use the "I could have been . . . but . . . " formula. Encourage the children to use puns in their oral language and to write various types of puns.

3.

Title: Writing Diaries

Objective: To keep daily records of imaginative and real events in chronological sequence.

Materials: Notebooks suitable for recording daily entries. These may be purchased commercially or constructed in school.

Procedure: 1) Read excerpts from various diary accounts. Suitable examples are obtainable from school and local libraries. Alternatively, record a personal diary account to use as an example.

2) Discuss diary entries. Consider how entries differ depending on the type of diary maintained. Point out distinctions between factual, imaginative, and personal diaries. Provide suitable examples of each.

3) Keep a class diary for a period of three to five days. Record some event chosen by the children, such as the weather or a simple experiment.

4) Here are some examples of types of diary activities:

Imaginative diary:
a) Invent a daily account of your life on board the *Mayflower*.
b) Invent a daily account of your experiences as a competitor in the recent Olympic games.

Personal diary:
a) Write a daily account of the important things that happen to you.
b) Write a daily account of personal matters and feelings.

Factual diary:
a) Record daily information relating to a scientific experiment you are conducting.
b) Record daily weather conditions.

5) Encourage each child to choose which type of diary he or she will keep for a given period of time. Agreement should be

reached beforehand about who, if anyone, will read the diaries that are personal.

Follow-up: 1) Dramatize the events in an imaginative diary account.
              2) Keep a class record of a plant-growing experiment.

4.

Title: Terse Verse Riddles.

Objective: To express a humorous idea in terse, two word rhymes.

Materials: Overhead projector and a set of terse verse riddles written for the occasion.

Procedure: 1) Prepare a transparency with examples of terse verse riddles, such as:
              a) What was the historic command given by Joshua at the Battle of Jericho? (Fall, wall!)
              b) What were Washington's last words as he crossed the Delaware River? (Float, boat!)
              c) What did the little outlaw say to the kindergarten teacher? (Reach, teach!)
        2) Place the terse verse riddles on the transparency so that the riddle stem can be exposed without revealing the answer:

           Example: What did the little cowboy say to his kindergarten teacher?
                             Reach, teach!

        3) Give several examples where the riddle and answer are revealed. Then expose only the riddle and encourage the children to supply the answer in terse verse. Several responses are possible.
        4) Elicit discussion about the characteristics of a terse verse response. They should note that terse verse rhymes, is humorous, is appropriate to the riddle stem, and that both words have the same number of syllables.
        5) When you are satisfied that the children are ready, have them write their own terse verse riddles. Provide some riddle stems to get them started.

Follow-up: 1) Have the children read their terse verse riddles to the class when they are ready.
              2) Have the children illustrate or dramatize their terse verse riddles.

5.

Title: Twig Game

Objective: To use langauge more precisely so as to develop effective descriptive writing.

Materials: Twigs of various sizes, shapes, and varieties.

Procedure: 1) Divide the class into groups of five or six students. Distribute a bundle of clearly distinguishable twigs to each group. Each group will, in turn, distribute one twig to each member of the group.

2) Instruct the children to describe their twigs as accurately, precisely, and completely as possible. Show them the usefulness of using their senses to analyze their twig to discover texture, shape, smell, size, taste, and other unusual features.

3) When the written descriptions are complete, trade the twigs and written descriptions with another group. The groups are to match each twig with its correct written description.

4) Have the groups evaluate the experience to determine how useful their descriptions were to the other group who did the matching of description to twig.

Follow-up: 1) Repeat the experience with different objects such as rocks, leaves, or types of grasses.

2) Discuss the reasons for using language precisely. For example, the language used to describe patents must be precise for practical reasons, whereas the language of poetry and prose must be precise for reasons of enhanced meaning, rhythm, and other similar factors.

6.

Title: Advertising and Choosing Real Estate

Objective: To make decisions based on research information and personal preference. To write descriptions of houses in advertising terms.

Materials: Real estate advertisements from a local paper; pictures of different types of houses; table of tax rates in surrounding cities and townships; educational materials distributed by local real estate companies, chambers of commerce, and utilities; road maps of the local area; advertisements by stores and shopping centers in the area; local newspapers; other similar information about the community.

Procedure: 1) Make a display of the materials you have accumulated prior to the formal introduction of the activity.

2) Present the activity to the children. Start with a description like this:

> Your family must move to a new home. You are given the responsibility of purchasing or renting the new home. Write a description of the sort of house you wish to buy or rent that will be suitable for a real estate advertising brochure. In looking for the type of house you wish to purchase, consider

these matters: price range you can afford; location of convenient schools, shopping centers, and other matters important to you; tax rates; transportation; job opportunities.

3) Make available the information and materials you have gathered for the activity. Suggest other sources which the children may investigate for further information. Allow the children to work together if they wish.

Follow-up:
1) Have the children construct models and drawings of their houses and display these along with their written work.
2) Invite a real estate broker to speak to the class either during or after the initiation of the project.

7.

Title: Two-Minute Mysteries

Objective: To write an orginal two-minute mystery story.

Materials: Envelopes containing clues relevant to the solving of a mystery, Encyclopedia Brown books, Sherlock Holmes books.

Procedure:
1) Read some mystery stories to the children. Younger children will appreciate and understand the Encyclopedia Brown stories by Sobol. Older children will enjoy the shorter Sherlock Holmes mysteries.
2) Discuss the essential elements of a mystery: the problem or mystery to be solved, the unraveling of the mystery through the discovery and interpretation of relevant and irrelevant clues, the explanation of how the mystery was solved.
3) Arrange the class into a circle to play a mystery solving game. Give instructions as follows:
   a) Each envelope contains a clue that will help you solve a crime. If you put all of the clues together correctly, you will be able to discover the criminal, the weapon used, the time of the crime, the place of crime, and the motive or reason for the crime.
   b) Hand out the clue envelopes to the children. Tell them they cannot pass their clues around or show them to anyone else, but they can share their clues verbally. When the group thinks they have the answer to all five questions, they may tell you. Say that you will tell them only if all five answers are right or wrong and that you cannot tell them which of the five answers is right or wrong. The children may organize their discussion in any way they wish.
4) After the game is finished instruct the children to work in groups to create a mystery similar to the one just played.
5) Invite the children to write individual mystery stories.

Follow-up: Have the children dramatize some of the mysteries they have written.

8.

Title: Fables and "Just So" stories

Objective: To write fables and "just so" stories using literary models.

Materials: Pictures of animals; *Just So Stories* by Rudyard Kipling, Doubleday, *Aesop's Fables* as retold by Ann McGovern, Scholastic Book Services.

Procedure: 1) Read "How the Camel Got His Hump" by Kipling. Follow this by reading "The Hare and the Tortoise" from *Aesop's Fables*.
2) Discuss the differences and similarities between these two stories. Children will likely notice that the fable teaches a moral lesson, whereas the "just so" story is a fantasy about how the camel acquired a particular physical feature.
3) Have each child choose a picture of an animal that interests him or her. Invite the children to write a "just so" story about how the animals they chose obtained a particular feature, such as "How the Giraffe Got Its Long Neck."
4) Have the children write a fable using the same animal they used for the "just so" story. Emphasize that this story has a different purpose and should have a lesson to teach.

Follow-up: Have the children share their stories with each other. Sometimes this activity is more interesting when done with groups of four or five students rather than with an entire class.

9.

Title: Using the Right Word

Objective: To improve word choice through the use of a thesaurus and dictionary.

Materials: A thesaurus for children (*In Other Words: A Beginning Thesaurus* by Greet, Jenkins and Schille, Scott-Foresman and Company); a dictionary for children.

Procedure: 1) Have the children write a story, poem, or other type of account. The next day have the children edit their writing.
2) Instruct the children to do these two things:
   a) underline words (usually nouns, verbs and adjectives) that are used over and over
   b) underline words that might have other suitable synonyms.
3) When they have established a short list of words, show them how to locate words in the thesaurus. Remind them to check

the definitions of substituted words to make sure the new word fits their story.

4) Rewrite the original piece of writing, inserting the new words.

5) This activity should initially be done in pairs to provide support for each other in editing and using the reference materials.

Follow-up: 1) Bring in a cartoon or newspaper article with specific words underlined. Have children use the thesaurus to find suitable substitutes for the underlined words.

2) Have children exchange stories and perform this same task on another child's writing.

10.

Title: I Seem To Be . . . But Really I am . . .

Objective: To write poetry which encourages the examination of personal feelings, thoughts, and behavior as it relates to how others see us.

Materials: Selected story material where the main character or characters are young people faced with a situation in which they behave differently in front of their peers as compared to how they feel inside. Such materials may be extracted from various types of youth literature, written by the teacher, or obtained commercially.

Procedure: 1) Read a selection in which the main character acts differently from the way he or she feels. For example, a boy joins a gang that steals cars, but secretly he feels that what he has done is wrong. A different type of situation would be one where a young girl acts aloof and overbearing towards her peers but secretly wishes to be friendly. These situations can be adapted to all age groups and can be tied to all types of common, conflicting experiences that children of all ages encounter.

2) Write these lines on the board:

I seem to be . . .
but really I am . . .

Encourage the children to complete these lines as a description of the story or situation previously read. For example, they might complete the story like this:

a) I seem to be cool because I hang out with some tough people, but really I am worried because I know that what I am doing is wrong.

b) I seem to be conceited and unfriendly, but really I am lonely and frightened.

Follow-up: Have the children write their own story materials that would be suitable for stimulating "I seem to be" poetry.

13

Teaching Comprehension in Reading Instruction

Reading is to the mind what exercise is to the body. Unfortunately, a good deal more is known about exercise than is known about reading. Reading may be the most complex task people have devised for themselves. The purpose of reading instruction is to improve comprehension. No task in teaching is more crucial. Few are more difficult to achieve.

The purpose of this chapter is to discuss some of the aspects of what is known about comprehension and to suggest some teaching techniques that have worked in classrooms and clinics. Major topics discussed include (1) guiding principles of comprehension instruction, (2) four components of reading comprehension, (3) purpose setting, prediction and reflective thinking in comprehension, (4) directing comprehension instruction through the directed reading thinking activity, and (5) evaluating comprehension instruction.

Guiding Principles of Comprehension Instruction

This section presents six guiding principles of comprehension instruction. The test of their validity is the extent to which teachers find them useful in teaching comprehension.

1. *Comprehension occurs when what is already known is related to new information obtained through reading.* The degree to which the reader integrates new information with what is already known determines the effectiveness of comprehension. The degree to which the reader is stimu-

lated to integrate new information with previous knowledge is influenced by how well comprehension instruction is directed. This suggests two teaching concerns. First, teachers must be aware of the limitations of what children already know so that confusion in the teaching process is kept to a minimum. If teachers are not aware of these limitations children will have a difficult time making sense of what they are reading. Second, comprehension instruction must be directed in ways that give opportunities to think about the various ways new information may be related to what is already known.

2. *The techniques of instruction, in combination with the underlying competence of the teacher, can have a positive effect on comprehension.* Some techniques of instruction are better than others. Some teachers are better at motivating and directing the instruction of children. Any technique of comprehension instruction which fails to facilitate the integration of previous knowledge with new information is inferior to any technique which does facilitate the integration of new information with previous knowledge. A teaching technique alone, however, is of little use. It must receive the breath of life from a teacher. The teacher recreates the technique with each teaching episode. The teacher's underlying competence is combined with the promise of the teaching technique—the magic occurs or fails to occur at this mysterious point.

3. *Comprehension instruction should teach readers to set their own purposes.* Purposes set by the teacher are an inadequate substitute for self-declared purposes. Self-declared purposes stimulate the desire to read, direct the quest for new information in specific channels, certify the reader's sense of competence, simulate the conditions which prevail in independent reading, and have a positive effect on comprehension, as Henderson's research has shown. (1)

4. *Readiness for comprehension is best facilitated through teacher questioning, not through teacher telling.* Typically, preteaching assistance consists of a narrative description of material background and preset purposes for reading. The intent is to stimulate interest and to build background presumed to be lacking in the reader. While the intent is understandable, the idea is unfortunate. Such procedures are inimical to stimulating interest and they do not make the best use of existing experience. While it is true that what is known in advance is what enables the reader to comprehend, the question is how to make best use of existing knowledge. Should readiness for comprehension be supplemented through telling, or is readiness for comprehension best facilitated through questioning which requires the reader to integrate what is known with what is about to be read? The research of Davidson (2) and Petre (3) support the latter conclusion.

5. *Comprehension questions should stimulate higher-level thinking rather than the recall of information.* Questions should prime the critical mind, not dull it by testing the extent of retention. The asking of questions is an art. The lawyer who cross-examines well does so through effective

questioning. Likewise, the teacher who directs comprehension instruction well does so through effective questioning. Questions are the teacher's lever on the pupil's mind. Without the lever the teacher can have little influence. If the wrong question is asked, or even the right question at the wrong time, growth is stymied and confusion or boredom can result. Much of comprehension instruction is devoted to the asking of trivial questions intended to stimulate recall of information after reading has occurred. Such questions test the memory but do not help the reader to make sense of what has been read. Smith (4) has wisely pointed out that recall questions should have a minor role in comprehension instruction. Useful comprehension questions must serve a broad purpose. They should require pupils to integrate what they already know with new information; they should engender educated guesses regarding outcomes; they should stimulate the reader to make inferences; they should direct inquiry regarding values, worthiness, and usefulness. If comprehension questions do not stimulate productive, intellectual responses that go beyond the information given, they will not significantly improve comprehension.

6. *Comprehension is a relative matter.* What constitutes comprehension varies from reader to reader. The ability to measure it and to teach it is limited because so little is known about what occurs in the brain. Teachers are probably more effective in teaching comprehension than they are given credit for. After all, many children *do* comprehend what they read. While much of the credit must be given to the child, a fair measure of credit may also be ascribed to the teacher.

7. *Reading and writing are extraordinarily complex tasks.* Each sentence contains whatever the writer explicitly said as well as what he or she may have intended to say. Readers inject their personality, knowledge, and experience into what they read. Consequently, every sentence read is also "read into." Conversely, every sentence written is also "written into." The result is that reading comprehension is highly personal and inevitably subjective. Even at the literal level, comprehension is never completely objective.

8. *Reading is a thinking process.* It is primarily implicit comprehension that is referred to when reading is thus described. Furthermore, there is a sense in which the complex referred to as intelligence is related to comprehension. In many respects, the operations and processes called comprehension are indistinguishable from the operations and processes called thinking. Lennon (5) states this proposition in the following way:

The intellectual operations or processes that it is common now to include in the notion of reading as a thinking process are indistinguishable from at least some of the operations and processes that we define as comprising "intelligence." In other words, it is inconceivable that a good test of reading as reasoning should not also be a valid measure of some aspects of the complex we term intelligence.

Four Components of Comprehension

Testing and teaching materials imply, or state explicitly, that there are twenty, forty, eighty, or more reading comprehension skills. Is this true? Certainly there is no empirical evidence of the existence of such a large number of separate measurable comprehension skills. On the contrary, research by Davis (6), Hunt (7), and others indicates that there may be from one to nine separate, measurable comprehension skills.

The large number of comprehension skills commonly identified are often nothing more than different names describing the same limited set of comprehension components. What has happened is that the descriptions used in materials have become the vocabulary of instruction. When a term is used often enough, people believe that the term describes something real. The labels are assumed to verify the reality. After a time nearly everyone accepts the descriptions as valid representations of reality.

Consider, for example, comprehension skills, commonly cited in tests and materials, such as "making inferences" and "drawing conclusions." Making inferences and drawing conclusions are often tested and taught as separate comprehension skills. Few people question whether they are indeed distinct. It is difficult to question the terminology that has been used for years. But still some questions must be asked. Is there a difference between drawing a conclusion and making an inference? No empirical evidence exists. Can one draw a conclusion without making an inference? It seems unlikely. Can questions be asked which require one of these operations exclusively? It is doubtful. Are making inferences and drawing conclusions parts of a more complex set of mental operations that are indistinguishable in testing and teaching? Apparently so. Is there a more general comprehension component under which both making inferences and drawing conclusions can be classified? I believe there is. Would a more limited set of comprehension components serve a useful instructional purpose? My purpose here is to persuade you that this is so.

Comprehension can be taught more efficiently and effectively if the teacher has an economical framework around which instruction can be organized. After all, teaching eighty skills is more difficult than teaching three. If there are indeed eighty, then teaching is impossibly complex. Where will the teacher find time to teach them all? Who is to be taught which skill? How will this be discovered? And if discovered, how will the instruction of eighty different skills to thirty different children be organized? Teachers saddled with unmanageable reading systems should ask these questions. They will be surprised to discover that much of the complexity can be eliminated by conceptualizing comprehension skills in a different way.

Analysis of research and a common sense interpretation of teaching experience suggests that reading comprehension can be classified into four components. Each of the components covers a broad spectrum of reading behavior. The components are overlapping and interrelated. Yet, it is possible to recognize at least one distinct characteristic of each. Furthermore, when comprehension is conceptualized within a more limited framework, it is possible, indeed necessary, to reorganize that set of eighty (or however many) so-called skills within this more economic scheme. It is essential that any comprehension scheme accommodate the traditional descriptive labels of reading comprehension skills since all texts, tests, and materials use them to identify reading comprehension skills. To make this accommodation requires common sense judgments as to where each of the eighty (or however many) skills fits within the more economic classification system described below.

The components of comprehension are (1) comprehension of explicit meaning, (2) comprehension of implicit meaning, (3) comprehension of word meaning, and (4) comprehension of aesthetic-appreciative meaning.

Comprehension of Explicit Meaning

This is the most basic of the comprehension components. It may be defined as the ability to understand, at a literal level, information clearly stated in the text. In traditional terminology, explicit comprehension may include locating information, following explicit directions, identifying supporting detail, recognizing stated sequence, finding explicit proof, and answering factual questions.

Normally, the comprehension of explicit meaning requires the reader to recall or recognize relatively small bits of information, though this is not always so. Explicit comprehension is often referred to as getting or knowing the facts. It is the easiest of the comprehension components to teach and the one most frequently taught. While it is usually regarded as the lowest in the hierarchy of comprehension components, it is important because it is part of the foundation on which higher level comprehension depends.

While explicit comprehension is important it should not be emphasized out of proportion to its relative contribution to the total process. Because it is relatively easy to teach and test, there is a temptation to devote a disproportionate amount of time to its development. Teachers should resist this temptation.

Explicit comprehension may be likened to the thinking component Guilford has called cognitive memory. (8) Cognitive memory is the understanding and retention of information in any form as a result of all types of experiences. Questions which require cognitive memory usually ask who? what? when? or where? Cognitive memory, like explicit comprehension, provides a background and foundation for further thinking. Cognitive memory and explicit comprehension appear to function in similar ways.

Comprehension of Implicit Meaning

This is the most sophisticated and perhaps the most important reading comprehension skill. It encompasses all those reading behaviors commonly labeled thinking, or reasoning, in reading. It may be defined as the ability to gain meaning, through reasoning at levels, beyond explicit meaning. In traditional terminology, implicit comprehension includes recognizing relationships, extrapolating information and ideas, generating predictions, contriving applications, evaluating the worth of information and ideas, understanding the organization of a passage, deriving principles, and so on. In short, comprehension of implicit meaning involves all those reading abilities that demand a thinking, productive, intellectual response to what is read. The ability to operate effectively at this level distinguishes the mere receiver of information from the user, the passive from the active reader, the indifferent from the motivated, and the dull from the bright.

Implicit comprehension is the most difficult to teach because it places significant intellectual demands on both teachers and children. Teaching implicit meaning requires thoughtful, purposeful questioning which stimulates children to use their reasoning abilities. Teachers must acquire a repertoire of questioning strategies and techniques for teaching implicit comprehension. Effective teaching of implicit comprehension demands careful preparation, a willingness to accept children's thinking, and the enjoyment of productive intellectual discussion.

Because the comprehension of implicit meaning is a difficult skill to teach or test, there is a danger of devoting an insufficient amount of time to its development. Teachers must schedule sufficient time for it as well as sufficient time to prepare themselves for teaching it.

The component that we have called comprehension of implicit meaning may be similar to the three thinking skills that Guilford has called convergent thinking, divergent thinking, and evaluative thinking. Convergent thinking is problem solving in situations where sufficient information is given so that reasoning is likely to lead to a specific answer or outcome. The emphasis in convergent thinking is toward achieving conventionally accepted answers to questions and problems. Divergent thinking is problem solving when several answers are possible. It is stimulated in situations where a limited amount of information is available. Divergent thinking may proceed in several directions leading to varying answers, solutions, or insights. Evaluative thinking is problem solving in relation to a value judgment. It is stimulated in situations where one decides if available information supports a carefully defined concept. Evaluative thinking focuses on questions of suitability, desirability, and worthiness of ideas and information. Convergent, divergent, and evaluative thinking require mental operations and processes similar to implicit comprehension.

Comprehension of Word Meaning

The mastery of word meanings is prerequisite to every level of reading comprehension. It may be defined as the ability to understand both the connotative and denotative meanings of words and phrases. Comprehension of word meaning is prerequisite to success at all levels of comprehension.

Word meaning is perhaps the most universally recognized component of reading comprehension. Research studies by Davis (6) and Hunt (7) identified a general verbal factor related to word meaning. In traditional terminology, word meaning comprehension includes knowledge of the denotative and connotative meanings of words, translation of figures of speech, idioms, slang, word origin, and other circumstances related to word meaning. At its simplest level, comprehension of word meaning requires an accurate translation and explanation of words. At its more complex levels it requires extracting the last morsel of hidden meaning, perceiving simple and complex relationships, and ferreting out subtle nuances of intent and tone.

Words are the repository of our experiences, the symbols of our thinking, the bearers of our concepts, the conveyors of our knowledge. Depth and breadth of word meaning depends largely on the quality of our experiences. Research and teaching experience shows that word meaning is crucial to reading comprehension. Teachers should make children aware of words by providing experiences which will enrich their store of available meanings.

Explicit, implicit, and word meaning comprehension are illustrated below. The questions used demonstrate both the distinctions and the similarities that exist among the components. The passage is a brief excerpt from a Sherlock Holmes story entitled "The Blue Carbuncle."

> I took the tattered object in my hands, and turned it over rather ruefully. It was a very ordinary black hat of the usual round shape, hard and much the worse for wear. The lining had been of red silk, but was a good deal discoloured. There was no maker's name; but, as Holmes had remarked, the initials "H.B." were scrawled upon one side. It was pierced in the brim for a hat-securer, but the elastic was missing. For the rest, it was cracked, exceedingly dusty, and spotted in several places, although there seemed to have been some attempt to hide the discoloured patches by smearing them with ink.
> "I can see nothing," said I, handing it back to my friend.
> "On the contrary, Watson, you can see everything. You fail, however, to reason from what you see. You are too timid in drawing your inferences."
> (9, p. 246)

Following are three sets of questions which are illustrative of the type of question one might use to elicit comprehension in the various categories described.

Explicit comprehension questions:

1. What is the object that Watson has been examining? (Answer: a black hat.)
2. Give four facts that descirbe the condition of the hat. (Answer: (1) it is lined with red silk, (2) it is cracked, (3) it is dusty, (4) it is spotted in several places.)

Notice that the explicit comprehension questions require the reader to locate, recognize, or recall literal information. One cannot help but observe that the questions, despite the fact that they are central to the passage, bear the unmistakable stamp of triviality. Techniques for locating explicit information quickly and accurately are needed, however, since relevant literal information is prerequisite to higher levels of comprehension. Acquiring this skill is no mean task. It requires diligence and straightforward thinking. The questions need not remain trivial. They can be transformed if subsequent questioning requires the information be used to perform higher level comprehension functions.

Two problems in the teaching of explicit comprehension have developed. First, an inordinate amount of time and attention is devoted to it. Estimates indicate that as much as 80 percent of reading instruction time is devoted to teaching explicit comprehension. Likewise, an examination of reading materials shows a tendency to focus too much attention on this skill. Such over-emphasis is not conducive to good reading instruction. Second, the connection between explicit comprehension and implicit comprehension is often neglected in teaching. Training in explicit comprehension should stress opportunities to apply literal information to higher-level comprehension problems. Simple acqui-sition and rehearsal of literal information has limited relevance, whereas the use of such information to solve more challenging and complex problems has a much wider use.

Implicit comprehension questions:
1. What does the condition of the hat suggest about the sort of person the owner may have been? (Answer: The owner may have been a per-son of foresight and self-respect, but is perhaps less so now than in the past.)
2. What does Holmes think that Watson has been too timid in drawing inferences? (Answer: Because while Watson has observed a number relevant facts about the hat he ends up saying, "I can see nothing." Actually he has seen everything but makes no attempt to use the information he has observed.)

Notice that both implicit questions require the use of explicit information but in a different way than the two explicit questions. The implicit questions require an interpretation or use of literal information to derive meaning the author has not stated directly. Consider, for example, the first implicit question. You may think the passage does not support the answer. Holmes, of course, would not agree with you. Nevertheless, thinking readers may indeed disagree about what constitutes a correct answer. Effective reading at the implicit level of comprehension only requires that the reader point to in-formation which logically may be construed to support an answer. Arriving at correct answers is only part of the goal of implicit comprehension training. Beyond correctness, an important purpose is to challenge pupils to use infor-mation in thinking ways. Inevitably this leads to disagreement. Good readers often reason to different conclusions and extrapolate different meaning from the same literal information. The goal of implicit comprehension is to train readers to reflect on probable and possible meaning of what has been stated. Such training must be given to all pupils, whether first graders or graduate students, whether mentally limited or bright. Such opportunities should be given daily and should be balanced with training in other comprehension skills.

Perhaps the most challenging problem in teaching implicit comprehension is that it demands a great deal of teacher involvement. A good question is not easily formulated. Reflection is required. On the other hand, asking an explicit question requires little effort. Discussion between and among pupils and the teacher is essential if reflective thinking is to occur. Someone must be prepared to challenge children's initial offerings, to question their reasoning, to demand their proof, to probe deeper than they may be willing to go on their own. Self-checking may be sufficient in some explicit comprehension exercises, but it is seldom satisfactory where implicit comprehension is concerned. Since teachers have a limited amount of time to devote to the teaching of reading, maximum use of what time is available should be devoted to teaching implicit comprehension rather than explicit comprehension.

Word meaning questions:

1. What is meant when the lining of the hat is said to be *discoloured?* (Answer: The original colour of the lining had faded or been stained through use.)
2. What is meant by the expression, "too *timid* in *drawing* your *inferences?*" (Answer: It meant that Watson lacked the confidence or boldness to make guesses about the probable meaning of the facts he had observed regarding the hat.)

The first word meaning question deals with a specific word while the second focuses on a lengthier expression. In teaching word meaning, primary stress should be placed on understanding the meaning of words in context. The contextual use of a word often conveys a subtle nuance or inference that goes beyond the definition given in the dictionary. The expression "too timid in drawing your inferences" could in fact be either a word meaning question or an implict comprehension question. The second word meaning question focuses on the meaning of *timid, drawing,* and *inferences.* An inference question would focus on whether Holmes was expressing an implied criticism of Watson's powers of intellect. The difference between a word meaning question and an inference question may be small or great depending on the form the question takes. This further illustrates an earlier statement that the skills of comprehension are not independent entities. Rather, they are overlapping and interrelated categories.

Comprehension of Aesthetic-appreciative Meaning

Lennon (5) has suggested a component of comprehension which he terms *appreciative meaning.* The empirical justification for this component is debatable, although the Davis (6) study seems to substantiate its existence. Logical analysis of the reading act justifies it as a probable comprehension component. Clearly, there is an affective dimension to reading which defies precise empirical measurement. One must account for the reading experience which derives pleasure from the beauty of written language, enjoying the sound of poetry or prose, the emotional exhilaration engendered by a poem, the impact of a tragic story, the unaccountable bias one may experience on reading an editorial, the humor of a joke. It seems reasonable to propose a component of comprehension called aesthetic-appreciative meaning.

Comprehension of aesthetic-appreciative meaning is defined as the ability to derive personal enjoyment and meaning from materials and to understand and appreciate the literary devices associated with the interpretation of mood, tone, beauty, humor and other affective elements associated with the written word. While comprehension at the aesthetic-appreciative level is personal and affective, it is not divorced from the normal reasoning processes associated with cognitive functioning. Aesthetic-appreciative comprehension requires the use of inference and thinking. It differs from the other comprehension components in emphasis and outcome, not in process.

An example of aesthetic-appreciative comprehension may be illustrated in the following story. A group of children had just completed the reading of a story entitled "Wild Dog." Near the end of the story the following passage appeared:

> He stroked the dog's velvet ears and cupped the dog's muzzle between his hands, shaking it in rough tenderness. He stroked the dog's body and then, very carefully, so that the dog might not know any moment of fright, he drew his revolver from his belt and pressed it to the trusting head. (10, p. 69)

This passage usually arouses a strong emotional response from young readers. Following the reading of this paragraph the children were asked, "Do you think the boy should kill the dog?" One child responded, "No, the dog trusted him and it would be cruel and disloyal to kill the dog." However, another child disagreed, saying, "Yes, I think he should shoot the dog. The boy loved the dog and knew that what he was doing was best for both him and the dog." Notice that both responses are dependent on a personal evaluation and are valid points of view even though the logic is based on personal criteria. At the aesthetic-appreciative level of comprehension responses are not right or wrong in the conventional sense. Thinking is required but answers are based on values and idiosyncratic criteria. Comprehension at this level often requires a value judgment rather than a logical judgment. Personal meaning, enjoyment, and appreciation are the principal outcomes at this level of comprehension. The *emphasis* is on the affective rather than the cognitive side of intellect.

Research on comprehension supports a distinction among the components called explicit, implicit, and word meaning comprehension. These three can be identified as separate, measurable components of comprehension. The evidence is less clear regarding aesthetic-appreciative meaning. It has been presented here as a probable fourth comprehension component.

All comprehension components are related and mutually interdependent. For example, the ability to derive implicit meaning presupposes that the material has been understood at the explicit level, comprehension of explicit and implicit meaning is dependent on word meaning, and so on. Every comprehension component is related at some level to every other component. The fact that comprehension components are closely related and overlapping is neither surprising nor distressing. Rather, it is reassuring since it suggests that instruction devoted to improving comprehension in one area may have a beneficial influence on comprehension in other areas.

The Relationship Between the Four Components of Comprehension and the Commonly Used Names of Reading Skills

Figure 1 is a chart listing the four components of comprehension. Listed under each of the four components are some of the common names used to describe comprehension skills. The list of common skill names is representative rather than exhaustive.

FIGURE 1
The Four Basic Components of Comprehension

EXPLICIT (Literal)	IMPLICIT (Reasoning)	WORD MEANING (Vocabulary)	APPRECIATIV (Affective)
Main idea (stated)	Inference	Denotation	Mood
Factual questions	Prediction	Connotation	Tone
Sequence (stated)	Application	Multiple meanings	Characterizatior
Following directions	Cause-Effect	Contextual meanings	Beauty
Restating information	Interpretation	Compounds	Humor
Finding proof	Evaluation	Synonyms	Values (personal
Recognizing details	Contrast	Antonyms	Feelings
Recalling details	Purpose setting	Homonyms	Opinion
Locating information	Comparison	Homographs	
	Organization	Root words	
	Generalization	Prefixes	
	Extrapolation	Suffixes	
	Recognizing propaganda	Word origin	
	Main ideas (implied)	Idioms	
	Drawing conclusions	Slang	
	Critical reading	Figures of speech	
	Creative reading	Classification	
		Metaphor	
		Simile	

There are four major components of comprehension. There is empirical evidence to substantiate these categories. Under each of the four components (or skills) are listed common terms often described as reading comprehension skills. These common terms do not correspond to separate reading skills. There is no evidence that they can be either measured or taught as separate entities. However, these terms do often describe the intent of an activity or a question. They are a legitimate part of the descriptive language associated with the teaching of reading. No harm is done by using the terms so long as it is understood that teachers are limited in their ability to teach them to children as separate and measurable skills of reading.

Current tests and materials list many comprehension skills. Some materials may list as few as twenty comprehension skills while others may list as many as eighty or more. The teacher must bridge the gap between the four components of comprehension and the common skill names encountered in testing and teaching materials. The following suggestions will help you relate your testing and teaching materials to the comprehension components described in this chapter.

1. *Study the definitions for each of the four comprehension components.* Be especially aware of the major characteristic of each component.
2. *Examine your reading materials and tests.* Make a list of the names of the skills they purport to teach or test. Determine which of the four comprehension components each of the skills can be listed under. Make a chart similar to Figure 1 substituting your own list of common skill names for each of the comprehension components.
3. *Examine the comprehension activities provided for teaching and testing the reading skills presented in your materials.* Determine the nature of the task the pupil is expected to perform on each skill. Ask yourself

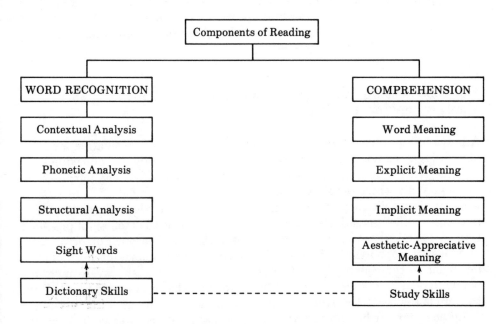

The two concerns in reading instruction are *word recognition* and *comprehension*. Word recognition has four sub-components: *Contextual analysis, phonetic analysis, structural analysis and sight words.* Comprehension has four subcomponents: *word meaning, explicit meaning, implicit meaning, and aesthetic-appreciative meaning.* Dictionary skills and study skills are related to both word recognition and comprehension, but in an indirect way as the broken line indicates.

questions such as: Does this skill activity require the pupil to deal exclusively with explicitly stated information? If so, that skill belongs under the explicit meaning component. Does the skill require the pupil to work with words or phrases? If so that skill belongs under the word meaning component. Does the skill require the pupil to reason with information at a level beyond the explicit information? If so that skill belongs under the implicit meaning component.

Remember that the name of a comprehension skill does not always accurately describe the task associated with it. For example, "finding the main idea" is a skill taught in nearly all reading materials. The task associated with this common skill name often requires an inference, since the main idea is usually not stated directly. If this is so, it would belong under the implicit comprehension component. In another instance "finding the main idea" may only require locating a sentence which states the main idea. In that case the activity may be an explicit one.

4. *When the preceding steps are completed, determine whether too much or too little emphasis is given to one component or another.* For example, if over half of the skill activities in your materials are devoted to explicit comprehension, the balance is not appropriate. You may make adjustments in your teaching to correct this deficiency. You may also wish to take this information into consideration when ordering materials in the future.

Purpose-setting, Prediction and Reflective Thinking in Comprehension Instruction

A prevailing practice in reading instruction is to provide motivation for reading through readiness procedures. Typically, these readiness procedures direct the teacher to summarize related background and set the purposes for reading. While these procedures may be faulted on a number of counts, their most glaring deficiency is that they seldom have the desired effect of motivating children to read. Perhaps one reason for this is that telling pupils what is to come and what to look for fails to stimulate imagination. Furthermore, it provides little opportunity for the children to make a personal intellectual commitment to the course of events in the material. A better way to motivate pupils to read is to reverse the traditional roles of the teacher and pupil. Have the pupils tell what the story or essay is going to be about. Motivation and comprehension are heightened when the reading lesson is directed in a fashion that allows pupils to set their own purposes for reading as Henderson's (1) research has shown.

How can a child tell you about a story not yet read? You must use a teaching format which requires children to examine what they already know and to use this knowledge to forecast where a story or essay is likely to go. Stauffer (11) calls this process a directed reading-thinking activity.

The directed reading-thinking activity is a teaching procedure useful for directing reading comprehension. It is a procedure usually associated with small group work but can be applied to individuals or even large groups of individuals. It has two major purposes. First, to teach children the skill of extracting information of predictive value from fiction or nonfiction material. Second, to provide a forum for group instruction that emphasizes higher level comprehension experiences that may be useful to pupils when reading on their own.

The practice of encouraging children to set their own purposes for reading through prediction can lead to growth in reading comprehension. When children are encouraged to set logical purposes for reading nonfiction materials and to make predictions regarding story outcomes when they are reading fiction, they may discover that the ideas of the author are different from their own. When readers make predictions, they establish a dialogue between themselves and the author. In order for the dialogue to be effective, the readers must regularly make decisions as to whether they will maintain, reject, or modify their speculations. During a directed reading-thinking activity, the business of the teacher is to guide the lesson so that dialogue between the child, the teacher, and other children will occur. Readers who know how to set a purpose for reading and to predict where the story or essay will go, have at their disposal an effective method for making accurate evaluations while they are reading. It is effective because it requires readers to examine the adequacy of their own thinking while they read.

Imagine that a group of children are reading an essay on "The Influence of Slavery on the South." One reader discovers statements which lead her to expect a certain conclusion. As she reads on, however, she finds her own conclusions are different from the author's even though she has only the author's evidence to go on. She must, in such an unresolved situation, maintain, reject, or modify either her own ideas or the author's. Whichever course is chosen will depend on the evidence, of course, but also on variables that are peculiar to the reader. If the reader has been guided to make predictions, she at least has a reason to place her own viewpoint beside that of the author. She has made predictions on the basis of information stated in the material and her own logical set.

In the case of fiction, predictions are based on the facts of the story and the reader's own formal literary set. For example, one can ask, "Where is a story which brings in a poor but beautiful peasant maiden and a charming prince likely to go?" As children gain a sense of conventional literary structure (and one way of gaining this is through the procedures being described) they will begin to put together the "two plus two" of story structure and come up with a number of ideas as to where such a story is likely to go, and how the facts of the story determine its outcome.

The intelligent use of questions is the key to comprehension. Open-ended questions are especially useful when you want to encourage the reader to think beyond the evidence currently available. The following questions are typical of the type that might be used to generate thoughtful predictions and reflective thinking:

1. What would happen if . . . ?
2. How do you think the author came to believe . . . ?

3. What sort of ending does the evidence suggest?
4. Based on what you have read, what do you think the author will say about . . . ?
5. Do you agree with the author's idea that . . . ?
6. Do you think . . . was the right thing to do?
7. Why do you think that . . . ?
8. What evidence do you have for your idea that . . . ?
9. What do you think about Tim's ideas that . . . ?
10. What sort of person would . . . ?

Questions like these focus thinking on broader issues and themes. They demand that the reader make sense of what is read. They encourage the reader to place his or her own thinking alongside that of the author. They give opportunity (9) for interaction between and among the readers. In short, they are more likely to evoke imaginative and reflective responses than questions which focus on the recall of information.

There is inherent in the procedures described the likelihood that the reader will sometimes make wrong decisions and evaluate information inaccurately. But mistakes, as Bertrand Russell, (12, pp. 79-111), John Stuart Mill (13, pp. 15-54), and others have pointed out, are part of human inquiry. Swartz (14) has argued persuasively that a useful philosophy of learning must view mistakes in a positive rather than in a negative fashion. Comprehension must be improved when opportunities to reflect, evaluate, and predict are the dominant theme of reading instruction. As children learn the process of inquiry through reading they will more and more recognize which facts are incidental and which are vital to the author's intent in nonfiction, or in the case of fiction, which literary structures are likely to determine what comes later.

Here are some steps in a directed reading-thinking activity which will help accomplish the aims alluded to above.

1. *The teacher asks the readers to descibe what will happen in the material about to be read.* This procedure is repeated at selected stopping points throughout the material.
2. *The teacher requires the readers to examine the evidence in the text carefully to determine its relevance to the announced purposes and predictions.*
3. *The teacher asks the readers to relate what they find in the text and illustrations to their announced purposes and predictions.* This is done to determine if the purposes and predictions were correct, incorrect, or partially correct; concomitantly, readers are asked to assess whether they have accomplished their purposes and what prevented or helped in the accomplishment of them. The children, not the teacher, determine the adequacy of the proof of accomplishment of purpose. The teacher's role is to use questions deftly to lead the children to the realization of their own accuracy or lack of it.
4. *The teacher chooses appropriate stopping points where the readers may confirm, modify, or reject the original predictions.*

5. *The teacher encourages readers to suspend final judgment regarding the accuracy of their predictions until all evidence has been examined.* The teacher's work is to bring the readers and the material together in a situation calculated to use the knowledge and experience of the readers in evaluating what is before them and what is about to be encountered.

6. *The teacher may determine that follow-up discussion centering around values, feelings, and beliefs is an appropriate way to conclude the lesson.* On the other hand, the teacher may wish to focus the discussion on the relevancy of predictions and purpose-setting. In some cases it may be best to have no follow-up discussion at all. What is done at the end is determined by the course of events throughout the lesson.

Directing Comprehension Instruction Through the Directed Reading-Thinking Activity

Introduction

Comprehension is the goal of reading instruction. While there are various ways to direct reading instruction, some seem to work better than others. An illustration follows of how the procedures described earlier worked with a group of children.

The story selected is entitled "An Old Letter." (15, pp. 176-180). The story concerns a discovery made by a young boy (Donald) and his mother (Mrs. Short) while going through the contents of some old boxes in their home. They discover a letter written by the boy's great grandfather. Affixed to the letter is a stamp on which is a picture of Benjamin Franklin. Donald decides he would like to enter the stamp in a contest sponsored by his class in school. The mother and boy decide to first check on the authenticity of the stamp with the local postmaster. The postmaster offers to purchase it and suggests that the stamp be placed in a glass covered container before it is taken to school. The story ends with the boy remarking that, in their excitement, he and his mother had forgotten to read the letter.

The story covers five pages of text and is illustrated with four pictures. The illustrations consume approximately 25 percent of the space and provide a pictorial background for concept development, prediction, and reflection.

Directed Reading-Thinking Dynamics

This story could be directed in several different ways. One must guard against a routinized approach to the presentation of a directed reading-thinking activity. Various learning sets can be created by varying the number of stopping points and the amount of information to which the student has access prior to making predictions. Variation not only makes the process more interesting but also makes the directed reading-thinking activity a more versatile tool for exercising thinking skills and forging reading comprehension.

The job of the teacher in the process is to bring the pupils and the materials together in a milieu calculated to use the knowledge and experiential background of the reader. All students are encouraged to set their own purposes by making their own educated guesses regarding possible outcomes. In this manner readers learn to deal with concepts in a thinking fashion, for they are asked to process information in terms of a purpose they have helped to establish. In this process the most active person is the student. The teacher's role is that of intellectual stimulator. Naturally, the teacher has a pertinent role but it is quite different from that of the reader. Readers must be given freedom to think, discuss, predict and, in the process, set their own purposes. This freedom motivates interest and encourages reflective thinking—together they have a positive effect on comprehension.

The concepts in this story are likely to be familiar to many children since it deals with stamp collecting. While most children are not stamp collectors per se many are collectors of baseball cards, bubble gum wrappers, coins, cars, and hundreds of other collectible items. Some children will also be familiar with the experience of searching through boxes of items that have been stored for some time. Finally, the settings of contests, hobby shows, and post offices are experiences that children universally have some prior knowledge of.

Five new words are introduced in this story. They are *stamp, Franklin, contest, post office*, and *postmaster*. It is almost certain that three of these words (*stamp, contest, post office*) will be in the speaking and listening vocabularies of most third graders. The other two words (*Franklin* and *postmaster*) will likely be familiar to a high percentage of third graders.

These five words are not to be pretaught or introduced prior to the reading of the story. To do so would deny pupils an ideal opportunity to encounter the words in a context where they can use their word attack skills. In most instances the words will already be known, therefore preteaching would be inefficient and unnecessary. Those who do not have these new words as part of their existing reading vocabulary may now use the word attack skills that teachers have been building over the years. Furthermore, to preteach the words would provide too many clues concerning story outcomes. As a result, conjecturing and hypothesizing would be based on information given by the teacher and not through reading and thinking.

Outlined below is an illustration of how this story was developed with a group of average third grade students. For brevity's sake only portions of student-teacher dialogue are recorded.

STEP ONE: *Making predictions and setting purposes from title clues only.*

1. Instruct pupils to turn to the table of contents to locate the title of the story.
2. After the title has been located and read, initiate the prediction and purpose-setting session with an open-ended question such as, "What do you think this story will be about?" or "What do you think will happen in this story?" You should expect predictions to be divergent at this point since only a limited amount of information is available upon which

An Old Letter

Donald Short and his mother were upstairs looking through some old boxes. They found old letters and papers. Some of the things were over a hundred years old.

"These boxes have been here a long time," said Mrs. Short. "This is one of the oldest turkey farms in Delaware.

"Here is a letter signed by your great-grandfather. His name was John Short. He mailed the letter to his sister, Mary Short."

"Look at the stamp," said Donald.

NOTE: Reprinted from *Into the Wind* by Russell Stauffer, Alvina Treut Burroughs, and Millard H. Black. Adapted from an original story by Crayce Krough Boller. © 1960 by Holt, Rinehart and Winston, Publishers.

"That is really an old stamp," said Mrs. Short.

"Who is that?" asked Donald, looking at the picture on the stamp.

"It looks like Franklin," Mrs. Short said. "Hold the letter under the light."

"Is it Franklin?" asked Donald.

"Yes, I'm sure it is," said Mrs. Short. "I've seen Franklin's picture many times."

Miss Mary Short
Happy Hill Farm
Middletown
Delaware

"This is an old letter," Mother went on. "It was mailed in 1847."

"May I take the stamp to school?" Donald asked. "I would like to share it with my friends. Also we are having a stamp contest. It's the only stamp I have, but it might win a prize."

"It's an old stamp all right," Mother said. "But we don't know if it's a real one. You should find out before you take the stamp to a contest."

"Why do you think it isn't real?" asked Donald. "It looks real to me."

"I don't believe stamps were used that long ago," Mrs. Short said. "When we go to town, we will go to the post office and find out."

In a very short time Donald and his mother were driving toward Middletown, Delaware. They stopped at the United States Post Office on Rope Street.

"We were cleaning out some old boxes," said Mrs. Short. "In one we found this old letter with a stamp stuck on it. Were stamps used that long ago?"

The postmaster invited Donald and Mrs. Short into his office. "Let's see what the books say," he said.

The postmaster took down an old book and started looking.

"Let me see the stamp again," he said.

"Yes, it's a real stamp," the postmaster added. "The first United States stamps were used in 1847. On the first stamp was a picture of Franklin."

"That's just like our stamp," Donald said. "This must be one of the first stamps."

"You've made a great find," said the postmaster. "What will you do with it?"

"I'm going to use it in the school stamp contest," replied Donald.

"That's a good idea," the postmaster said. "But take good care of it. You could sell that stamp for a lot of money."

"I'll take good care of it," said Donald. I'll get a box with a glass top. Then I'll put the letter in the box so that everyone can see the stamp."

"Another good idea," the postmaster said. "I'm sure you'll win a prize in the contest. If you ever decide to sell the stamp, come to the post office and let me know. I'll buy it."

The postmaster invited Donald and his mother to come back again some time.

They thanked him and left the post office.

Suddenly Donald turned and said to his mother, "We were so busy thinking about the stamp. We forgot to read Great-grandfather's letter!"

to base conjectures. Divergent responses are the teacher's boon. The importance of divergent reactions as a legitimate process has been well established by psychologists and educators.

3. Be sure that children have sufficient time to think and reflect during the prediction and purpose-setting session. Make every effort to involve each child in this initial discussion.

4. Guard against injecting your own ideas and value judgments into the discussion. You should remain neutral during the purpose-setting and prediction period. Your comments should be designed to draw out the students' thinking.

Following are some of the purposes and predictions made by four pupils in a group of third grade students when this story was directed in the manner outlined above.

Mark: I think the story will be about a letter that was lost in the post office for a long time and then delivered later.

Teacher: That's an interesting idea, Mark. How long ago do you think the letter was lost?

Mark: Twenty or thirty years, maybe.

Pat: I think it could be a letter that is worth a lot of money.

Teacher: Why do you think that?

Pat: Well, the title says it's an old letter and old letters sometimes have important things in them.

Walt: I think it could be a letter that is worth a lot of money, too.

Teacher: You agree with Pat then?

Walt: Yes.

Dick: It could be an old letter written by some famous person like Lincoln or Washington. If it is, they could sell it to a museum or someone.

Teacher: How old would you guess that the letter is, Dick?

Dick: Maybe a hundred years old.

Several students were asked the question, "How old do you think the letter is?" Estimates ranged from 20 to 300 years. It should be noted that the teacher's role revolved around the asking of open-ended questions. When the teacher commented on a student's prediction, it was worded to draw out an elaboration from the student. Student predictions and purposes were always honored. The weakest was accepted as well as the strongest, the plausible along with the implausible. When a student is willing to agree with another student's prediction this response should be accepted. A pupil can be asked why he or she accepts the other pupil's prediction. At other times, as students become familiar with the process, the teacher may encourage each to venture a prediction of his or her own.

STEP TWO: *Examine illustrations and read text on pages 213-14.*

1. Direct the children to open their books to page 213.
2. Remind children not to look ahead in their books until directed to do so.

Some critics suggest that this notion stifles children's interest and desire to read. This is neither true nor is it a valid criticism. Such criticism ignores the fact that this is a *directed* lesson prepared by the teacher and designed for a specific instructional purpose. This purpose can best be accomplished by planning specific stopping places where instructional goals are realized. There are, obviously, many reading situations which you can provide to allow children to proceed at their own pace. The DRTA is not that place.

3. While the reading is in progress, you should carefully observe the pupils to note difficulties or to acknowledge requests for help. Visit with the pupils individually during the silent reading to provide encouragement or to give guidance.

STEP THREE: *Appraisal of predictions and purposes: maintaining, modifying, or rejecting original purposes and predictions.*

1. Begin the discussion by asking questions such as "Who was right?" or "Did you find the answers to the questions you raised?" Sometimes a simple nod of the head will suffice as a cue for the students to begin the appraisal and readjustment period. This is especially true when the students and teacher are quite familiar and comfortable with the nuances of the DRTA.

2. Quickly check with the students to see how they have dealt with their original purposes and predictions. A simple question can get the process started. For example, "Well, Gail, were you right in what you said was going to happen?" If the student thinks that she has found the answer to her prediction or purpose. Ask her to tell why she thinks she was right. Conversely, it may be desirable to ask a student why she thinks she was wrong. When this situation arises, it is quite appropriate to say, "Well, Gail, take another look at what you read and see if you can find the answer to the prediction you made." Most likely some pupil in the group will suggest this too.

3. It is useful to ask students to orally reread the lines that prove the validity of their predictions. Students must learn the necessity of citing evidence to support their assumptions or to withhold judgment until sufficient evidence is available. If the teacher and the group do not demand proof of the validity of a student's predictions, critical evaluation during the reading act is less likely to occur. Of course, it is not necessary to request oral rereading of lines with every prediction. To do so would be pendantic and boring. It is important, however, over a period of time, for you to allow each student an opportunity to exercise this skill. The practice of oral rereading to prove predictions gives validity and purpose to the oral reading act. Oral reading should be part of the DRTA process but only under the circumstances described.

4. Students should be given an opportunity to adjust their predictions and purposes. You will recall that the original predictions made by the

group of third graders were in response to a title clue only. At this stage each student has had an opportunity to view two illustrations and has read two pages of the story. The students should now be capable of rejecting or modifying earlier predictions, and of refining and extending other predictions. Predictions should now begin to converge on the focal point of the story since a fair number of clues regarding possible and plausible outcomes have been introduced in the two pages of text.

Following is a typical response from one student in the group described earlier:

Dick:	I was wrong about its being a letter from a famous person.
Teacher:	What did you read that makes you think you were wrong?
Dick:	Well, it said the letter was written by Donald's great-grandfather.
Teacher:	Read the lines that tell who wrote the letter.
Teacher (to entire group):	While Dick is reading the lines that prove his point the rest of us will close our books and listen. Then I want you to decide if he read the right lines. Be sure to keep your finger in the book so you can find your place again.

The other students in the group were given an opportunity to consider their original predictions in terms of their accuracy, use of clues, and so on. Then each student was allowed to maintain, modify, or reject his or her original purpose and prediction. At this point in the story the reader has a fair amount of information. It can be seen below that the predictions and purposes differ from the author's. The students' predictions still represent use of story facts and student knowledge and experience.

Mark:	Now I think Donald will take the stamp to school and he'll win first prize in the stamp contest.
Pat:	I think he may take it to school, too, but he may lose it and then find it again. If he loses it his mother will be mad unless he finds it. I still think it will be worth a lot of money.
Teacher:	The stamp or the letter?
Pat:	The stamp.
Walt:	I think Mark is going to be right.
Teacher:	What do you think of Pat's idea?
Walt:	Well, I don't think he'll lose it but she could be right about the stamp being worth a lot of money.
Teacher:	Why?

The reader should note how student predictions have shifted in emphasis. It is obvious that students readily use their knowledge and background of experience in projecting possible outcomes. The students in this group were familiar with contests, stamp collecting, the value of old stamps, and mother's anger when something is lost. Finally, it can be seen that the purposes and predictions reveal comprehension of the events and concepts in the story. There-fore, it is unnecessary to ask the group to retell story events. Nor is it necessary to ask them to recall irrelevant details. This common practice is of doubtful value under any circumstances. It is lethal to the development of reading-thinking skills.

STEP FOUR: *Direct students to read to the end of the story on page 217 (fol-low-up).*

1. After directing the extension and refinement of purposes and predic-tions, tell the students to read to the end of the story.
2. Observe the reading, noting student reactions, and provide help where needed.
3. Word recognition help may be given to pupils individually while they are reading silently. The student should always be reminded to follow the appropriate self-help steps before you provide help. If some students are unable to avail themselves of the help you provide, tell them the word and make a mental note to deal with this problem in the follow-up session or at a later time. Do not distract the entire group by interjecting a word recognition lesson for the entire group in the middle of the DRTA process.
4. When all students have completed the reading of the story, initiate the final discussion period by asking an open-ended question such as, "Did you find the answer to your question?" or "Were you right about what you said?" This is also an appropriate time to allow the student to read aloud the lines that confirm or disprove original predictions.
5. Follow-up activities may include such things as word recognition prac-tice, vocabulary meanings, projects, writing, or discussions, and may vary according to instructional needs. You should not feel that every DRTA needs a follow-up activity, however. It is sometimes appropriate to help students discover those clues which may have misled them or which they may not have used to best advantage. It is also important to help the students realize that although their predictions were not con-firmed they may, nevertheless, have been quite as good as the author's own outcomes.

Adapting to Content-Type Reading

It is necessary that pupils receive training in how to deal with nonfictional dis-cursive material: natural sciences, social sciences, biological sciences, and mathematics. This training can be initiated in the primary grades with suitable materials. It is good to teach the process in a so-called reading class because the preoccupation of both the teacher and the pupil can be with acquisition of read-ing efficiency rather than with a grade in a subject.

Pupils will need to learn to read with specific purposes in mind when read-ing content-type material just as they did when reading fiction. To know what you are after is still the crux of the reading learning act. The act of discovery, backed up by a teacher who checks on the discoveries made, is the heart of the act. This is especially urgent since the reader now has a double obligation—to assimilate and retain the ideas and to use them in future occasions as they fit into longitudinal and in-depth refinement of an area of knowledge.

In content area reading, it is imperative that the readers learn to take advantage of all clues or sources of information. They read words; they also read pictures, maps, graphs, charts, and so on. Each pictorial presentation may be worth a thousand words and they must be read. Accordingly, pupil reading must be more penetrating and thus, thinking more judicious than ever before.

A marked difference in directing the reading of content materials is that the teacher needs to channel pupil thinking. This channeling is done along major concept lines—time or historical, space or geographical, people or social, numbers or numerical, and so on. In addition, during comprehension check time, teacher inquiry into major concepts is essential. New vocabulary and concepts take on scholarly significance. This is so because the reading is done to thoroughly understand, to assimilate, to remember, and to use.

Evaluating Direct Comprehension Instruction

Some teachers may succeed immediately with the directed comprehension procedures described. Others will have difficulty making them work. Whether things go well or badly, you should evaluate your teaching performance. One of the ways to do this is to make an audiotape or videotape recording. This will enable you to analyze your performance thoroughly. If you do not have the time or equipment for tape recording, evaluation must be accomplished by less formal means. The checklist, which appears at the end of this section, is a useful informal instrument for evaluating teaching performance in direct comprehension instruction. Here are five general guidelines to keep in mind when evaluating comprehension instruction:

1. *Do not become discouraged if your first efforts are failures or only modest successes.* Implementing new techniques requires practice and patience. When an idea doesn't work well, the first impulse is to reject the idea. Instead, examine the manner in which the idea was applied. Did I understand the idea well enough? Why didn't it work for me when it has worked for others? What can I do to make the idea work? This sort of analytical question will enable you to make a genuine examination of the worth of a new idea.

2. *Give as much effort to understanding the philosophy behind the comprehension instruction as you do to mastering the techniques required to teach it.* Use of techniques without understanding their purposes places severe limitations on their usefulness. Teachers need, perhaps above all things, a basic understanding of what they believe about reading instruction. This understanding must be based on knowledge gained through formal training, reading, and teaching experience.

Teaching based on inadequate knowledge is likely to mislead rather than to enlighten. The bibliography for this chapter contains excellent resource material for gaining an extended background on directed comprehension instruction.

3. *Use the directed reading-thinking procedures with children of different reading levels, backgrounds, interests and abilities.* The variety of teaching conditions which different children present will improve your understanding of the procedures and their purpose. Challenging teaching problems will occur more often when different kinds of circumstances are deliberately sought. Facing these challenges directly will, in the long run, help you to master the techniques.

4. *Use a variety of materials for directing comprehension instruction.* Begin a collection of fiction stories that have interesting plots and unique endings. you will find such stories particularly suitable for motivating interest. A wide variety of nonfiction materials should also be used.

5. *Apply the directed reading-thinking procedures in listening and viewing activities.* Instead of always having pupils read the materials, you may occasionally read to them. Presenting materials as a directed *listening* thinking activity provides instructional opportunities not possible with the directed *reading* thinking activity. For example, it is possible to group pupils whose reading levels are completely dissimilar when doing a directed listening lesson. This, of course, is not possible with the directed reading lesson since pupils who participate in group directed reading instruction must be able to read whatever materials are used. In addition to using the procedures in listening and reading you may use them in viewing experiences with filmstrips or movies.

When using directed reading-thinking procedures it is useful to have some informal means of appraising your performance. Following is a check list covering seven areas related to direct comprehension instruction. After directing a reading lesson, fill out the checklist or have a colleague who has observed your teaching fill it out. Use the check list to compare your performance over a span of eight to twelve weeks.

CHECKLIST FOR DIRECTED COMPREHENSION INSTRUCTION

1. What comprehension components were your questions intended to stimulate?
   _____ Explicit comprehension
   _____ Implicit comprehension
   _____ Word meaning comprehension
   _____ Aesthetic-appreciative comprehension
2. Which of the following question stems were used while directing the DRTA?
   _____ What do you think . . . ?
   _____ What would happen if . . . ?
   _____ Why do you suppose . . . ?
   _____ How does your idea apply to . . . ?

_____ The story said . . . How do you feel about . . . ?

_____ Why do you think the author said . . . ?

_____ What sort of ending does the evidence suggest now?

_____ Based on what you've said, what do you expect the author will say about . . . ?

_____ Would you like to change your mind now that you've read this far?

_____ Can you prove that your prediction was right?

_____ What leads you to that conclusion?

3. Did you encourage pupils to

_____ maintain their original predictions?

_____ modify their original predictions?

_____ reject an earlier hypothesis?

_____ accept, modify, or reject someone else's idea?

4. Were stopping places in the story

_____ used to control the flow of events and information in the material?

_____ used to discuss earlier ideas?

_____ used to set new purposes and predictions?

_____ used too frequently?

_____ used too infrequently?

_____ chosen to heighten interest in story outcome?

5. How did you respond to pupils' ideas, purposes, and predictions?

_____ Accepted with positive comments or other signals

_____ Accepted with neutral comments or other signals

_____ Used to elicit further comments and ideas

_____ Rejected by manner, tone, or word

_____ Used to encourage interaction between and among participants

_____ Used as a basis for stating your ideas and opinions

6. What activities did you engage in while pupils were reading silently?

_____ Encouraged and guided pupils who demonstrated some need

_____ Provided some word recognition help for pupils

_____ Provided some assistance in comprehension

_____ Conducted business not related to the DRTA itself

7. What is your estimate of pupil response to the DRTA?

_____ They appeared motivated and interested.

_____ They appeared listless and uninterested.

_____ They used their experience and knowledge to predict well.

8. What activities were used to conclude or follow-up the lesson?

_____ Asked questions to stimulate reflective thinking

_____ Asked questions regarding the meaning of words in context

_____ Asked pupils to evaluate the effectiveness with which they used information in their predictions

_____ Directed a word recognition exercise stemming from the lesson

_____ Directed a writing activity stemming from the lesson

9. What steps could you take to improve future performance?

SUMMARY

There are eight guiding principles of comprehension instruction: (1) comprehension occurs when what is already known is related to new information obtained through reading; (2) the techniques of instruction in combination with the underlying competence of the teacher can have a positive effect on comprehension; (3) comprehension instruction should teach readers to set their own purposes; (4) readiness for comprehension is facilitated through teacher questioning, not through teacher telling; (5) comprehension questions should stimulate higher level thinking rather than recall of information; (6) comprehension is relative and varies from reader to reader; (7) reading and writing are extraordinarily complex tasks which inevitably makes comprehension highly personal and inevitably subjective; and (8) reading is a thinking process.

The four components of comprehension are explicit comprehension, implicit comprehension, word meaning comprehension, and aesthetic-appreciative comprehension. Explicit comprehension is the ability to understand, at a literal level, information clearly stated in the text. Implicit comprehension is the ability to gain meaning through reasoning at levels beyond the explicit meaning. Word meaning comprehension is the ability to understand both the connotative and denotative meanings of words and phrases. Aesthetic-appreciative meaning is a logical rather than an empirical category associated primarily with the affective side of intellectual functioning.

Purpose-setting, prediction, and reflective thinking are an important part of the directed reading-thinking lesson. Its purpose is to motivate reading and to encourage children to examine what they already know and to use that knowledge to forecast in which direction a story or essay is likely to go.

An illustration of how a directed reading-thinking lesson could be directed was described in detail.

Five ideas for evaluating teaching performance are presented along with a checklist for assessing teaching performance on a directed reading-thinking activity.

REFERENCES

1. Henderson, Edmund H. "A Study of Individually Formulated Purposes for Reading in Relation to Reading Achievement Comprehension and Purpose Attainment." Unpublished doctoral dissertation, University of Delaware, 1963.

2. Davidson, Jane L. "The Quantity, Quality, and Variety of Teachers' Questions and Pupils' Responses During an Open-Communication Structured Group Directed Reading-Thinking Activity and a Closed-Communication Structured Group Directed Reading Activity." Unpublished doctoral dissertation, University of Michigan, 1970.

3. Petre, Richard M. "Quantity, Quality, and Variety of Pupil Responses During an Open-Communication Structured Group Directed Reading-Thinking Activity and a Closed-Communication Structured Group Directed Reading Activity." Unpublished doctoral dissertation, University of Delaware, 1970.

4. Smith, Frank. **Comprehension and Learning.** New York: Holt, Rinehart and Winston, 1975.

5. Lennon, Roger. "What Can be Measured?". Edited by Russell G. Stauffer and Edmund G. Henderson. **The Science and Philosophy of Reading: The Role of Tests in Reading,** vol. 9. University of Delaware School of Education, Reading-Study Center, 1961.

6. Davis, Fredrick B. "Fundamental Factors of Comprehension in Reading." **Psychometrika** 9 (1944): 185–97.

7. Hunt, Lyman C. Jr., "Can We Measure Specific Factors Associated with Reading Comprehension?" **Journal of Educational Research** 51 (1957): 161–71.

8. Guilford, J. P. "Intellectual Factors in Productive Thinking." Edited by J. Ashner and C. E. Bish. **Productive Thinking in Education.** Washington, D.C.: National Education Association, 1965.

9. Doyle, Sir Arthur Conan. **The Complete Sherlock Holmes.** Doubleday and Company, Inc. (no copyright date)

10. Cottrell, Mackenzie. "Wild Dog." Edited by Helen Miller and Nell Murphy. **Let's Read: Book 1: Reading for Fun.** New York: Holt, Rinehart and Winston, 1953.

11. Stauffer, Russell G. **Directing the Reading Thinking Process.** New York: Harper and Row, Publishers, 1975.

12. Russell, Bertrand. **Philosophical Essays.** New York: Simon and Schuster, 1968.

13. Mill, John Stuart. **On Liberty.** New York: Appleton-Century-Crofts, 1947.

14. Swartz, Ronald. "Mistakes as an Important Part of the Learning Process," **The High School Journal** 59 (March 1976): 246–57.

15. Stauffer, Russell G., Burrows, Alvina Treut, and Black, Millard H. **Into the Wind.** Philadelphia, Pennsylvania: John C. Winston Co., 1960. (permission rights held by Holt, Rinehart and Winston, New York)

14

Teaching Word Recognition

Word recognition is a term used to describe the skills needed to pronounce written words. The skills of word recognition include contextual analysis, phonetic analysis, structural analysis, and sight recognition. These four skills are used singly and in combination to aid in the pronunciation of words and the gaining of meaning. The mature reader must also learn to use the dictionary as a means to confirming pronunciation and meaning. Strictly speaking, using the dictionary is not a word recognition skill per se any more than using an index is a comprehension skill. Dictionaries and indexes represent resource material where word recognition and comprehension skills may be confirmed or aided. However, for organizational convenience, dictionary skills are briefly discussed in this chapter.

Beginning readers have the most need for word recognition skills since they must use them most often. Of course, the reading act is not complete when accurate pronunciation has occurred. There must also be understanding of word meaning. Word recognition and word meaning normally occur together. When they do not, either word meaning is inadequate and must be discovered, or word recognition is inaccurate and must be corrected. Since word recognition skills and knowledge of word meaning are interdependent, a continuing goal of reading instruction is to simultaneously expand sight recognition vocabulary and knowledge of word meanings. Meaning is the dominant theme of reading. Therefore, we must constantly be aware that word recognition skills are used not merely to pronounce words but to gain meaning.

Guiding Principles for Teaching Word Recognition

Discussing "principles" is sometimes thought to be an academic throwaway having little useful purpose. This need not be so. The following principles represent my philosophy and guide my practice. They may also serve as useful guidelines for teachers.

1. Meaning *is the principal goal of instruction in word recognition.* Therefore, any word recognition practice which hinders its attainment should be avoided. For example, looking for small words in larger ones is not only ineffective as an aid to pronunciation, but it also hinders meaning. Similarly, exaggerated pronunciation of sounds (*buh-uh-tuh* for *but*) hinders recognition and thus interferes with meaning.

2. *Distinguishing one speech sound from another and one letter from another is prerequisite to more advanced word recognition skills.* The technical terms for these two prerequisite skills are auditory discrimination and visual discrimination. Both may be taught concurrently and should precede systematic instruction in advanced word recognition skills. For some pupils it may be desirable to continue training in auditory discrimination after systematic instruction in word recognition has begun.

3. *Only word recognition rules that have a high degree of usefulness should be taught.* Usefulness is dependent on two conditions. First, the rule should apply to a substantial number of common words useful in the elementary grades. A rule that works 90 percent of the time but only applies to *20* words is not useful. Other means for teaching the *20* words should be used. Second, a rule must hold true in about 75 percent of the instances to which it is applicable and should apply to a substantial number of words. How useful, for example, is this common rule? *When there are two vowels side by side, the long sound of the first one is heard and the second is usually silent.* (When two vowels go walking, the first one does the talking.) This rule hold true about 30 percent of the time (Bailey (1), Clymer (2), Emans (3)). Readers would be misled seven times out of ten if they applied this rule. It is not a useful rule because the percentage of times it holds true is too low even though it applies to a substantial number of words.

4. *Focus on application rather than memorization when teaching word recognition rules.* Knowing what a rule says is less important than knowing how to use it. Help children apply rules by providing words which exemplify a given rule. Lead children to search for the common element in the words through inductive questioning. When they have discovered the common element, help them formulate the rule in their own words. Then have them search for words in other materials which exemplify the rule. They may also note exceptions. While inductive teaching is an effective way to learn rules, direct instruction need not be avoided. On the contrary, sometimes direct instruction is more efficient. A

limited number of useful (75 percent) word recognition rules may be taught using both inductive teaching methods.

5. *Instruction in word recognition must be balanced and integrated.* Its components are not independent but interrelated. Balanced instruction requires that appropriate emphasis be given each major component. Integrated instruction requires unified teaching for contextual, phonetic and structural analysis. Thus, when an unknown word fails to yield to contextual analysis, the learner automatically employs the next relevant component. While there is an implied sequential order for applying the components of word recognition, in practice their application should be integrated into a single act.

6. *Diagnosis directs instruction in word recognition.* It may be formal or informal. Formal diagnosis uses testing instruments to measure achievement, monitor progress, and inform instruction. These instruments typically include standardized tests, informal inventories, and teacher-made tests. A less formal type of diagnosis arises from assessment of daily instruction. The latter form of diagnosis is dependent on the teacher's judgment as to how instruction is progressing and what adjustments should, therefore, be made.

7. *Word recognition skills are reinforced through writing.* The skills required to read a word are the inverse of those required to write or spell it. Writing is a natural and productive way to extend many of the lessons taught in word recognition. The natural connection between reading and writing should be reflected in instruction. Failure to integrate these natural allies of literacy is perhaps the single greatest failure of modern reading instruction.

8. *Word recognition instruction should be tied directly to meaningful reading experiences.* Word recognition should not be taught in an isolated set of drills unrelated to reading books and other material. When a lesson has been taught, an opportunity to read should follow. This focuses attention on the purpose of word recognition instruction and provides practice in using what has been taught in a reading context. In football, fundamentals are taught so they may be used in the game. Without the game, the fundamentals are meaningless. In reading, the fundamentals serve the same purpose.

9. *Word recognition instruction should proceed from the whole to the parts, not from the parts to the whole.* The sounds that letters represent should not be taught in isolation. Rather, they should be taught in the context in which they appear in words. Teaching isolated speech sounds is more abstract, adds the extraneous "uh" to letter sounds, and makes blending more difficult.

Contextual Analysis

Contextual analysis is the ability to determine the correct pronunciation or meaning of a word as a result of using surrounding linguistic and visual clues.

The richer the linguistic and visual context, the more likely the reader is to derive the correct pronunciation or meaning of an unknown word. For example, the missing word is easy to predict in this sentence: "The cowboy jumped on his ____ and rode away." Even the readers who do not have *horse* in their sight vocabularies are likely to use context to correctly pronounce the missing word. Sometimes the surrounding context of a word is topographical or visual as in this symbol ◯ . The visual context immediately suggests the word *stop*.

Contextual analysis is based on principles similar to the cloze procedure. Closure is the tendency to fill in a missing part to make a meaningful whole. Closure occurs when a reader uses context to derive pronunciation and meaning. The reader fills in the missing word or words by making predictions based on linguistic information and inference. Semantic, syntactic, phonetic, structural, and visual features of language are used. These linguistic and visual features are combined in various ways to derive word pronunciation and meaning.

Context is not always helpful in deriving pronunciation or meaning. Three major circumstances may prevent readers from using context effectively. First, readers may be poorly equipped to use context clues. Second, the surrounding linguistic and visual context may be weak. Third, the reading material may be too difficult.

Poorly trained readers may resort to random guessing rather than using the surrounding information and inferential thinking that are needed in contextual analysis. Teachers must know what linguistic clues are likely to be useful and provide specific training in the use of these word recognition and meaning aids. There are many context clues in language which may aid the reader.

McCullough (4) has listed eight such clues including pictorial illustrations, experience, comparison and contrast, synonyms, summary, mood, definition, and verbal clues. Ames (5) has suggested a more extensive list which overlaps some of McCullough's categories. He lists fourteen context clues: (1) experience with language and familiar expressions, (2) modifying phrases and clauses, (3) definition or description, (4) words connected in a series, (5) comparison and contrast, (6) synonym clues, (7) time, setting, and mood, (8) referents or antecedents, (9) association clues, (10) main idea and supporting details, (11) question-answer pattern of a paragraph, (12) preposition clues, (13) nonrestrictive clauses or appositive phrases, (14) cause-effect patterns.

Certain context clues are more useful than others. Rankin and Overholzer (6) studied Ames' classification scheme. They found that the easiest context clues for intermediate grade children were words connected in a series, modifying phrases and clauses, experience with language and familiar expressions, cause-effect patterns, and association clues. The most difficult were nonrestrictive clauses or appositive phrases, main idea and supporting details, comparison or contrast, and question-answer pattern of a paragraph. Emans (7) has suggested several contextual analysis exercises based on the cloze procedures which are useful for combining phonetic analysis with contextual analysis. He has suggested the following types of exercises: (1) supplying the beginning letter, (2) showing the length of the word, (3) giving the beginning and ending letters, and (4) giving only the consonants in the blank space.

Reading materials should be rich in context. The closer the match between the words and the reader's vocabulary the better. Basal readers use controlled vocabularies to achieve this goal. They want the printed words to match the vocabulary of the reader. This goal is admirable but has sometimes resulted in unnatural language and impoverished content particularly in beginning reading materials. Fortunately, this is less so now than in the past. One of the advantages of a language experience approach to beginning reading is that children's language assures an appropriate match between printed words and language competence. Stauffer (8, p. 269) speaks of the importance of a rich context in beginning reading materials in this statement:

> The context at all levels, but especially at the primary level, should be rich linguistically as well as perceptually. The language used should be appropriate and arranged syntactically in orderly fashion. Pictures, illustrations, maps, and graphs should be planned so as to support and facilitate understanding or communication.
>
> In the use of the language experience approach each of the conditions is met. The language context is the product of the child. Since what he produced served to communicate it was of special quality. The illustration prepared by the child to accompany his dictation provided the child's perceptual-conceptual context.

The natural patterns of language must be present in instructional materials if instruction in contextual analysis is to succeed. Otherwise beginning readers will be unable to use their language and meaning skills to best advantage. Language such as, "Dan can fan Nan" or "Look! Look! Come here. Come here Spot" lacks the natural flow and meaning of children's conversation. Such language does not provide enough support for contextual analysis to operate. Language experience provides a natural correction for this deficiency by using the child's language. Basal materials can accomplish a similar goal by using more natural language in beginning readers.

Finally, in order to use context clues, the reading material must not be too difficult for the reader. If the reading material is at the independent or instructional level of the reader, context clues can be used effectively. If the material is at the frustration level of the reader, contextual clues are less likely to be useful. Using context clues requires knowledge of the meaning and pronunciation of an overwhelming majority of the words in the passage. Too many unknown words overwhelm the reader. The usual criteria for an instructional level is that 94 to 98 percent of the words must be known. However, Pikulski (9) has found that some readers can sustain a slightly lower percentage of unknown words and still maintain satisfactory comprehension. Recognition of the importance of proper placement of children in materials is essential to all types of word recognition training. This is particularly true for teaching contextual analysis.

Phonetic Analysis

Definition

The term *phonetic analysis* has become synonymous with a similar term *phonic analysis*. While there is some pedantic debate about which term is correct, *phonetic analysis* is the one we shall most often use here. Phonetic analysis is the act of associating speech sounds with certain letters that represent speech sounds and blending these letter-sound relationships together to pronounce words. The purpose of teaching phonetic analysis is to enable readers to use letter-sound relationships to pronounce words not known at sight. Of course, meaning is the goal of reading and phonetic analysis is only one more means to that end. Phonetic analysis would normally be used along with contextual and structural analysis. It is not an isolated but an integrated skill used to derive pronunciation so that meaning may be realized.

In most approaches to beginning reading instruction, children start with an initial sight vocabulary. Once readers have acquired a small sight vocabulary, phonetic analysis is taught so that skill in sounding and blending unknown words may be acquired. Phonetic analysis should start with sight words and proceed to an analysis of word parts. It is possible, of course, to teach letter-sound relationships as isolated elements unrelated to known words and then synthesize these parts into whole words. This is not, however, the approach recommended in this book. Most basal and language experience approaches to reading instruction start with sight words and teach letter-sound relationships from known words. Thus, the process goes from the whole to its parts rather than going from the parts to the whole as in synthetic phonics instruction.

Guidelines for Teaching Phonetic Analysis

Whatever combination of sounding and blending techniques are used certain guidelines should be observed.

1. *Auditory discrimination should precede and accompany the teaching of phonetic analysis.* Some children need relatively little training in auditory discrimination while others require instruction over an extended period of time.
2. *Stress the use of contextual analysis in conjunction with the initial sound that begins an unknown word.* The beginning letter is the most common word recognition clue used by children. Combining context with the initial letter is often enough to correctly predict the word.
3. *Initiate phonics instruction with words derived from experience charts and individual experience stories.* Auditory discrimination activities can be informally conducted following the reading of a group or individual story. Later, as children learn sight words from their stories, other phonetic and structural analysis activities can also be incorporated into

the teaching program. Experience charts and stories are an excellent place to begin word recognition activities since the words that appear in these stories are certain to be in children's oral vocabularies.

4. *Avoid extraneous and exaggerated sound in the pronunciation of word parts.* Sound and blend words parts smoothly and continuously. The time interval between word parts should be kept as short as possible. When illustrating blending, say the whole word first and then say it successively more slowly until each part is distinct but not distorted. Then reverse this process and gradually reconstruct the whole word.

5. *Phonetic analysis activities (and other word recognition exercises as well) should be limited to short periods of time, not exceeding fifteen or twenty minutes.*

6. *Integrate the teaching of phonetic analysis with the other major word recognition skills.* Phonetic analysis is only one type of word clue. When teaching phonetic analysis, simultaneously teach other significant word recognition clues such as context, length, starting letters, or structural parts.

7. *Many phonic elements appear in initial, medial, and final positions.* Teach the phonic elements in their various positions.

8. *Provide extensive reading practice in materials at independent and instructional levels to facilitate transfer of word recognition skills.* Much effort is wasted by failure to reinforce skills already taught. Reading is the best way to reinforce skill teaching.

9. *Teach a step-by-step strategy for pronouncing words that are unknown.* When an unknown word is encountered in reading, a child must know instinctively what the best steps are that will lead to correct pronunciation and meaning.

Sequence for Teaching Phonic Elements

Teachers are sometimes lead to believe there is a "correct" and "incorrect" sequence for teaching phonetic analysis. This is not so. First, there is little empirical evidence to direct sequence decisions. Second, the task is exceedingly complex. The most complex variable is the learner. An optimal sequence for one learner may not be optimal for another. Another complexity is the English language. Even the most stable linguistic element, the single consonant letter, presents difficulties. There are twenty-one consonant letters. Many consonant letters have two or three common spellings (/k/: c, k, ck; /s/ : s, c, ss) and two or three less common spellings (/k/: ch, cc, cq; /s/ : z, sc, ps). A given consonant letter may appear in initial, medial, and final positions and may do so with varying frequency. In spite of these complexities the consonants are more regular than the vowels. Regardless of the complexities, sequence decisions must be made. Since there is no scientific way of precisely determining what is best, one must proceed on the basis of logic, bits and pieces of research evidence, and a modicum of arbitrariness. The following sequence represents more of the former than the latter.

Sequence for Phonetic Analysis

1. Visual discrimination of words and letters
2. Auditory discrimination of speech sounds
   a. Rhyming words
   b. Beginning single-letter consonant sounds
   c. Ending single-letter consonant sounds
   d. Consonant digraphs
   e. Consonant blends
   f. Long vowel sounds
   g. Short vowel sounds
3. Letter-sound relationships
   a. Single consonants
   b. Consonant digraphs
   c. Consonant blends
   d. Phonograms and consonant substitution
   e. Single-letter short vowels
   f. Single-letter long vowels
   g. Vowel digraphs
   h. Vowel diphthongs
   i. Double consonants
   j. *R*-controlled vowels
   k. Silent *e*
   l. Silent letter combinations
   m. Unusual consonant spellings
   n. Unusual vowel spellings

This sequence does not imply simple chronological order. For example, visual and auditory discrimination can be taught concurrently. Once a child has learned two or three sight words and can discriminate a few letters and sounds (steps 1 and 2), the relationship between the letters and sounds (step 3) should be taught. In other words, it is not necessary to learn all of the elements in steps 1 and 2 before the third step is taken for any given phonic element.

Phonic Rules

Much discussion centers around the question of teaching phonic rules (or generalizations as they are often called.) There are two questions to be considered. Should phonic rules be taught? If so, which phonic rules should be taught? The second question has been partly answered by research while the first question is still being debated.

Clymer (2) conducted a study to determine the usefulness of forty-five generalizations as applied to a list of 2,500 words. His purpose was to determine whether the forty-five generalizations aided or hindered in the pronunciation of a particular word. Accordingly, Clymer calculated a "percentage of utility" for each of the generalizations. He found that of thirty-seven phonic generalizations, only nine met the criteria of 75 percent utility. Emans (3), Bailey (1), and Burmeister (10) conducted similar studies using much larger lists of words. Their findings, while not matching Clymer's in every detail, were substantially the same. Many word recognition generalizations have too many exceptions to justify their inclusion in a reading curriculum.

The studies cited above inform us that low utility generalizations should not be taught. They do not directly answer the questions of whether high utility generalizations should be taught. It would seem reasonable, however, to include a limited number of high utility generalizations in the reading curriculum. A useful list of high utility phonic generalizations is one recommended by Spache and Spache (11, p. 473). After considering various studies they recommended the following set of phonic generalizations as a defensible minimum.

At the preprimer level

1. When the letter *c* is followed by *o* or *a*, the sound of *k* is likely to be heard.
2. When there is one *e* in a word that ends in a consonant, the *e* usually has a short sound.

At the primer level

3. When *y* is the final letter in a word, it usually has a vowel sound. At the first reader level:
4. When *c* is followed by *e* or *i*, the sound of *s* is likely to be heard.
5. When *c* and *h* are next to each other, they make only one sound.
6. When two of the same consonants are side by side, only one is heard.
7. *Ch* is usually pronounced as it is in *kitchen*, *catch*, and *chair*, not like *sh*.
8. The *r* gives the preceding vowel a sound that is neither long nor short.
9. In these double vowel combinations, the first vowel is usually long, and the second silent: *oa*, *ay*, *ai*, and *ee*.

Sounding and Blending

The major task in phonetic analysis is to determine the sounds that letters represent and to blend them together to achieve conventional pronunciation of words. In order to pronounce a word using phonetic analysis, the separate parts of a word must be sounded and then blended together. Sounding and blending are taught in different ways.

Perhaps the oldest technique is letter by letter sounding and blending. In this technique the word *rat* would be pronounced in three parts. The reader is taught to pronounce the *r*, *a*, and *t* sequentially and separately. A major difficulty with this technique is that *extraneous sounds* are often attached to each word part. The resulting pronunciation may be grossly distorted, sounding like this: *ruh ah tuh*. Since sounding and blending is a difficult task to begin with, the addition of extraneous sounds makes the task even more difficult.

Another technique for sounding and blending is to combine the initial consonant and the following vowel as a unit and then to blend this unit with the following consonant. In this technique the word *rat* would have two parts to be sounded and blended, as in *ra-t*. The advantage of this technique is that it is easier to avoid extraneous sounds during the blending process. Furthermore, it may help prepare the way for analysis of syllables in multisyllabic words. Its limitation is that it is difficult to know what sound to give the initial vowel since the sound of a vowel often depends on the letters that follow it, as in *ca-k* (*e*).

Still another technique combines initial consonants with phonograms. Using this substitution technique the phonogram *ent* would be blended with different consonants. For example, the phonogram *ent* when combined with *b*, *c*, *d*, *k*, *l*, *p*, *r*, *s*, *t*, *v*, and *w* produces the following set of related words: bent, cent, dent, Kent, lent, pent, rent, sent, tent, vent, and went. Substitution simplifies the blending and sounding task because it reduces the number of parts to be sounded and blended. It is also a good way to deal with vowel variation since the entire vowel phonogram, rather than the separate vowel sound, is taught. When phonograms are taught, a vowel is always combined with one or two consonants. Using substitution and phonograms is an excellent alternative for children who have difficulty with vowel sounds—particularly those having difficulty distinguishing vowel sounds. Its major limitation is that it applies mainly to one syllable words. However, it also applies to many syllables within multisyllabic words.

Steps in Teaching a Phonic Element

There are various ways in which a phonic element, or any word recognition element, might be taught. The steps vary depending on whether the approach is inductive or deductive. The following three steps illustrate how a phonic element might be directly taught rather than discovered. The example illustrates the teaching of the *st* blend.

1. *Production and illustration.* The teacher produces and illustrates the elements directly. The child listens and observes.
   a. "Listen to these two words: *star*, *stone*. *Star* and *stone* begin with these two letters." (Teacher writes *star* and *stone* on the board and underlines the *st* blend in each word.
   b. "Now, listen to these two words: *stick*, *store*. *Stick* and *store* begin with the sound you hear in these two letters." (Teacher writes *stick* and *store* on the board and underlines the *st* blend.)
2. *Identification and recognition.* This step extends the first step. The teacher discovers whether the learner has understood step 1. The learner is required to identify and recognize what has been taught in step 1.
   a. "I'm going to say two words. Tell me which word begins like *star*, *stone*, *stick*, and *store*. Listen to the words: *stop*, *black*. Which word

begins like *star*? After the learner makes an oral response, the teacher writes the two words on the board and says, "Yes, *stop* begins like *star, stone, stick* and *store.*"

b. If the child responds incorrectly, the teacher says: "Listen again: *stop*, and *black. Stop* begins like *star.* (*Start* and *stop* are written on the board and the *st* is underlined. The teacher then returns to step 1.)

3. *Production and application.* The learner produces and applies what has been taught in step 1 and step 2. This is done by producing a relevant example of what has been taught (step 1) and what has been recognized and identified (step 2).

a. "Give me a word that begins like *star, stamp, stone,* or *stick.*" The words are written on the board after the child has given a correct example. If the example is correct, the presumption is that the child has learned what has been taught. However, the teacher should ask for other examples. The element should be followed up in context and should be taught again later for reinforcement.

b. If the child cannot produce a correct example, the teacher may return to step 2 or in some instances to step 1.

Strategy for Applying Word Recognition Skills

As word recognition skills develop, children must use them in reading materials at an instructional level. If the materials are at an instructional level, some unknown words will be encountered, but not so many that frustration overwhelms the learner. This kind of circumstance is a favorable one for applying word recognition skills. If children were to read only materials where few unknown words were encountered, there would be little opportunity to apply the growing word recognition skills.

Children should learn and practice a specific set of steps for pronouncing unknown words. Unfortunately, the two most common strategies that children articulate are either, "I sound it out," or "I skip the word." A specific and workable strategy that incorporates the major components of word recognition is needed. The strategy must be taught and it must be learned if planned and orderly learning is to occur. If learned, it will improve the chances of accurate pronunciation and the consequent attainment of meaning. The following is a five step strategy that has proved useful in classrooms and clinics.

WHAT TO DO WHEN I DON'T KNOW A WORD

1. *Read to the end of the sentence and note other clues.* (This is a contextual strategy to make the reader aware of the surrounding linguistic and pictorial environment. The stress here is on meaning.)
2. *Say the first part of the word.* (This is usually one or two consonant letters or a vowel and a consonant. This is a phonetic analysis strategy.)
3. *Say the middle and last part of the word.* (This is often a combination of

phonetic and structural analysis. Particular stress should be placed upon determining the word ending and the root word.)

4. *Think of a word almost like the unknown word.* (This is a substitution strategy and emphasizes the use of analogous word parts to derive word pronunciation.)

5. *Ask the teacher or consult another source such as a dictionary.* (Once one has exhausted the limits of contextual, phonetic, and structural analysis one must either consult a dictionary or another person who knows the word—usually the teacher. Whether one chooses to consult the teacher, another student, or the dictionary should depend on the level of the youngster, the reading circumstance (independent or directed reading), and the teacher's classroom policies.

Structural Analysis

Structural analysis is the visual examination of words to discover component parts which may lead to pronunciation and meaning. Children must learn the pronunciation of parts of words and the effect each part has on meaning. Using structural analysis, the reader divides a word such as unkind into its two structural parts, the prefix *un* and the base word *kind* (which also correspond to its two syllables). Once a structural element has been identified, the reader may use a combination of contextual, phonetic, and structural skills to pronounce the word and get its meaning. As word recognition skill increases, reliance on breaking words into their structural parts is reduced. Blending parts of words into wholes is done rapidly and smoothly. Finally, the word is instantaneously recognized as a sight word. Structural analysis involves the recognition of inflected forms, derived forms, compound words, and syllables.

Inflected Forms

Inflected forms are used to indicate person, tense, number, possessive case, comparison, and present and past participle. Inflected endings include *s, es, ed, ing, er, est, t,* and *en.* Once children have become familiar with root words they need to learn what happens to roots when endings are added. There is no need to teach the terminology, but children should learn the derived endings and understand how, when, and why these endings are added to words. Examples of various types of derived forms are presented below:

Person	I, me; he, him; she, her
Tense	need, needs, needed, needing
Number	boy, boys; woman, women
Possessive	Tom's, ours, theirs
Comparison	kind, kinder, kindest
Participle	falling rain

Derived Forms

A derived word is formed when a prefix or suffix is added to a root word. Words such as *unhappy, happiness, unhappily* are derivatives of the root word *happy*. Root words form the foundation of a vocabulary. They are the language element to which other word parts are affixed. A prefix is a word part attached to the beginning of a root word which produces a derivative word. A prefix normally forms a syllable by itself and always modifies the meaning of the root word to which it is attached. A suffix is a word part attached at the end of a root word which produces a derivative or inflected word. A suffix usually forms a syllable by itself and always modifies the meaning of the base word to which it is attached.

Meaning is central in the analysis of derived words. Children should be taught that the meaning of a root word remains stable. However, the addition of an affix (prefix or suffix) modifies the meaning of the root word. This often results in a derived word with a meaning quite distinct from the root word. Knowledge of the meaning of some of the most common prefixes, suffixes, and root words is one way of expanding vocabulary. A relatively small number of root words, prefixes, and suffixes will help children recognize the meaning of thousands of new words that are derivatives of familiar root words. The learning of these key word parts should come about through direct instruction accompanied by wide reading. A variety of vocabulary building exercises may be used. Words learned in vocabulary exercises will not be mastered, however, unless they are subsequently encountered in reading, and used in speaking and writing.

Below is a list of prefixes, suffixes, and base words which are common in the English language. The list is suggested by Dawson and Bamman (12, pp. 160-61) in *Fundamentals of Basic Reading Instruction*.

Common Prefixes

ab-	off from, away	absent, abscond
ad-	to, toward	admit
co-, con-, com-, col-, cor-	together, with	context, correlate
de-	away, down, out of	depart, demote
dis-	not, opposite	disclaim
ex-	out of, formerly	extend, ex-president
in-, im-, il-, ir-	in, not	inhuman
pre-	before	precede
pro-	forward	proceed
re-	back, again	return, rerun
un-	not, opposite	unhappy

Common Roots

dic, dict	to say, speak	predict
duc, duct,	to lead	conduct
fac, fec, fic,		
fect, fly		
fer	to bring, carry	transfer
mit(t), miss	to send	transmit
pend	to hang	suspend
pos, pon	to put	deposit, expose
scrib, script	to write	prescription
speci(t), spic	to look	inspector
ven(t)	to go, come	convention
vert, vers	to turn	reverse

Common Suffixes

-able	capable of, worthy	lovable
-ance, -ence,		
-ancy, -ency	act or fact of doing, state, quality, condition	allowance
-er, -or	person or thing connected with, agent	teacher, auditor
-ful	full of, abounding in	thankful
-less	without, free from	worthless
-ly	like, characteristic of	queenly
-ment	state or quality of	amazement
-tion, -sion, -xion	action, state, result	tension, adoption

Compound Words

A compound word is formed when two or more words are combined. Each part of a compound word can be a useful clue in structural analysis since the spelling of each part is retained. Compounded word parts represent both a visual and a meaning unit. While a compound word has its own meaning, the compound form contains elements of meaning from each of its individual components. Thus, both *basket* and *ball* are partly descriptive of the meaning of the compound word *basketball*. They contribute to, but do not completely define the compound form.

Compound words should be analyzed visually to help determine pronunciation. The individual parts are pronounceable units and an aid to meaning. Some teachers have extended the principles that apply to compound words to words in general. This has resulted in teaching children to look for small words in larger words. The strategy is weak because, unlike the component parts of compound words, small words do not normally contribute to the meaning or pronunciation of larger words. While the practice may occasionally aid pronunciation, more often it distorts both pronunciation and meaning. For example, the word *thinking* contains the following small words in this sequence: *thin, in, ink, kin, king,* and *in.* Of these six words, only *ink* aids in the pronunciation of *think.* None of the six words are related to the meaning of think. The words, *kin,* and *king* cross the boundaries of the root and the suffix and *in* distorts the ending digraph *ng.* The goal of word recognition is to achieve accurate pronunciation in order to gain meaning. The practice of searching for little words in big words is destructive of both of these goals.

Syllabication

A syllable is a unit of speech containing one vowel sound forming either a whole word or a word part. A syllable may have a variety of letter-sound combinations including a vowel only, a vowel-consonant (s) combination, a consonant (s)-vowel combination, or a consonant (s)-vowel-consonant(s) combination. Beginning at the third grade level, reading materials tend to have a larger percentage of words with more than one syllable. Since multisyllabic words are less obviously related to known words, structural analysis is a useful aid in analyzing unknown words.

The role of syllabication in structural analysis is controversial. Much of the controversy centers around the teaching of syllabication rules. Unquestionably, many rules for syllabication are either too complex or fail the test of usefulness. Groff (13) has concluded that the teaching of syllabication generalizations is hardly worth the effort since they are primarily useful as spelling conventions rather than as word analysis aids. He also suggests that syllabication may be largely intuitive since many children seem able to syllabicate prior to learning the rules. Harris (14, p. 337) hints at a similar conclusion in the following statement.

> It is probably unwise to spend much time on rules of syllabication below the sixth grade, and even in secondary school such rules are not very helpful. Bright children can learn such rules easily and tend to apply them with judgment, but slower children are often more confused than helped by them.

An examination of the Clymer (2), Emans (3), Bailey (1), and Burmeister (10) studies on phonic generalizations shows that some syllabication rules do meet the test of usefulness. However, the question of whether they should be taught is not resolved in these studies. Our opinion is that a small number of high utility rules can be taught. Their application as spelling and writing conventions is not necessarily a hindrance to word analysis. If the interrelationship among the language arts is regarded as beneficial their usefulness as spelling and writing conventions may be regarded as a strength. A small number of high utility rules may be useful in word analysis for some children. Children who already possess an intuitive ability to apply syllabication principles need not be taught these rules. The few rules that are taught should be simply stated and taught by both inductive and deductive methods. The following rules are suggested.

1. Every single vowel or vowel combination indicates a syllable except for the final *e*.
2. Divide between the prefix and a base word.
3. Divide between the suffix and a base word.
4. Divide between two consonants when there is a vowel on both sides of the consonant. However, do not divide consonant digraphs and blends.
5. Divide before the consonant in a C-le pattern (pad/dle, lit/tle).

Sight Words

A sight recognition vocabulary consists of words that can be pronounced instantaneously at sight. A sight recognition vocabulary is built up through previous reading experiences. The beginning reader has either a small sight recognition vocabulary or none at all. During the beginning stages of developing a sight recognition vocabulary, ways must be found which give the child an opportunity to reinforce the learning of words. An initial sight recognition vocabulary is partly developed through the use of phonetic, structural, and contextual analysis skills and partly developed through the learning of whole words independent of word analysis.

Sight words are learned through a combination of visual clues including configuration or shape, length, unique features, and letter combinations. Sight words clues should not be taught in isolation but combined with other word analysis skills. For example, *house* and *horse* are not distinguishable by shape, length, or unique features. Context undoubtedly helps the reader to distinguish *house* from *horse* even though both words may be in the reader's sight vocabulary. Even mature readers are occasionally confused by words such as *through* and *thorough*. When such words are mispronounced in context the mature reader rereads to get the contextual meaning and searches for other word recognition clues. A combination of phonetic, contextual, and structural clues are used in such instances.

Since beginning readers have a small sight recognition vocabulary they must use contextual, phonetic, or structural analysis skills more often than a mature reader. The more children read, the more likely they are to develop a large sight vocabulary. Of course, English has too many words for anyone to know every word by sight. Therefore, other word recognition skills are needed throughout a reader's lifetime. Even so, the final goal of word recognition instruction is instantaneous recognition of the maximum number of words. Mature readers use phonetic and structural analysis only when an unfamiliar word is encountered or when an unusual arrangement of words causes momentary confusion.

There are a number of methods used to teach sight words. One of the most common is to associate words with pictures. Workbooks and picture word cards are widely used to teach sight words. Children are sometimes encouraged to memorize a story and thus learn the words in this fashion. One of the most popular methods of teaching sight words is the flash card. While this method is popular, most experts agree that it is not a useful practice. One major objection to flash cards is that the isolated drill provides little opportunity to connect words with meaning. Another difficulty is that words may be associated with irrelevant clues such as an ink stain on the flash card. Word cards may be better used *after* words have been initially encountered and learned in context.

The language experience approach is an ideal way of learning sight words. In this approach, words that have been remembered from dictated stories are recorded on small cards. The sight words learned from dictated stories differs from those learned in basal materials. Basal materials present a common core of vocabulary that all pupils are expected to master, albeit at different rates. While no common set of words are taught in a language experience approach, a common set of words is, nevertheless, acquired due to the natural redundancy of certain words. In addition to the common words, a wide range of other words are also learned. Because children have different abilities, language, and interests, a percentage of sight words are unique to any given child.

The sight words learned from dictated stories are usually kept in a small container and used in various reading and writing activities. The following list contains some of the ways that sight words may be reinforced. These ideas can be applied to sight words learned through basal materials and other sources.

1. Have children exchange words and teach each other words that one child knows and the other does not.
2. Have children use their words to make short phrases, sentences, and brief stories.
3. Have children alphabetize their words.
4. Have children classify their words. Categories may include naming words, action words, people words, short words, long words, scary words, and so on.
5. Have children work in pairs to write phrases, sentences, and brief stories.
6. Have children classify words according to various phonetic, or structural elements. For example, words that end in *-ed* or *-ing*, words that start like *cat*, or words that end like *pig*.
7. Have children spontaneously tell a story about a given word selected from their known words.
8. Have children paint, illustrate, or dramatize their words.
9. Have children trace their words in various ways. For example, words can be traced in sand, on textured paper, or with a crayon.
10. Have children find their words in other sources such as magazines, trade books, and newspapers.
11. Have children make a dictionary illustrating words that are often used in writing.
12. Have children write their words in a special script such as italic script, fancy printing, and cursive manuscript.

Dictionary Skills

Dictionary skills are an aid to word recognition, not a word recognition skill per se. Through the resourceful use of a dictionary, one may find information regarding meaning, pronunciation, spelling, usage, and word histories. Training in the use of a dictionary is necessary since it is the most reliable means of confirming pronunciation and meaning. However, a dictionary cannot be used until the rudiments of word recognition have been learned. Therefore, dictionary usage is not a word analysis skill per se, but rather a resource wherein comprehension and word recognition skills are applied. Upon finding a word in a dictionary one must use contextual, phonetic, or structural analysis skills to discover a word's pronunciation and to read its meaning.

While it is useful for children to know how to use a dictionary, we have perhaps been naive in our expectations regarding children's use of them. It is naive to expect casual readers, particularly children, to make frequent use of the dictionary. Even mature readers seldom do so. Still, one cannot find treasure without the tools for recovering it. Hence, children should be acquainted with the dictionary's treasures and equipped with the tools to search them out. An outline of the basic dictionary skills would include the following:

1. Locating a word
   a. Knowledge of alphabetical order by first, second, third, fourth, and fifth letter
   b. Dividing the dictionary into thirds (front, middle, and back)
   c. Using guide words
2. Understanding entry words
   a. Regular entry words
   b. Special entry types (different spellings, cross-referenced entries, entries which are word parts, entries spelled alike, run-in entries, and run-on entries)
3. Pronunciation
   a. Pronunciation key
   b. Consonant symbols
   c. Vowel symbols
   d. Stress (primary, secondary, weak)
   e. Variant pronunciations
   f. Homographs
4. Meaning
   a. Order of definitions
   b. Finding the right meaning
   c. Using the context
   d. Understanding illustrative material
   e. Informal slang and idiomatic usage
   f. Synonyms
   g. Special circumstances (capitalized words, special plurals)
5. Spelling
   a. Finding a word you can't spell
   b. Variant spellings
   c. Spelling inflected forms
   d. Using a spelling chart
   e. Breaking a word for writing

6. Abbreviations
   a. Common abbreviations
   b. Specialized abbreviations
7. Word histories
   a. How and where to locate them
   b. How to read them
   c. Abbreviations used in word histories

SUMMARY

The nine guiding principles of word recognition are (1) meaning is the principal goal of instruction in word recognition, (2) auditory and visual discrimination are prerequisite to more advanced word recognition skills, (3) only word recognition rules that have a high degree of usefulness should be taught, (4) when rules are taught, the focus should be on application, not memorization, (5) instruction in word recognition must be balanced and integrated, (6) diagnosis directs instruction in word recognition, (7) word recognition skills are reinforced through writing, (8) word recognition instruction should be tied directly to meaningful reading experiences, and (9) word recognition instruction should proceed from the whole to the parts, not from the parts to the whole.

The four components of word recognition are contextual analysis, phonetic analysis, structural analysis, and sight word recognition. Contextual analysis is the ability to determine the correct pronunciation or meaning of a word as a result of using the surrounding linguistic and visual environment in which words appear. Phonetic analysis is the act of associating speech sounds with certain letters that represent speech sounds and blending these letter-sound relationships together to pronounce words. Structural analysis is the act of visually examining words to discover component parts which leads to pronunciation and meaning. Finally, sight recognition vocabulary are those words that can be pronounced instantaneously at sight. A sight recognition vocabulary is built up through the use of visual clues including configuration, length, unique features, letter combinations, and reading practice.

Dictionary usage is not a word recognition skill, but rather a resource wherein comprehension and word recognition skills are applied and confirmed after the rudiments of contextual, phonetic, structural analysis, and some sight words have been acquired.

REFERENCES

1. Bailey, Mildred Hart. "The Utility of Phonic Generalizations in Grades One Through Six." **Reading Teacher** 20 (February 1967): 413–18.
2. Clymer, Theodore. "The Utility of Phonic Generalizations in the Primary Grades." **Reading Teacher** 16 (January 1963): 252–58.

3. Emans, Robert. "The Usefulness of Phonic Generalizations Above the Primary Grades." **Reading Teacher** 20 (February 1967): 419-25.

4. McCullough, Constance. "Context Aids in Reading." **Reading Teacher** 11 (April 1958): 225-29.

5. Ames, Wilbur. "The Development of a Classification Scheme of Contextual Aids." **Reading Research Quarterly** 2 (Fall 1966): 57-82.

6. Rankin, Earl and Overholzer, Betsy. "Reaction of Intermediate Grade Children to Contextual Clues." **Journal of Reading Behavior** 1 (Summer 1969): 50-73.

7. Emans, Robert. "Use of Context Clues." In **Reading and Realism: Proceedings International Reading Association.** Part 1. Edited by J. Allen. Newark, Delaware: International Reading Association, 1969.

8. Stauffer, Russell G. **Directing the Reading-Thinking Process.** New York: Harper and Row, Publishers, 1975.

9. Pikulski, John. "A Critical Review: Informal Reading Inventories," **Reading Teacher** 28 (November 1974): 141-51.

10. Burmeister, Lou E. "Usefulness of Phonic Generalizations," **Reading Teacher** 21 (January 1968): 349-56.

11. Spache, George D., and Spache, Evelyn B. **Reading in the Elementary School.** Boston: Allyn and Bacon, Inc., 1973.

12. Dawson, Mildred A., and Bamman, Henry A. **Fundamentals of Basic Reading Instruction.** New York: David McKay Co., Inc., 1963.

13. Groff, Patrick. **The Syllable: Its Nature and Pedagogical Usefulness.** Portland, Oregon: Northwest Regional Educational Laboratory, 1971.

14. Harris, Albert J. **How To Increase Reading Ability.** 5th edition. New York: David McKay Company, Inc., 1970.

Appendix A

The following list of books is appropriate for reading to children or for children to read. It is reprinted with permission of the publisher and the author from *Elementary English*, "Instant Enrichment", by Marie E. Taylor. Copyright February, 1968, by the National Council of Teachers of English.

Kindergarten

Angelo the Naughty One, by Helen Garrett. Viking, 1944. Children love this story about a boy who hates to take baths.

Angus and the Ducks, by Marjorie Flack. Viking, 1944. A favorite picture book about a sassy little Scotty. Other books in the series are **Angus Lost** and **Angus and the Cat.**

Bedtime for Frances, by Russell Hoban. Harper, 1960. A badger child tries to delay bedtime just as other children do.

The Biggest Bear, by Lynd Ward. Houghton, 1952. A Caldecott Medal Book about a boy's pet bear cub that becomes overwhelming when he grows up. **Nic of the Woods,** by the same author, is equally successful as a dog story.

Blueberries for Sal, by Robert McCloskey. Viking, 1948. Anticipation is strong in this story about Sal and her mother, and little bear and his mother, getting all mixed up while gathering blueberries.

Contrary Woodrow, by Sue Felt. Doubleday, 1958. About kindergarten and Valentine's Day.

The Country Bunny and the Little Gold Shoes, by DuBose Heyward. Houghton, 1939. A favorite Easter story.

Curious George, by H.A. Rey. Houghton, 1941. Only one of many monkey stories: "Curious George Flies a Kite," "Curious George Learns the Alphabet," "Curious George Goes to the Hospital," and others.

Daddies, by Lonnie C. Carton. Tender, amusing rhymes about daddies and their children.

Edith and Mr. Bear, by Darr Wright. Doubleday, 1964. All the Darr Wright books are highly recommended by one of our staff.

George and the Cherry Tree, by Aliki. Dial, 1964. One of the few simple picture books available for seasonal demand.

The Happy Lion, by Louise Fatio. McGraw, 1934. All the people who visited the zoo were the lion's friends until he got out of the cage. More titles in this series.

Make Way for Ducklings, by Robert McCloskey. Viking, 1941. A family of mallard ducks makes their home in the middle of Boston. Outstanding Caldecott Award book.

May I Bring a Friend? by Beatrice S. De Regniers. Atheneum, 1964. Children are carried away as each successive caller at the queen's tea party is more ridiculous. Rare illustrations and delightful rhymes.

No Roses for Harry, by Gene Zion. Harper, 1958. Indomitable Harry knows no self-respecting dog would wear a sweater with roses, even one knitted by Grandma.

Paddy's Christmas, by Helen Monsell. Knopf, 1942. A bear story with the subtle meaning of Christmas.

Read-to-Me Storybook, by the Child Study Association of America. Crowell, 1947. Excellent collection of contemporary stories for young children.

The Red Balloon, by Albert Lamorisse. Doubleday, 1957. An imaginative picture book that leads to discussion.

Rosebud, by Ed Emberly. Little, 1966. Delightful turtle story.

Swimmy, by Leo Lionni. Pantheon, 1963. Like **Rosebud,** a book for sharp eyes. **Inch by Inch,** by the same author-illustrator, uses the concept of size.

Told under the Blue Umbrella, by the Association for Childhood Education International. Macmillan, 1933. Excellent collection of recommended stories for children.

First Grade

Andy and the Lion, by James Daugherty. Viking, 1938. Andy, who likes to read about lions, meets one on his way to school. The thorn pulling episode is a modern version of **Androcles and the Lion.**

Babar and Father Christmas, by Jean deBrunhoff. Random, 1949. A fine introduction to the other Babar books. Children squeal when Babar falls through the roof.

The Five Chinese Brothers, by Claire Bishop. Coward, 1938. A modern classic. Exaggeration and repetition delight youngsters.

The Gift of Hawaii, by Laura Bannon. Whitman, 1961. A little Hawaiian boy has "a great big love for his Mamma."

Hailstones and Halibut Bones, Mary O'Neill. Doubleday, 1961. Intriguing book of verse that invites creativity with color.

Jeanne-Marie Counts her Sheep, by Francoise. Scribner's, 1951. A simple story, picture, counting book.

Katy No-Pocket, by Emmy Payne. Houghton, 1944. An amusing story of how a mother kangaroo solves the problem of having no pocket.

Madeline's Rescue, Ludwig Bemelmans. Viking, 1953. The little girl from the boarding school in Paris is rescued from the River Seine by a dog "that kept his head." Distinctive illustrations in all the Madeline books that read in rhyme.

Nine Days to Christmas, by Marie Hall Ets. Viking, 1959. A Caldecott book about a Mexican Christmas, introducing the pinata.

A Pocketfull of Cricket, by Rebecca Caudill. Holt, 1964. A quiet story about a boy's affection for his pet cricket and the first day of school.

Red Is Never a Mouse, by Eth Clifford. Bobbs, 1960. A book of color.

Ski Pup, by Don Freeman. Viking, 1963. Hugo, a Saint Bernard rescue dog, accidentally becomes a ski dog.

The Snowy Day, by Ezra Jack Keats. Viking, 1962. An experience in visual perception. A little boy tries out the snow.

The Story about Ping, by Marjorie Flack. Viking, 1933. A little duck in China does not wish to get a spank if he is the last one on board.

Time of Wonder, by Robert McCloskey. Viking, 1957. One can feel the fog and the other sensations of beach life at the ocean.

Where the Wild Things Are, by Maurice Sendak. Harper, 1964. A very imaginative monster book about a little boy who gets even after being sent to his room.

Whistle for Willie, by Ezra Jack Keats. Viking, 1964. Willie's day is full of the small discoveries made by all children.

Second Grade

And to Think That I Saw It on Mulberry Street, by Dr. Seuss. Vanguard, 1937. Nonsense rhyme about a street where the ordinary becomes the extraordinary.

"B" is for Betsy, by Carolyn Haywood. Harcourt, 1939. The day-by-day incidents in the Haywood books make them completely realistic and entertaining. Good readers will enjoy reading them at the end of the year.

The Bears on Hemlock Mountain, by Alice Dalgliesh. Scribner's, 1952. Everyone told Jonathan there were no bears on the mountain. Suspense mounts as Jonathan crosses the mountain.

Brighty of the Grand Canyon, by Marguerite Henry. Rand, 1953. This story of a lone burro found by an old prospector has magnificent drawings of the Grand Canyon.

Charlotte's Web by E.B. White. Harper, 1952. The gentle friendship of a pig, a spider, and the little girl who could talk to animals.

Clown Dog, by Lavinia Davis. Doubleday, 1961. A boy defends his dog in a new neighborhood until his pet becomes a hero by discovering an orphaned fawn.

Crow Boy, by Taro Yashima. Viking, 1955. A shy Japanese boy is recognized by his classmates through his teacher's understanding.

Down, Down the Mountain, by Ellis Credle. Nelson, 1961. Two Blue Ridge Mountain children want creaky-squeaky shoes more than anything else in the world.

Easter in November, by Lilo Hess. Crowell, 1964. A surprise Easter story about an unusual breed of chickens that hatches colored eggs.

Lentil, by Robert McCloskey, Viking, 1940. Lentil's harmonica saves the day. Illustrations large enough to be seen by the class.

Little Runner of the Longhouse, by Betty Baker. Harper, 1962. A much needed, easy treatment of Iroquois life.

Marshmallow, by Clare T. Newberry. Harper, 1942. A pet cat cannot understand when a little white bunny comes to live at his home. Exceptional illustrations, fine story.

Mike's House, by Julia Sauer. Viking, 1954. Most second graders have been introduced to **Mike Mulligan and His Steam Shovel,** by Virginia Burton, and will chuckle at this story of a boy who makes no compromise with any other book.

Millions of Cats, by Wanda Gag. Coward, 1928. How does a little old woman choose one from millions of cats?

Reindeer Trail, by Berta and Elmer Hader. Macmillan, 1959. "How the fleet-footed reindeer brought to Alaska by the friendly Lapps save the Eskimos from starving."

The Story of Helen Keller, by Lorena Hickel. Grosset, 1958. This version of a great lady's life is simple enough to be enjoyed by second and third grades.

Tom Tit Tot, illustrated by Evaline Ness. Scribner's, 1965. The comic illustrations fit the "gatless" girl in this refreshing variation of Rumplestiltskin.

Two is Company, Three's a Crowd, by Berta and Elmer Hader. Macmillan, 1965. Fine to use when the geese are migrating. The story of how Big John and his wife feed a few and soon have more than they can handle.

Third Grade

The Borrowers, by Mary Norton. Harcourt, 1953. If you can't find your stamps or thimbles, the Borrowers are probably using them for pictures or footstools. One third grade constructed a home for the little people.

The Courage of Sarah Noble, by Alice Dalgliesh. Scribner's, 1954. The true story of a brave little girl who, in 1707, went with her father into Indian territory.

Dancing Cloud, The Navajo Boy, by Mary Buff. Viking, 1957. Excellent story of Navajo life with striking full-spread illustrations.

The Enormous Egg, by Oliver Butterworth. Little, 1956. Young Nate Twitchell finds an oversized egg in his chicken nest that hatches into a baby dinosaur and complications.

Henry Huggins, by Beverly Cleary. Morrow, 1950. All the Henry books enthusiastically recommended.

Homer Price, by Robert McCloskey. Viking, 1943. Each chapter is its own story. **The Doughnuts** and **Super Duper** are samples of the humor.

The Indian and the Buffalo, by Robert Hofsinde. Morrow, 1961. This author has given us much authentic Indian material.

The Limerick Trick, by Scott Corbett. Little, 1960. Kerby needs to write a Limerick to win a contest. A chemical mixture solves one problem but leads to another when Kerby finds he can't stop rhyming.

The Light at Tern Rock, by Julia Sauer. Viking, 1951. Excellent Christmas reading. A boy learns patience the hard way when he is forced to spend Christmas tending the lighthouse beacon.

Little House in the Big Woods, by Laura Ingalls Wilder. Harper, 1953. The entire Wilder series, depicting the author's childhood in the mid-west, is highly rated and always enjoyed.

Little Navajo Bluebird, by A.N. Clark. Viking, 1943. A fine picture of present-day Navajo life.

Mary Poppins, by P.L. Travers. Harcourt, 1962. Remarkable things happen when Miss Poppins blows in as the new Nanny.

The Matchlock Gun, by Walter Edmonds. Dodd, 1941. Historical fiction set in the Mohawk Valley during the French and Indian War. A boy is left to protect the family when the father answers the call for help from a settlement under attack.

The Nightingale, by Hans C. Andersen; illustrated by Harold Berson. Lippincott, 1963. A fine retelling of a favorite story.

The Nutcracker, translated by Warren Chappell. Knopf, 1958. An excellent selection for Christmas. May be used with the music.

The Otter's Story, by Emil Liers. Viking, 1953. Like **The Beaver's Story,** recommended as an absorbing, unsentimental animal story.

Paddle-to-the-Sea, by Holling C. Holling. Houghton, 1941. An Indian boy carves a toy canoe and launches it in the waters of northern Canada. The story traces its journey through the Great Lakes, over the Falls, into the Atlantic. Striking illustrations showing landscape and industry native to the area.

Tatsinda, by Elizabeth Enright. Harcourt, 1963. A fantasy with weird creatures, strange names, and a little girl pursued because she is different.

A Weed Is a Flower: The Life of George Washington Carver, by Aliki. Prentice, 1965. Fine introduction to biography.

Fourth Grade

Away Goes Sally, by Elizabeth Coatsworth. Macmillan, 1934. Sally moves from New England to Maine wilderness in the original house trailer—a log cabin on runners.

The Bee Man of Orn, by Frank Stockton. Hold, 1964. A man wishes to live his life. The surprise ending delights the children.

The Children of Green Knowe, by L. M. Boston. Harcourt, 1955. A beautifully written fantasy. Children will differ about what is real and what is imagined.

Chitty-Chitty-Bang-Bang, by Ian Fleming. Random, 1964. A magic car becomes a boat airplane when the family escapes from gangsters. Highly recommended.

Ice King, by Ernestine Byrd. Scribner's 1965. Sensitive story of a friendship between an Eskimo boy and a bear orphaned by hunters.

The Magic Bed-Knob, by Mary Norton; in **Bed-Knob and Broomstick.** Harcourt, 1957. Sheer fantasy about English children and their magician friend who gets the book off to a fine start when she falls off her broomstick and sprains her ankle.

Mama Hattie's Girl, by Lois Lenski. Lippincott, 1953. This regional book gives meaning to the place of the Negro in the North and South and is also excellent for the relationship between child and grandmother.

Misty of Chincoteague, by Marguerite Henry. Rand, 1947. A captivating horse story that begins with Pony Penning Day, still held on Chincoteague Island.

The Moffats, by Eleanor Estes. Harcourt, 1941. A family story full of humorous incidents. The Halloween chapter is hilarious.

Navajo Sister, by Evelyn Lampman. Doubleday, 1956. Excellent tale about the adjustment necessary when Navajo children leave the reservation for boarding school.

Pippi Longstocking, by Astrid Lindgren. Viking, 1950. A Swedish story about an uninhibited little girl who lives by herself and does only what she pleases in very unusual ways.

The Shy Stegosaurus of Cricket Creek, by Evelyn Lampman. Doubleday, 1955. George is the dinosaur who escaped extinction.

Strawberry Girl, by Lois Lenski. Lippincott, 1945. A realistic story about a family of Florida Crackers; strong regional background.

Stuart Little, by E. B. White. Harper, 1945. This mouse-man has been a "smash" in one fourth grade. "Good for the first day of school."

Wind in the Willows, by Kenneth Grahame. Scribner's, 1961. A classic that few children will enjoy unless it is first shared aloud.

The Witch of Blackbird Pond, by Elizabeth Speare. Houghton, 1958. Excellent background of Puritan America and the witchcraft movement. A Newbery medal winner.

Young Mark Twain and the Mississippi, by Kane Harnett. Random House, 1966. One of the excellent Landmark Series.

Fifth Grade

And Now Miguel, by Joseph Krumgold. Crowell, 1953. Authentic picture of sheep-raising in New Mexico and a boy who longs to become a man.

The Animal Family, by Randall Jarrell. Pantheon, 1965. A mystic story of a woodsman, a mermaid, and the animals. Like **The Children of Green Knowe,** children will puzzle over the story.

Call it Courage, by Armstrong Sperry. Macmillan, 1940. A South Sea Island boy, shamed by the tribe, redeems himself by his bravery. Adventure at its best.

The Complete Peterkin Papers, by Lucretia Hale. Houghton, 1960. The uninhibited Peterkin family finds solutions peculiar only to them. Ridiculous humor.

Farmer Boy, by Laura Ingalls Wilder. Harper, 1933. "Good to show how people lived before modern conveniences." Early New York state.

The Gold-Laced Coat, by Helen Fuller Orton. Lippincott, 1934. Fine to read before a field trip to an early American fort. This setting is Ft. Niagara.

The Island of the Blue Dolphins, by Scott O'Dell. Houghton, 1960. Based on the actual life of the sole inhabitant of the island, this Newbery winner has had great appeal for intermediate grades.

Li Lun, Lad of Courage, by Carolyn Treffinger. Abingdon, 1947. A courageous boy proves himself by achieving the impossible on a mountain.

Miss Pickerell Goes to Mars, by Ellen MacGregor. McGraw, 1951. Miss Pickerell shuddered at the thought of a Ferris wheel or stepladder. Her jaunt on a spaceship is a complete surprise. One of many in a series.

Pancakes-Paris, by Clair Bishop. Viking, 1947. A realistic story about a typical friendship between a French boy and American soldiers during World War II. A little French vocabulary.

Shadow of a Bull, by Maia Wojciechowska. Atheneum, 1964. The future is decided for the nine-year-old son of a famous bull fighter when he is born. A fine treatment of a child's reaction to public pressure in a setting rare to children's literature. A Newbery Award winner.

The Talking Tree, by Alice Desmond. Macmillan, 1949. A fine book for the study of Alaska; about totem poles and a young Tlingit Indian who must reconcile past with present.

Twenty and Ten, by Claire Bishop. Viking, 1952. Twenty school children in France befriend ten Jewish children fleeing from the Gestapo during World War II.

Sixth Grade

Adam of the Road, by Elizabeth Gray. Viking, 1942. An interesting picture of life in 13th century England.

Aunt America, by Marie Halun Block. Atheneum, 1963. Life behind the Iron Curtain. Children need to understand the concepts of freedom.

The Bronze Box, by Elizabeth Speare. Houghton, 1961. An unusual setting portraying the hatred of the Jews for their Roman conquerors during the time of Christ. Used before Easter each year by one fifth-grade teacher. A Newbery Medal book.

The Christmas Carol, by Charles Dickens. Many editions. The descriptive flavor of Dickens' words are not heard in the television versions.

The Door in the Wall, by Marguerite deAngeli. Doubleday, 1949. A crippled boy, despairing in a society of medieval knighthood, triumphs over his handicap. Excellent background for monastic and feudal study. A Newbery winner.

Follow My Leader, by James Garfield. Viking. A boy adjusts to his blindness at the age of eleven.

The Incredible Journey, by Sheila Burnford. Little, 1961. Fascinating adventure of a motley group of animals traveling together.

It's Like This, Cat, by Emily Neville. Harper, 1963. Sophisticated sixth graders will enjoy this story of New York City and a boy who never quite understands his parents, and vice versa. A Newbery book.

The Loner, by Ester Wier. McKay, 1963. Excellent character study of a boy who travels with migrants until he meets "Boss" and desperately wants to please her. Fine picture of sheep raising.

Martin Rides the Moor, by Vian Smith. Doubleday, 1965. A wild pony is the salvation of a boy deafened by an accident.

Onion John, by Joseph Krumgold. Crowell, 1959. A close friendship develops between the boy and the town junk man. Excellent human relations; humorous but realistic.

Second Hand Family, by Richard Parker. Bobbs, 1965. An up-to-date treatment of teenage interests. Concerns a group who play rock and roll. Enjoyed by preteens.

The White Panther, by Theodore Waldeck. Viking, 1951. A fast-moving story about a panther stalked by man and beast because he was born white.

A Wrinkle in Time, by Madeleine L'Engle. Farrar, 1962. Science fiction at its best; concerns children involved in the fourth dimension.

Appendix B

Bibliography of Books for Modeling Literary Forms

The following children's books are useful for modeling specific literary forms. This bibliography was compiled by Dr. Jane M. Bingham, Associate Professor of Education, Oakland University, Rochester, Michigan, and is used with her permission.

Behn, Harry. **The Far Away Lurs**. World, 1963. Grades 6–7. (Setting, metaphor, simile, point of view, plot structure).

Bonsall, Crosby. **I'll Show You Cats**. Harper, 1964. Grades K–1. (Mood, point of view, exaggeration).

Brown, Marcia. (Illustrator). **Three Billy Goats Gruff**. Harcourt, 1957. Grades K–1. (Sequence, climax, surprise, theme, folktale).

Burch, Robert. **Queenie Peavy**. Viking, 1966. Grades 5–6. (Character development, symbolism, point of view, setting).

Burton, Virginia Lee. **The Little House**. Houghton-Mifflin, 1942. Grades 1–2. (Personification, theme, setting, plot, mood).

Burton, Virginia Lee. **Mike Mulligan and His Steam Shovel**. Houghton-Mifflin, 1939. Grades 1–2. (Foreshadowing, personification, fantasy).

Cleary, Beverly. **Henry Huggins**. Morrow, 1950. Grades 3–4. (Humor, characterization, plot).

Cunningham, Julia. **Drop Dead**. Pantheon, 1965. Grades 4–5. (Symbolism, allegory, character development versus delineation).

Dalgliesh, Alice. **The Courage of Sarah Noble**. Scribner's 1954. Grades 2–3. (Symbolism, character development, setting).

DeJong, Meindert. **Hurry Home, Candy**. Harper, 1956. Grades 4–6. (Symbolism, style, point of view).

Forbes, Esther. **Johnny Tremain**. Houghton-Mifflin, 1946. Grades 6–7. (Character development, setting, plot structure, theme).

Grahame, Kenneth. **The Wind in the Willows**. Scribner's 1933. Grades 5–6. (Metaphor, simile, symbolism, personification, theme, humor).

Hunt, Irene. **Across Five Aprils**. Follett, 1965. Grades 4–5. (Historical fiction, plot, character development, dialogue and authentic speech, setting, theme).

Keats, Ezra Jack. **The Snowy Day**. Viking, 1962. Grades K-1. (Realism, alliteration, foreshadowing).

Krumgold, Joseph. " . . . **and now Miguel.**" Crowell, 1953. Grades 4–5. (Point of view, theme, mood, symbolism, humor, character development).

Langton, Jane. **The Boyhood of Grace Jones.** Harper, 1972. Grades 6–7. (Theme, characterization, symbolism, point of view, setting).

Lexau, Joan. **Me Day.** Dial, 1971. Grades 1-2. (Mood, point of view, dialect, foreshadowing, setting.).

Lindgren, Astrid. **Pippi Longstocking.** Viking, 1950. Grades 2-3. (Humor, characterization, dialogue).

Mathis, Sharon Bell. **Sidewalk Story.** Viking, 1971. Grades 3-4. (Dialogue, setting, characterization).

Miles, Miska. **Annie and the Old One.** Little-Brown, 1971. Grades 3-4. (Cadence, point of view, metaphor, setting, symbolism, theme).

Miles, Miska. **Hoagies's Rifle-Gun.** Little-Brown, 1970. Grades 3-4. (Characterization, dialect, theme, symbolism).

Milne, A. A. **Winnie-The-Pooh.** E. P. Dutton, 1926. Grades 2-3. (Humor, metaphor, simile, personification, point of view, cadence, characterization).

Mosel, Ariene. **The Funny Little Woman.** Dutton, 1973. Grades 1-2. (Plot, theme, folktale, characterization).

Neville, Emily. **It's Like This Cat.** Harper and Row, 1963. Grades 6-7. (Dialogue, mood, point of view, theme, setting, plot, character development versus delineation).

Newberry, Clare. **Marshmallow.** Harper and Row, 1942. Grades K-1. (Mood, point of view, simile).

Parish, Peggy. **Thank You, Amelia Bedelia.** Harper and Row, 1964. Grades 1-2. (Figurative language, humor, character delineation).

Piatti, Celestino. **The Happy Owls** /Atheneum, 1964. Grades 1-2. (Theme, characterization, figurative language).

Potter, Beatrix. **The Tale of Peter Rabbit.** Warne, 1903. Grades K-1. (Theme, characterization, climax, style, cadence).

Sandburg, Carl. **Abe Lincoln Grows Up.** Harcourt, 1956. Grades 5-6. (Biography, point of view, style, setting).

Sendak, Maurice. **Where the Wild things Are.** Harper and Row, 1963. Grades K-1. (Fantasy, symbolism).

Spear, Elizabeth. **Witch of Blackbird Pond.** Houghton-Mifflin, 1958. Grades 6-7. (Character development, setting, symbolism, point of view).

Sperry, Armstrong. **Call It Courage.** Macmillan, 1941. Grades 4-5. (Theme, point of view, symbolism, setting, style, plot structure).

Steptoe, John. **Stevie.** Harper and Row, 1969. Grades 1-2. (Dialect, setting, theme).

Sterling, Dorothy. **Mary Jane.** Doubleday, 1959. Grades 4-5. (Theme, character development, setting, point of view).

Stolz, Mary. **The Bully of Barkham Street**. Harper and Row, 1963. Grades 4-5. (Point of view, character development, plot structure).

Stolz, Mary. **A Dog on Barkham Street**. Harper and Row, ¹960. Grades 4-5. (Point of view, character development, plot structure).

Travers, Paula. **Mary Poppins**. Harcourt, 1934. Grades 3-4. (Humor, point of view, character development).

Trevino, Elizabeth Borton. **I, Juan de Pareja**. Farrar, 1965. Grades 6-7. (Theme, description, characterization, historical fiction).

Viorst, Judith. **The Tenth Good Thing about Barney**. Atheneum, 1971. Grades 1-2. (Theme, characterization, dialogue).

White, E. B. **Charlotte's Web**. Harper and Row, 1952. Grades 3-4. (Theme, characterization, dialogue, description, fantasy).

White, Edgar. **Sati**. Lothrop, 1973. Grades 2-3. (Flashback, cadence, setting, diction).

Weir, Ester, **The Longer**. McKay, 1963. Grades 5-6. (Theme, setting, symbolism, characterization, dialogue).

Wojciechowska, Maia. **A Single Light**. Atheneum, 1968. Grades 6-7. (Theme, setting, symbolism, characterization, dialogue).

Wyatt, Edgar. **Cochise: Apache Warrior and Statesman**. McGraw, 1953. Grades 4-5. (Characterization, theme biography).

Yates, Elizabeth. **Amos Fortune**. Dutton, 1950. Grades 4-5. (Symbolism, setting, theme).

Zolotow, Charlotte. **Sleepy Book**. Lothrop, 1958. Grades K-1. (Cadence, structure, point of view).

Appendix C

The following children's books or series of books are useful for doing patterned writing (see chapter seven).

Blossom, Budney. **A Kiss Is Round.** H. W. Wilson Co.

Barry, Katharina. **A Bug Is to Hug.** Harcourt, Brace and World.

Browne, Margaret Wise. **Where Have You Been?** Harper and Row.

Cameron, Polly. **"I Can't," said the Ant.** Scholastic Book.

Charlip, Remy. **What Good Luck! What Bad Luck!** Scholastic Magazine.

DeRegniers, Beatrice Schenk. **May I Bring A Friend?** Atheneum.

Einsel, Walter. **Did you Ever See?** Scholastic Magazine.

Emberly, Barbara. **Drummer Hoff.** Prentice-Hall

Emberly, Ed. **The Wing on a Flea.** Little, Brown and Co.

Heide, Florence. **Some Things Are Scary.** Scholastic Books.

Heilbroner, Joan. **This Is the House Where Jack Lives.** Harper and Row.

Joslin, Sesyle. **What Do You Say, Dear?** Scholastic Books.

Karp, Laura. **Opposites.** World Publishing Co.

Krass, Ruth. **A Hole Is to Dig.** Harper and Row.

Krass, Ruth. **Mama, I Wish I Was Snow.** Scholastic Books.

Krauss, Ruth and Johnson. **Is This You?** Scholastic Books.

Martin, Bill, Jr. **Brown Bear, Brown Bear.** Holt, Rinehart and Winston.

Martin, Bill, Jr. **David Was Mad.** Holt, Rinehart and Winston.

Martin, Bill, Jr. **Instant Readers Series.** Holt, Rinehart and Winston.

Martin, Bill, Jr. **Ten Little Caterpillars.** Holt, Rinehart and Winston.

Memling, Carl. **Hi, All You Rabbits.** Parents' Magazine Press.

O'Neil, Mary. **Hailstones and Halibut Bones.** Scholastic Books.

Schulz, Charles. **"Happiness Is . . . "** Determined Productions Inc.

Schulz, Charles. **"Love Is . . . "** Determined Productions Inc.

Sendak, Maurice. **Chicken Soup with Rice.** Scholastic Books.

Seuss, Dr. **One Fish, Two Fish.** Random House.

Sullivan, Joan. **Round Is a Pancake.** Holt, Rinehart and Winston.

Udry, Janice. **A Tree Is Nice.** Harper and Row.

Walker, Barbara. **I Packed My Trunk.** Follett.

Wright, H. R. **A Maker of Boxes.** Holt, Rinehart and Winston.

Appendix D

Story Starter Books

The following children's books are useful as story starters for creative writing.

Burton, Virginia Lee. **The Little House.** Houghton-Mifflin Co.

Domanska, Nanina. **If All the Seas Were One Sea.** Macmillan Co.

Emberly, Barbara. **One Wide River to Cross.** Prentice-Hall.

Holland, Ruth. **A Bad Day.** David McKay Co.

Gaeddert, Lou Ann. **Noisy Nancy Norris.** Doubleday and Co.

Jacobs, Leland and Elinor Johnson. **See Saw, I Wish I Were A Rabbit.** Charles Merrill Co.

Kaufman, Joe. **Big and Little.** Golden.

Krauss, Robert. **Whose Mouse Are You?** Macmillan Co.

Lenski, Lois. **I Like Winter.** Henry Z. Walck, Inc.

Lionni, Leo. **Inch by Inch.** Astor-Honor Inc.

Longman, Harold. **Watch Out! How to be Safe and Not Sorry.** Parents' Magazine Press.

Rees, Ennis. **Gillygaloos and Gally Whoppers.** Abelard Schuman. Simon, Mina and Howard. **If You Were an Eel, How Would You Feel?** Follett.

Slepian, Jan and Ann Seidler. **The Hungry Thing.** Follett.

Smith, Dorothy Hall. **The Big Little Book.** Harper and Row.

Tresselt, Alvin. **White Snow, Bright Snow.** Lothrup, Lee and Shepard Co.

Tresselt, Alvin. **A Thousand Lights and Fireflies.** Parents' Magazine Press.

Appendix E

Bibliography of Books on Children's Writing

Arnstein, Flora. **Poetry and the Child.** New York: Dover Publications Inc., 1962. Describes how to create a favorable climate for writing, evaluating poetry to be read to children, and the values of writing poetry. Presents good ideas for stimulating reluctant children to write poetry.

Burgess, C., T. Burgess and others. **Understanding Children's Writing.** New York: Penquin Books, 1973. Uses children's writing to illustrate concepts about the writing process. Shows how children's writing reflects their language, thought, and experience.

Burrows, Alvina, D. D. Monson and Russell Stauffer. **New Horizons in the Language Arts.** New York: Harper and Row Publishers, 1972. A general language arts book emphasizing the language experience approach to reading instruction. Contains excellent material on written composition.

Burrows, Alvina, D. Jackson and D. Saunders. **They All Want to Write.** New York: Holt, Rinehart and Winston, 1964. Discusses a wide range of writing topics. Contains excellent examples of children's writing used to illustrate specific writing concepts.

Clegg, Alec. (ed) **Enjoying Writing.** London: Chatto and Windus Educational, 1973. An anthology of children's writing and art solicited from schools in the West Riding, Yorkshire, England. The children who contributed to this anthology range in age from eleven to eighteen. Unfortunately, this anthology does not contain Clegg's reflections on the teaching of writing that were so effective in **The Excitement of Writing.**

Clegg, Alec. (ed) **The Excitement of Writing.** New York: Schocken Books, 1972. An outstanding anthology of children's writing solicited from schools in the West Riding, Yorkshire, England. Includes detailed descriptions of the circumstances under which the writings were produced.

Hennings, Dorothy G. and Barbara Grant. **Content and Craft: Written Expression in the Elementary School.** Englewood Cliffs, New Jersey: Prentice-Hall, Inc., 1973. An excellent book covering the full range of topics in writing. Covincingly illustrates ways to help children select, structure, and revise their writing.

Holbrook, David. **Children's Writing: A Sampler for Student Teachers.** Cambridge, England: Cambridge University Press, 1967. An anthology of children's writing organized into exercises designed to help teachers analyze the content and meaning of children's writing.

Hourd, Marjorie and Gertrude Cooper. **Coming Into Their Own**. London: Heinemann Educational Books Ltd., 1959. An anthology of children's writing drawn from the top class of a mixed county primary school of which one of the authors was head teacher. Contains an excellent descriptive and critical account of the children's writing.

Koch, Kenneth. **Wishes, Lies, and Dreams: Teaching Children to Write Poetry**. New York: Chelsea House Publishers, 1970. An excellent book containing many imaginative ideas for poetry writing. Describes how the author guided children's poetry writing experiences in a New York City public school.

Mearns, Hughes. **Creative Power: The Education of Youth in the Creative Arts**. New York: Appleton-Century-Crofts, 1929. The seminal book on creative teaching written in an engaging and readable style. Mearns foreshadows an entire genre of books on creative education by touching on every significant concept and controversy extant in the field of creative writing.

Petty, Walter and Mary Bowen. **Slithery Snakes and Other Aids to Children's Writing**. New York: Appleton-Century-Crofts, 1967. A good resource book of ideas for creative writing. Contains useful suggestions on how to make writing an enjoyable activity.

Pratt-Butler, Grace. **Let Them Write Creatively**. Columbus, Ohio: Charles E. Merrill Publishing Co., 1973. Discusses creative writing including such topics as verbal and nonverbal forms of expression, poetry writing, and techniques for encouraging writing among primary and intermediate age children.

Stauffer, Russell. **The Language-Experience Approach to the Teaching of Reading**. New York: Harper and Row Publishers, 1970. Presents the language experience approach to reading instruction, including a specific chapter on the role of creative writing in the language experience approach. An excellent discussion of the beginning stages of creative writing.

Witucke, V. **Poetry in the Elementary School**. New York: William C. Brown Publishers, 1970. Discusses the implications of using poetry with children. Lists sources of poetry, ways to evaluate poetry, and suggestions for a program of poetry for children.

Wolsch. Robert. **Poetic Composition through the Grades**. New York: Teachers College Press, 1970. An excellent account of the nature of poetic composition. Gives a detailed description of how to start the poetic composition process with children, how to develop precision with language, and how to share the written product.

Appendix F

Bibliography of Articles on Creative Writing

Bachrack, B. "Dirty Words in the Classroom." Elementary English, 48 (December 1971), 998-99. Presents ideas for broadening language power. Describes how children start by compiling synonyms for **dirty** and end up using a thesaurus.

Burrus, D. and I. Lohmann. "Composition Is Speech Written Down." **Instructor**, (March 1972), 55-56. Describes a longitudinal study showing how the language experience approach facilitates language growth.

Clapp, H. "Teach Writing Creatively." **Instructor**, 80 (January 1971), 63-64. Excellent discussion of reasons for teaching writing and ways of stimulating and maintaining interest in writing.

Cline, Sister D. "Developing Middle-Grade Children's Creativity through Poetry." **Elementary English**, 48 (November 1971), 843-48. Focuses on the importance of recognizing and encouraging the creative impulse in children. Emphasizes poetry as a satisfying means of self-expression.

Davis, G. "A Delicate Balance". **Elementary English**, 49 (April 1972) 596-99. Describes an experience in short story writing with eighth grade children.

Dehaven, Edna. "A Questioning Strategy Model for Creative Writing". Elementary English, 50 (September 1973), 959-60. Suggests that a feeling of involvement is paramount in encouraging reluctant children to write. Suggests ways to expand children's concept development and thinking ability.

Ellis, L. S. "Creating a Climate for Writing". **Elementary English**, 49 (October 1972), 90102. Discusses freedom and spontaneity in fostering written expression. Makes suggestions for enhancing the physical environment of the classroom and the teacher-child relationship and gives ideas for developing interest in writing.

Fleming, F. L. "Creative Communication in the Elementary Grades". **Elementary English**, 48 (May 1971), 482-88. Suggest ways to foster creative thought and expression. Emphasizes the need to develop divergent thinking abilities in children.

Hall, M. W. "Poetry in the Primary Grades". **Elementary English**, 49 (October 1972), 889-93. Annotates twenty sources of children's writing. Emphasizes the value of children's writing as a means of stimulating writing among other children.

Harris, J. "What Writers Advise on the Teaching of Creative Writing". **English Journal**, 60 (March 1971), 345-52. Indicates that professional writers feel that teachers should be the catalyst in guiding children to personal discoveries about writing. Writers also warn against emphasizing mechanics over content.

Humphrey, J. W. and S. R. Redden. "Encouraging Young Authors". **The Reading Teacher**, 25 (April 1972), 643-51. An excellent collection of practical writing ideas for classroom teachers. Contains a good description of the uses of book-making for stimulating writing.

Kaufman, W. "The Inhibited Teacher". English Journal, 60 (March 1971), 382-89. Argues that teachers' rigid, traditional behaviors prevent many children from freely expressing their ideas.

Larson, R. L. "Rhetorical Writing in Elementary School". **Elementary English**, 48 (December 1971), 926-31. Suggests that rhetorical writing (writing directed at a particular audience for a specific purpose) is not sufficiently emphasized in school writing experiences. Gives ways to encourage rhetorical writing.

McPhail, A. "Children's Language Development—Its Relation to Creative Writing." **Elementary English**, 49 (February 1972), 242-44. Suggests that oral language development encourages creative writing and that writing facilitates language growth. Links language development and critical thinking to creative writing.

MacPhee, A. "Children's Writing". **CITE Newsletter**, 5 (October 1971), 14-26. Interesting discussion of writing as a source of evidence about children's understanding, perceptions, and attitudes. Types of children's writing are classified in a manner congruent with stated objectives for writing.

Shapiro, P. P. and B. J. Shapiro. "Two Methods of Teaching Poetry Writing in the Fourth Grade". **Elementary English**, 48 (April 1971), 225-27. Comparative study of two methods of teaching the writing of poetry. One method is described as "free" and the other as "semi-structured". Concludes that the semi-structured method fostered greater growth in poetry writing.

Stroh, N. K. "How a Diary Encouraged Creative Writing". **Elementary English**, 46 (October 1969), 769-71. Good description of the uses of diary writing as an outlet for creative expression. Suggests ways to encourage children to write about themselves on a daily basis.

Swynehardt, M. and C. Hatlestad. "Extending Children's Appreciation of Book Illustration through Creative Activity". **Elementary English**, 49 (February 1972), 235-39. Excellent resource article describing language encounters based on illustrations in children's books. Advocates the use of art and drama in creative writing.

Wieger, M. "Found Poetry". **Elementary English**, 48 (December 1971), 1002-1004. Tells how the author sent students to "find" poetry in prose and encouraged them to rearrange the words to emphasize the poetic feeling and rhythm of the prose.

Index

Experiences (continued)
  use of, in writing, 2
  and words, 49

Feelings, use of in writing, 172
Field, Rachel, 170
Filmstrips, use of, 40
Format, for writing, 156, 157
Fortunata, 174
Freeman, Don, 180
Frost, Robert, 91

"Galoshes," 132, 175
Grades, use of in evaluation, 84-87
Grammar
  during child's dictation, 28
  and grading, 84
  use of, in writing, 157-60
Groff, Patrick, 241
Group stories, 28
Guilfoile, Elizabeth, 180
Guilford, J.P., 200, 201

Hahn, Harry, 92
Hailstones and Halibut Bones, 172
Hammond, Dorsey, 106, 155
Handwriting ability, and writing, 155-56
Hanna, P. and J., 106
Harris, Albert J., 241
Haywood, Carolyn, 180
Heide, Florence, 174
Hemingway, Ernest, 71
Henderson, Edmund, 106, 107, 197, 208
Henry, O., 169
Holidays, as ideas for writing, 182
Huckleberry Finn, 183
Hughes, Ted, 49
Hunt, Lyman C., Jr., 199, 201
Hymes, Lucia, and James L., 175

Ideas, for writing, 164
  One hundred seventy-two brief ideas, 166-88
Imitation
  of language models, 16, 17, 76-81
  and learning to write, 65
    close, 66
    creative modeling, 69-71
    loose, 67-68
  models for, 71-76

"Jabberwocky," 92
Japanese poetry forms, 69, 141, 144-46
Johnny Tremain, 183
Journal, keeping a, 153

Keen Edge, The, 54
Kipling, Rudyard, 194
Kitt, Tamara, 184

Lady With the Dog, The, 168
Language. *See* Oral language

Language acquisition, 22
  behaviorist theory of, 9-10, 17
  cognitive theory of, 12-13, 17
  environmental influence in, 15-18
  nativist theory of, 11-12, 13, 17
  stages of, 13-15
Language and thought, 7-9
Language experience approach *See also* Experiences, 25.
Language Master, 36
Language power, and poetry, 130-36
Lee, Doris, 31
Lenneberg, Eric H., 11
Lennon, Roger, 198, 204
Letter-sound association, 154
Letter writing, 181
Libraries, use of, 3-4
Listening
  reading to children, 73
  and writing, 161-62
London, Jack, 65, 71, 72, 153, 168
Lowth, Bishop Robert, 158

McCullough, Constance, 230
McGovern, Ann, 194
McNeill, David, 11, 16
Martin, Bill, Jr., 3, 78, 79, 166, 174
Materials
  commercial spelling, use of, 111, 113, 115
  reading, 3
    selecting appropriate ones, 74
  for word recognition, 231
Maugham, Somerset, 65, 71, 72, 153
Meaning
  of language, 17
  and reading, 227, 228
Mearns, Hughes, 1, 52, 59, 130
Metaphors, 70, 137
Mill, John Stuart, 210
Music, use of ideas for writing, 182

O'Neill, Mary, 172
Oral language, and reading and writing
  governed by rules, 21
  immediate gratification, 20
  natural v. unnatural, 18
  little stress in, 19
  versus written, 18
  and writing, 57, 161
Overholzer, Betsy, 230

Patterned stories, 79-80
Patterned writing, and imitation, 67
Peterson, Holly and John, 178
Petre, Richard M., 197
Pflaum, Susan W., 14
Phonetic analysis
  guidlines for teaching, 232
  rules, 234
  sequence for teaching, 233-34, 236
  sounding and blending, 235
  word recognition, 207, 237